Land of 10,000 Plates

Land of 10,000 Plates

Stories and Recipes
from Minnesota

Patrice M. Johnson

MINNESOTA
HISTORICAL
SOCIETY PRESS

Image Credits: page 16: Maddi Bazzocco, Unsplash; page 23: Sorin Gheorghita, Unsplash; page 66: Jason Leung, Unsplash; page 75: Caroline Attwood, Unsplash; page 80: Nadine Primeau, Unsplash; page 115: Jenna Hamra, pexels.com; page 162: Shelley Pauls, Unsplash; page 173: Sophie Nengel, Unsplash

mnhspress.org

The Minnesota Historical Society Press is a member of the Association of University Presses.

Manufactured in the United States of America.

10 9 8 7 6 5 4 3

∞ The paper used in this publication meets the minimum requirements of the American National Standard for Information Sciences—Permanence for Printed Library Materials, ANSI Z39.48–1984.

International Standard Book Number

ISBN: 978-1-68134-168-2 (paper)

Library of Congress Cataloging-in-Publication Data
Names: Johnson, Patrice M, author.

Title: Land of 10,000 plates : stories and recipes from Minnesota / Patrice M Johnson.

Description: Saint Paul, MN : Minnesota Historical Society Press, [2020] | Includes index. | Summary: "From Minnesota's newer culinary traditions—Hmong hotdish—to its oldest—nourishing wild rice—*Land of 10,000 Plates* explores far and wide, experiencing the festivals, communing with revelers, and celebrating the foodways that define the northland"—Provided by publisher.

Identifiers: LCCN 2020024473 | ISBN 9781681341682 (paperback)

Subjects: LCSH: Cooking, American—Midwestern style. | Cooking—Minnesota. | International cooking. | LCGFT: Cookbooks.

Classification: LCC TX715.2.M53 J64 2020 | DDC 641.59776—dc23

LC record available at https://lccn.loc.gov/2020024473

To Macaroni & Alligator,
for teaching me how to tell stories

to my mom, dad, & sisters,
for encouraging me to imagine

& for Minnesota, Mnisota,
that your waters remain clear and clean

Introduction · 2

Life Beneath the Snow · 9

New Year's Eve Fondue · 12

Snow Days · 15

Hotdish Culture: Tater Tot Nation · 17

Diary of a Minnesota Congressional Delegation
Hotdish Competition Judge · 24

Meat Raffle · 30

A Swede in Minnesota
Makes Sunday Gravy · 38

Ice Fishing · 46

Vasaloppet · 51

Competitive Souping · 53

Consider the Radish, &
Other Signs of Renewal · 63

Fish Fry · 69

Finding the Warmth · 77

Maple · 80

Jell-O Salad · 84

Jell-Epilogue · 88

Field Day · 91

Graduation · 92

Lazy Heat · 97

Taking 'er Easy for All Us Sinners · 100

Rainy Days & Front Stoop Food · 105

The Fourth of July · 109

Up North, aka To the Lake · 116

Farmers Market · 120

Crayfish Boils · 126

The Main · 130

Pizza Farms: Which Came First, the Pizza or the Farm? · 137

Corn Creeping · 142

It Ain't Over Til the State Fair · 145

Butter Head · 156

Jerry's Kids · 160

Apples · 162

Back to School Biscuits · 166

Diwali · 168

Honey · 172

Booya · 176

Commercials · 181

Friends Thanksgiving · 184

Wild Rice · 190

Hope · 192

Acknowledgments · 198

Index · 200

Passing Seasons · 196

Land of 10,000 Plates

Introduction

I love food so much that by the time I was two years old I had an imaginary friend named Macaroni. My earliest memories are of the daily rituals my family created around our meals, and the seasonal celebrations we enjoyed that always had a food focus. I am a Minnesotan, born with appetite for food and life.

Writing stories about food and culture allows me to delve into the delicious as well as issues of identity, belonging, and community. In the North we mix our food rites with the seasons, and this mix tells a compelling and occasionally quirky story.

There are the things people who aren't from here might know about. SPAM, the Green Giant, Creamette macaroni, Gold Medal and Pillsbury, Totino's Pizza Rolls, Betty Crocker, General Mills, and Nordic Ware Bundt cake pans are all famous Minnesotans—characters, companies, or products. So is Paul Bunyan. (Sorry, Maine. He's ours. And keep your hands off Babe.)

Then there are the things people who aren't from here don't know about. Whether it is meat raffles, ice fishing, butter heads, booyas, or wild ricing—life in the North is a seasonal adventure.

Minnesota winter can be bitter, weeks strung together with snow days and two-hour school delays. Blustery cold builds a hardy character and a craving for hotdish. Meat raffles and ice fishing both entertain and feed us.

Spring arrives, eventually, with Easter egg hunts that sometimes take place across snowy yards and parks. Maple syruping and Lenten fish frys nudge us into spring's warmer weather. We see promise of life as ramps and radishes replace white landscapes with green.

Summer is brief but full. Bounty is to be had at local farmers markets; the heat drives everyone outside to grill dinner and city folks "up north" to convalesce at cabins and lake homes. Crayfish boils and pizza farms lure us into sticky summer days and mosquito-laden nights.

Autumn smells first of abundance and then of decay. Falling leaves and overnight frosts remind us that the whole cycle is about to begin again. We celebrate at fairs where the biggest pig and princess busts carved from butter are equally honored. As the sun retreats, we harvest wild rice or throw a booya, and the kids return to school.

To live fully, we don't simply endure the seasons; we thrive because of them. Our seasons represent the people of this region: vulnerable yet resilient. Our seasons and their celebrations are the cycles that reassure us of normality in a chaotic world. As global warming changes our normal, we cling to the rituals of our region.

Woven into those seasons are our (occasionally odd) celebrations where food and community are so entwined we hardly notice the peculiarities. These celebrations connect us to place, climate, and each other. These are the rituals that make life in the North entertaining and tasty.

When I was a kid, we never asked what was for dinner. The smell coming from our kitchen told us what we were about to eat. Mom rotated the menus with favorite standbys: SPAM and potato hot-dish ("She fed a family of seven with one can!" my oldest sister, Cheryl, recalls), Swiss steak, and tuna noodle. Weekends brought frozen pizza, tacos, and burgers. Cheryl could eat more burgers and tacos than anyone else in our house, including Dad. Family legend is rich with tales of the Saturday night she ate four cheeseburgers in one sitting, along with a stack of homemade french fries and a chocolate malt.

Sunday nights Mom rested, like God. We fended for ourselves with peanut butter toast and canned fruit. We five sisters fought over dumb things like who would be the first to dip their knife into a fresh jar of Skippy or Jif, and who would get the lone halved cherry that rested atop the can of fruit cocktail. These were the rare competitions that Mom didn't decide by having us draw the short stick. (She broke one toothpick in half, then blended it with four unbroken sticks and held them at the same height in her clasped hand—one part mom, one part magician. We'd take turns drawing. The short stick was either the winner or the loser, depending on what we were fighting over.)

Our mandatory weekday breakfasts consisted of french toast, hot cereal, cold cereal drowning in whole milk, Bisquick pancakes, or scrambled eggs. I hated eggs and spent one winter pushing them through the space between the kitchen nook table and the wall. I don't recall what happened when the eggs were discovered, but it couldn't have been pleasant for anyone.

I also hated vegetables, and was always on the lookout for ways to hide them on my plate (under baked potato skin, beneath globs of ketchup, mingling with uneaten gravy), and for a few nights I got away with cramming as many bites into my mouth as possible, then excusing myself from the table so I could spit them out in the bathroom. Most nights I was not successful at hiding uneaten bits of overcooked canned peas or mushy carrots and spent hours at the table, alone, with a vegetable-loaded plate in front of me until finally I willed myself to chew and swallow so that I could get on with life.

There was buttered popcorn for Saturday night's TV lineup of *Mary Tyler Moore* and *Bob Newhart*. Cheryl directed us to eat one kernel at a time while she scooped her entire hand into the bowl and giggled at our misguided obedience. To this day I am compelled to eat my popcorn kernel by kernel, savoring each buttery, salty nibble.

On hot summer days, Mom would fry chicken early in the morning, and I'd sneak into the kitchen hoping for a bite of the fried liver. She'd slice the lump in half and remind me

3

that no one should eat too much liver because that's where the chicken's toxins were stored. We ate the fried chicken with good potato salad loaded with Miracle Whip and boiled eggs.

We rarely went out to eat, but somehow I learned about commercial sandwiches and immediately respected this dish that had everything I wanted all on one plate: meat, gravy, bread, potatoes, and a pickle.

I was never indifferent about meals. Every occasion, whether celebratory or mundane, was made glorious or horrid because of the food, and what that food represented. We always ate together: breakfast and lunch at the kitchen nook, supper in the dining room, and snacks in front of the TV and Mary Tyler Moore on Saturday nights.

It can be difficult not to romanticize a good childhood. Not everything was perfect, but our food always connected us.

· · ·

As I wrote this book, my panic about global warming intensified. In Minnesota we are especially vulnerable to any forces that shift the way we farm, fish, and flourish. Climate change and the resulting unpredictable weather experienced across the planet trigger heavy spring flooding, extended droughts, invasive species, fluctuating inconsistent seasons, and risk of pandemics. All wreak havoc on the way we produce and harvest food. Adding to the crisis are decreasing Farm Bill assistance to family farms, failing dairy and specialty farms, loss of farmland and wildlife habitats, and continued pesticide and herbicide overuse. Blame politicians, corporations, greed, or ignorance: we all suffer when we lose precious resources such as clean air, clean water, and clean energy.

Panic morphed into an urgency to document the way of life I've always loved and assumed would never end: a day out on a pristine fish-filled lake, a walk in the evening snow, and farmers markets abundant with every color and flavor of the seasons.

On a crisp, clear autumn morning, I sat in a hipster coffee shop in Northeast Minneapolis at a small table across from chef and television host Yia Vang. The first time I met Chef Yia, he was demonstrating how to make Hmong hotdish at the Minnesota State Fair. I was immediately drawn to his storytelling, and especially appreciative of his take on that Minnesota staple, tater tot hotdish. Yia epitomizes charisma, and as he spoke to me about food and culture, I wanted to buy whatever he was selling, maybe join his cult of sanity. I felt a little bit better about the world, and even more determined to testify about Minnesota's (and Minnesotan) excellence.

Yia speaks about Hmong food as a philosophy rather than a list of ingredients. Hmong food tells a cultural story: "Where we've been, where we are, and where we are going." He explained that as the Hmong people migrate they learn from their new neighbors and adopt regional fare. In Minnesota that fare includes local vegetables, like plenty of roots in the cool months, and meats such as pork and beef. It also includes regional specialties like hotdish.

"There is a soul component to hotdish. For Hmong people that is the ethos of our food, the soul and love aspect. We can make a Hmong version that reflects that soul. I take it kind of seriously." Yia described his Hmong approach to hotdish: "What is hotdish? A base of root vegetables and whatever else we have. That is soul food in the North: root vegetables keep us alive all winter. My gravy"—which Yia makes with Hmong sausage and coconut milk—"is southeast Asia."

"Hotdish was created out of necessity. How do I feed a family of ten with one pound of meat? That is also the Hmong narrative. Cultures are not that different. Food is fluid. Within the Hmong culture we can take any ingredient and make it into Hmong food. Hotdish tells the story of struggle and poverty, and that makes it soul food."

Yia described a noodle dish he ate a lot when he was a kid: "I hated it. There wasn't enough meat." Yia didn't realize his family couldn't afford a lot of meat and resented the vegetable-heavy meals he was served. He longed for the luxury of an entire slab of meat. "The first thing I wanted to cook was meat loaf!"

"When you are young, you don't want to be like your parents, but then you grow up and become them. They are a part of me. The sooner I accept that and let it sink in, the more I understand it. I love the way they love because they are the people who showed me how to love. I reflect them, and the more I look at my parents, the more I see my own reflection." Yia explained that many people think of love as filling up, and he gently placed his hands around a coffee cup. Then he mimed coffee spilling out of the cup: "That's how my mom loves. Her loves spills over, out of the cup, off the table." He went on to describe his young nephew's insatiable appreciation of Yia's mom's egg rolls. "One morning he tells my mom he wants egg rolls, and I come to their house and my mom is rolling them and my dad is frying them. They made a hundred egg rolls because my nephew had a craving."

Yia's parents also pitch in making food for Yia's chef adventures. Mama Yang's Hot Sauce has earned acclaim from celebrity chefs as well as regulars at Yia's food truck. In fact, her sauce is so popular that she makes thirty gallons a year to keep him supplied. Yia's dad's sausage won a best sausage award, and his parents' egg rolls and buns also delight diners at Union Hmong Kitchen.

"This is my parents' story," he said. Yet, early on, Yia got some complaints when Hmong diners claimed his food was not authentic. "I want to make food that my parents like to eat but not necessarily the way they prepare it." He reiterated,

5

"Food is fluid. There is no right or wrong way to use cilantro. Asian people don't own the Thai chili. If my parents were living here in the North forty years ago, how would they cook using what's around them? No one can define the word *authentic*. Food moves forward because of immigration and because of the beautiful group of refugees we have around here. The techniques I use to cook this food come from my fine dining experiences. My parents cook old style."

Yia's dad is a hero. He fought in a war, and in coming to America sacrificed everything for his family, including a position of honor in his village: "He could have lived like a king if he stayed in Laos." This knowledge changes Yia's view of the world. "When a guy like that," Yia said, referring to his father, "is nonchalant about his sausage winning a contest, while others might feel conceit, I am humbled. [My parents] never want to take credit for their food," which is one of the reasons Yia loves to tell their story.

"This is my mom and dad's food. Here is the story of my people. My goal is to tell the story of my mom and dad. If you also see Hmong culture through the food, it is a plus. We care about the story of our food, and we should know about the 'why' of it."

Yia spoke about food trends being nothing new. "Nose to tail? We call that a Tuesday," he laughed. "There is a cultural ebb and flow of trend. Look at fish sauce. Credit has to be given to the right culture." Yia's definition of appropriation is when white culture claims to have discovered something new without giving credit to the culture it comes from. Pay homage to those cultures by *giving* them a voice, he urges, don't *become* their voice.

"Every dish has a narrative. I may not agree with someone politically, but I can have empathy. We talk a lot about how we disagree, but we agree on much. People all have the same feelings of love, pain, loss, envy, grief. Pain doesn't discriminate. That is where we connect, at the soul level." And food, Yia believes, is the ultimate equalizer. "Food and weather are the two things people rally around regardless of politics, race, culture, sexuality. Food is more than sustenance. If we put aside what makes us different and see how we agree, we can sit down and have a great conversation."

Speaking with Yia renewed my own gratitude and resolve. As the nation continues stumbling down divisive paths, solutions are buried under rhetoric. To survive we need to take action as individuals. Plant more trees, stop using plastic, be kind to one another, and return to conversations about the things that matter to all of us. The place to begin difficult conversations is where we agree. When all else fails, sit down together over a delicious hotdish.

Minnesota Hmong Hotdish

SERVES 9–12

Chef Yia demonstrated this recipe at the Minnesota State Fair.

For the curry sauce

2 tablespoons canola oil
½ cup chopped white onion
1 tablespoon chopped galangal
1 tablespoon chopped fresh ginger
1 tablespoon chopped garlic
1 tablespoon minced lemongrass
2 Thai lime leaves

⅓ cup red curry paste (Mae Ploy brand)
2 tablespoons smoked paprika
Korean chili flakes (optional; to taste)
2 quarts (8 cups) coconut milk (Chaokoh brand)
salt

Add oil to a deep pot over medium heat and add onions, galangal, ginger, garlic, lemongrass, and lime leaves. Stir in curry paste, paprika, and chili flakes (if using), reduce heat to medium-low, and cook until fond (brown crust) forms on the bottom of the pan; be careful not to burn the aromatics. Stir in the coconut milk and let sauce simmer for 15 to 20 minutes. Pour mixture into blender or food processor fitted with a metal blade and puree. Pour through a fine-mesh strainer. Discard solids.

If you want a thicker sauce, return sauce to pot and reduce over medium heat. Season with salt to taste.

NOTE
You will have leftover curry sauce. Use it all week long to flavor chicken, fish, pork, or vegetables: cook the protein and vegetables directly in the curry and serve over rice.

For the hotdish

vegetable oil
1 pound Hmong sausage (Lowry Hills Meats), or substitute ground pork
1 cup chopped turnips
1 cup chopped carrots
1 cup chopped white onion

1 cup chopped parsnip
salt and pepper
3 cups curry sauce
1 (16-ounce) bag tater tots
cilantro, green onions, lime wedge for serving

Grease a 13x9–inch (3-quart) casserole dish; set aside. Heat oven to 375 degrees.

In a large skillet or sauté pan over medium-high heat, add 1–2 tablespoons oil and the sausage and cook for 15 minutes (or until meat is no longer pink), stirring frequently to break up the sausage.

Place pork in a large bowl. Add a little more oil to the skillet along with the turnips, carrots, onions, and parsnips; season with salt and pepper and cook until tender. Add the pork to the vegetables, then add the curry sauce. Stir well to combine.

Fill prepared pan with vegetable-pork mixture. Top with tater tots. Bake for 30 minutes. Serve with chopped cilantro, chopped green onions, and a wedge of lime (squeeze the lime over tater tots).

Life Beneath the Snow

The color of night changes with the first snowfall. Light reflects from the white outdoors into my bedroom, and I wake surrounded by soft blue. The first snowfall has a smell, a glow, and a quiet comfort.

Our neighbor works the night shift and sometimes arrives home before dawn to shovel a path in the backyard for their Boston Terriers. The familiar rasp and scrape, rasp and scrape is the cadence that lulls me back to sleep. My dreams are clean landscapes, calm and inherited from this place I call home: North.

I am hypersensitive about the vernacular used by Minnesota's meteorologists. I bristle when these weather reporters use subjective terms like *bad, bleak, severe, threatening,* or *inclement* when describing cold temperatures and snow. Unless it is sunny and seventy-five, Minnesotans are bombarded with negativity about our weather, as if Minnesota winter is shocking and unnatural. As if we should hide away in our homes or move to Florida to escape our frozen wasteland. What's worse is how contagious a bad attitude about weather is. A recent weather report describing the warmest winter on record was followed by the elated anchors extolling the fact that our local temps were finally above zero.

In 2015 *Washington Post* writer Christopher Ingraham wrote that Red Lake Falls, Minnesota, was "the absolute worst place to live in America," after a USDA map ranked America's counties by climate and scenery. The offended citizens of northern Minnesota invited Ingraham up to experience for himself the absolute worst place to live in America. Ingraham was so impressed with what he saw that he moved to Red Lake County with his family. He has since embraced our coldest season, and his words in a January 2020 piece about thriving during winter resonated with me:

> Winter's future is uncertain. By the end of the century many of us Up North may have to trade in our skis for mud boots and our snowmobiles for ATVs, while our Christmases fade from white to brown. In a rapidly warming climate, winter is something to be cherished. I'd even say there's a moral obligation to get out and enjoy it while we can, before it melts away. A half-century from

now, when my grandchildren ask me what winters were like when there was still ice at the North Pole, the last thing I want to tell them is, "I don't know—I stayed inside because it was too cold."

Ingraham and I are not alone. Askov Finlayson is a Minneapolis fashion brand founded by brothers (and former Minnesota governor Mark Dayton's sons) Andrew and Eric Dayton. They established a "Keep the North Cold" campaign aimed not only at educating us about how climate change impacts our state, but also at celebrating cold winters. They sell outdoor apparel built for a cold climate (because you cannot celebrate the cold unless you are dressed properly) and are committed to giving 110 percent of the company's climate cost to organizations that are striving to combat our climate crisis (because you cannot celebrate the cold if it no longer exists).

When I was a kid, I spent cold winter afternoons riding a shaggy pony named Tammy across frozen fields, galloping through snowdrifts, and refusing to come inside until my frostbitten feet were so painful I could hardly walk out of the barn. I was never a great skier, but I loved the outfits, and as a teen I'd strap on a pair of ancient cross-country skis to toddle about the neighborhood. Cross-country skiing is called Nordic skiing now, and I'd lose my Scandinavian cred if anyone ever witnessed my endeavors. Biking in the winter was my favorite pastime for years, and I recall one morning when windchills were negative thirty and a guy passing me in his car rolled down his window to shout insults at me for being out enjoying myself. Today, nothing much beats the joy of taking an evening winter walk with my husband when feathery flakes envelop us. Our boots crunch on top of the snow, our breath comes out wispy in the cold air, and the whole world sparkles with potential when you live inside a snow globe.

But my love of outdoor winter activities is probably not the story you came here to read. The gist of this narrative is that I love Minnesota winters. But I don't love winter just because I love the cold. I also love winter because of the food.

New Year's Eve Fondue

On New Year's Eve Mom took out the special fondue plates with the sections for dipping sauce, and we fried steak bites in hot oil. Each plate was a different color, and the tops of our fondue forks matched the colors of our plates. I filled each plate divot with a different sauce and waited impatiently for the steak to come out of the fondue pot.

It wasn't until I was in college that I discovered cheese fondue. I quickly realized cheese fondue was easier to pull together and clean up than fried meat, and soon Gruyère replaced grease in my fondue pot. Rarely do I revisit Mom's fried fondue, but when I do, I vow to myself I'll make it more often. There is room for both at my table.

Regardless of the fondue base, I always serve a light salad on the side as well as good crusty bread and plenty of wine.

Steak Fondue

SERVES 4

canola, grapeseed, or peanut oil
1 pound filet mignon, tenderloin,
   or sirloin, cut across grain into
   1½-inch cubes and patted dry

salt and pepper
sauces for dipping (recipes follow)

Pour oil into fondue pot according to manufacturer's instructions. Heat oil to 375 degrees (to test oil, drop a small cube of bread into pot; it should turn brown but not burn in less than a minute).

Generously season steak cubes with salt and pepper and then skewer using fondue forks and place in hot oil. Cooking time varies: 25–30 seconds for rare, 30–35 seconds for medium, and 45–60 seconds for well done. Remove from heat and cool slightly before transferring to a table fork, dipping, and eating.

Curry Dip

MAKES ABOUT 2 CUPS

FAY LEYDEN

1½ cups mayonnaise
1 tablespoon grated onion
2 teaspoons curry powder
½ teaspoon dry mustard

½ teaspoon salt
pepper and hot pepper sauce
   (Tabasco) to taste

Mix all ingredients in a small bowl; cover and refrigerate for 2 hours or more before serving.

Steak Sauce

MAKES ABOUT 1 CUP

½ cup ketchup
zest and juice from 1 orange
2 tablespoons cider vinegar
1 tablespoon Dijon-style mustard
1 tablespoon brown sugar

2 teaspoons Worcestershire sauce
¾ teaspoon garlic powder
1 tablespoon butter, cold
salt and pepper

In a small saucepan, whisk together ketchup, orange zest and juice, vinegar, mustard, brown sugar, Worcestershire, and garlic powder. Place over medium heat and bring to a simmer. Simmer gently for 5 minutes. Remove from heat and whisk in butter. When butter is melted, season to taste with salt and pepper.

Gjetost and Hard Cider Fondue

SERVES 4–6

Whey cheese is technically not cheese: it is a dairy product made from the by-product of cheesemaking. The Nordic countries have several versions: gjetost (goat's cheese), brunost (brown cheese), and mesost (whey cheese). Gjetost is a Norwegian cheese made from caramelized whey and cream. It is made from goat and/or cow milk products and has a sweetness and a fudge-like consistency that, if you didn't grow up eating it, might blow your mind when you first taste it. It is most common as a sandwich or crispbread topping, but a cooking class student of mine told me about the whey cheese gravy her family makes to serve alongside their Christmas Eve meatballs. The gravy's combination of gjetost and sour cream was too intriguing not to try, and I've been making it ever since.

There are too many variations to cheese fondue to count, but none matches this cozy Nordic fondue. I add cream cheese to replicate the tang of the gjetost gravy's sour cream and replace the wine in common cheese fondue with local hard apple cider, dry rather than sweet.

I was at our neighborhood wine store conferring with my wine guy, Mark, about this recipe. I explained that I wanted a dry hard cider for a gjetost fondue. Another customer sidled up to us. His eyes brightened and he exclaimed, "Gjetost! That's Norwegian goat cheese!" I described the fondue, and the gentleman asked, "What is your address?" I think he'll approve of this dish even more once he tastes it.

> **NOTE** *I used organic dry cider from Keepsake Cidery in Dundas, Minnesota. The cider has a bright, earthy apple flavor.*

4 teaspoons cornstarch
1 tablespoon cider vinegar
1¼ cups hard apple cider, dry not sweet
1 large shallot, minced
1½ cup grated gjetost cheese (or similar caramelized whey)
1 cup grated Gruyère

4 ounces cream cheese
generous pinch fresh ground nutmeg
pinch pepper
1 loaf good crusty bread (such as French baguette), cut into 1-inch cubes
assorted fruits for dipping (such as apples, pears, grapes, and orange sections)

Stir together cornstarch and vinegar in a small bowl until cornstarch dissolves; set aside. Combine hard cider and shallot in a heavy pot or saucepan; simmer over medium heat 2 minutes. Remove from heat and stir in all of the cheese until melty and well combined. Stir in cornstarch mixture and return pot to medium heat. Stir until cheeses melt into a smooth sauce and mixture begins to simmer and thicken slightly. Season fondue with nutmeg and pepper.

Transfer to fondue pot and keep warm. Serve with bread cubes and fruit.

> **NOTE** *If cider is too hot when cheese is added, there is a risk of the mixture breaking. If fondue breaks or clumps, add a few additional tablespoons of warm cider. Use a whisk to break any cream cheese lumps.*

Snow Days

The first time I heard of windchill was my sixteenth birthday. It was negative sixty outside on that January evening, and I was all set to go to a boyfriend's hockey game when my mother's good sense prevailed. I spent my sweet sixteen at home on a Saturday night. Saturday is bad timing for windchills. But nothing beats a good old-fashioned Snow Day.

A Snow Day is that official declaration of a snowfall so deep, so heavy, so wonderful that snow plows can't keep up and buses cannot push through it, and a free day, an unexpected vacation, is bestowed upon every kid within the vicinity of the blizzard. (Except for those suckers in the districts that stay open. Woe to those kids living in the inner city where the schools never seem to close.) A snow day is not the same thing as a pathetic two-hour delay (why bother?), not a "buses will be delayed but we expect to start on time," but an ENTIRE DAY.

Every mom and dad listened to WCCO. The "Old Person Station," I called it. WCCO read the snow day list before any other station, so we kids accepted Boone and Erickson's slow articulation of the endless alphabetical lineup of closings and delays. Patiently we'd wait to hear the name of our school, and when it was reported we'd let out wild hoots and hollers while running around the house in jubilant celebration.

This particular snow day ritual makes it impossible to go back to bed once a snow day is declared. Your nerves are rattled, your voice is hoarse from screaming with joy, and the fresh snow beckons. Nowadays kids have alerts texted directly to their mobiles. I wonder if the delayed gratification of waiting to hear your school name makes news of a snow day more exciting, or if the rarity of the event these days is plenty enough to whip modern kids into a snow-induced frenzy.

Regardless of how you receive the news, snow days are rites of passage in the North. Kids spend the morning shoveling and the afternoon harnessed to sleds and skates and skis. A good snow day is complete with mugs of hot chocolate. Swiss Miss is the universal choice, unless your older siblings dabble in cookery and can make real hot chocolate.

There is no single best thing about snow days: the ritual of waiting to hear your school announced, the luxury of a surprise vacation, the hard work and play, the comfort of hot chocolate, and the camaraderie that comes with it. Rosy cheeks and snow-burned skin, the odor of wet wool against your face, tracks of melting snow from the entry to wherever a kid pulls off her boots, and mittens warming over the radiator—all familiar comfort to children from Minnesota.

Hot Chocolate

SERVES 2

⅓ cup water
3 tablespoons cocoa powder
2–3 cups whole milk
½ vanilla pod
sugar
**marshmallows, whipped cream, and/or
chocolate shavings for serving**

In a medium saucepan, bring water to boiling;
whisk in cocoa powder. Reduce heat to
medium and add milk and vanilla pod, stirring
to combine; heat but do not allow to scald or
boil. When milk is hot, add sugar to taste. Pour
into mugs and garnish with marshmallows,
whipped cream, or chocolate shavings. (If you
are a kid, find the stash of maraschino cherries
your parents hide in the back of the fridge and
add one to your mug.)

Hotdish Culture: Tater Tot Nation

Arguments about what defines a hotdish versus a casserole abound. I always thought hotdishes must contain a can of cream-of-something soup because that was what I grew up with. Now I understand that hotdishes and casseroles are relatively identical, and the category simply denotes where the cook comes from. I come from a hotdish family, and therefore casseroles rarely appear on my table (the exception is tuna noodle, which is either called tuna noodle casserole or simply sans designation).

Around Minnesota, hotdish competitions are part of our culture. Neighborhoods, offices, schools, and churches host friendly contests where home cooks spar for the title "Best Hotdish." Even fancy restaurants and acclaimed chefs are part of the fun. The Lexington, a supper club in the capital city, throws the "Fancy Hotdish Competition" as part of the St. Paul Winter Carnival festivities. The event is complete with paired cocktails and local celebrity judges. The hotdishes contain components like smoked salmon, colossal stuffed tater tots, braised beef, and duck fat. Canned soup is a rare ingredient in the fancy hotdish domain.

Canned soup was considered a convenience food when it began rolling into grocery stores across America around the turn of the last century, first as a luxury item for the wealthy, and then by the start of World War II as an economical addition to American tables.

In 2016 *Food & Wine* credited Mankato, Minnesota's *Grace Lutheran Ladies Aid Cookbook* for publishing the first hotdish recipe in 1930. The concoction included ground beef, Creamette brand elbow macaroni, and canned peas. In 1934 Campbell's introduced their condensed creamed soups. When our great-grandmothers and grandmothers reached for the cans to bind their hotdishes, an entire new food group was created.

Campbell's cream-of-something was particularly popular, and remains so, mixed with some ground meat, vegetables, and a starch. Edie Schmierbach defined hotdish (or hot dish) in the Associated Press: "To qualify as a hot dish, recipes should call for a combination of protein (tuna for example), a canned vegetable (peas are popular), a starch (maybe mashed potatoes) and a binding sauce (perhaps a can of cream of mushroom). For crunch, cooks may add tater tots, chow mein noodles or crushed potato chips."

I define hotdishes as containing a protein, starch (tater tots are common but not mandatory), usually a vegetable (canned, frozen, or fresh), and binder (canned cream-of-something soup is common, but again, not mandatory). Recipes that call for canned cream soup can also be made with the following substitute.

Cream-of-Something Soup Substitute

REPLACES 1 (10.75-OUNCE) CAN CONDENSED SOUP

2 tablespoons butter
2 tablespoons very finely chopped white onion
¼ teaspoon salt
¼ teaspoon pepper

2 tablespoons all-purpose flour
1 cup whole milk (broth or ½ cup milk plus ½ cup broth can also be used for a lighter soup), at room temperature

For mushroom soup add:
⅓ cup finely chopped mushrooms

For celery soup add:
½ cup finely chopped celery

Melt butter in a large skillet over medium heat. Add onions (and mushrooms or celery, if using), salt, and pepper, and stir to coat with butter. Cook for 3 to 5 minutes, or until vegetables are just tender. Add flour and continue cooking, stirring or whisking constantly to avoid lumps, for an additional 2 minutes. Slowly add half of liquid, stirring or whisking to make a smooth texture. Add remaining liquid and bring to a simmer. Simmer and continue stirring until mixture is thickened, about 5 minutes. Remove from heat and use as a cream of soup replacement in recipes.

No-Can Tater Tot Hotdish

SERVES 9–12 (DEPENDING ON HUNGER LEVELS
AND HOW BLUSTERY IT IS OUTSIDE)

For the sauce

2 tablespoons butter
2 tablespoons all-purpose flour
1 tablespoon Dijon-style mustard
2 cups whole milk, just warm

1 cup shredded Monterey Jack cheese
½ teaspoon pepper
pinch fresh ground nutmeg

Add butter and flour to a saucepan and place over medium heat. Whisk constantly as butter melts and blends with flour. Add mustard and continue whisking for 3 to 5 minutes. Slowly whisk in milk so that the mixture is completely blended. Remove from heat and stir in 1 cup cheese and seasonings. Set aside.

For the filling

1 tablespoon butter
10 ounces mushrooms, chopped
1 medium white or yellow onion,
     chopped (about 1 cup)
1 pound lean ground beef or turkey

1 teaspoon fresh thyme
2 medium zucchinis, chopped
     (about 2 cups)
2 tablespoons tomato paste
salt and pepper

In a large skillet, melt butter over medium-high heat. Add mushrooms and onions and cook until the mushrooms begin to release their liquid and onions are soft and translucent, 5 to 7 minutes. Make space in middle of skillet and add ground meat and thyme. Increase heat to cook (not steam) meat. Cook, stirring, for about 8 to 10 minutes, using spoon or spatula to break up meat and combine with vegetables. Add zucchini and tomato paste and mix well; cook an additional 2 minutes. Season with salt and pepper.

For the topping

1 pound frozen tater tots
½ cup shredded Monterey Jack cheese

To assemble

Heat oven to 350 degrees. Generously grease bottom and sides of a 13x9–inch (3-quart) casserole dish. Add filling and top with all but ½ cup of the sauce. Top evenly with tater tots, reserved sauce, and ½ cup cheese. Cover with foil and bake for 30 minutes. Remove foil and continue baking 20 minutes or until cheese is melted and golden. Let hotdish stand for 10 minutes before serving.

No-Can Fish and Noodle Hotdish

SERVES 12

16 ounces thin egg noodles
3 tablespoons butter
3 tablespoons all-purpose flour
½ cup finely chopped bell pepper
½ cup finely chopped white onion
1 teaspoon Old Bay Seasoning
2 cups warm chicken broth
1½ cups whole milk, warmed
½ cup crème fraîche (see page 128)
½ cup shredded Parmesan cheese

8 ounces smoked fish (such as trout, whitefish, or salmon), bones and skin removed and fish broken into coarse pieces
1 cup frozen peas
fresh ground nutmeg
zest of 1 lemon
2 cups crushed plain potato chips
Everything Bagel Seasoning (optional)
fresh dill and chives for garnish

Heat oven to 350 degrees. Generously coat a 13x9–inch (3-quart) casserole dish with nonstick spray.

Fill a large stockpot with generously salted water and bring to a boil. Add noodles and cook to al dente according to package directions. Drain and set aside.

In a large stockpot, melt butter and whisk in flour, bell pepper, onions, and Old Bay. Whisk over medium-low heat until well blended; mixture may clump, but continue cooking and whisking for 3 to 5 minutes. Slowly add broth and milk, whisking constantly until sauce is well blended. Bring to a low simmer, whisking constantly, and cook 3 minutes or until sauce thickens. Remove from heat and stir in crème fraîche and Parmesan.

Gently fold in fish, peas, and noodles. Place in prepared baking dish and top evenly with nutmeg to taste, lemon zest, and potato chips. Cover and bake 30 minutes; uncover, sprinkle generously with Everything Bagel Seasoning if desired, and bake an additional 5 to 10 minutes or until chips are just toasted golden. Let hotdish rest for 10 minutes before serving. Garnish with fresh dill and chives.

SPAM Potato Hotdish

SERVES 4

SPAM is one of those Minnesota products that we are both proud and sheepish to claim as ours. When Minnesotans hear that Hawaiians eat more SPAM than we do, we might step up our consumption a little bit so as not to be shamed for shunning our hometown luminary. There is even a SPAM Museum in Austin, Minnesota, where Hormel reigns supreme. SPAM is a canned pork product with a name mysteriously derived. Perhaps it means SPiced hAM, or Special Processed American Meat.

Arriving home just before supper, I always knew when it was SPAM hotdish night. The aroma coming from the kitchen was intoxicating to a hungry kid who had spent her afternoon playing in the snow.

4 medium Yukon Gold or
   russet potatoes
1 (12-ounce) can SPAM
2 tablespoons butter
¼ cup finely chopped white onion
¼ cup finely chopped celery
2 tablespoons all-purpose flour

2½ cups whole milk, warmed
1 cup shredded cheese (Gruyère or
   Cheddar works great)
salt, pepper, and nutmeg
½ cup panko breadcrumbs

Heat oven to 350 degrees. Grease an 8- or 9-inch square cake pan; set aside.

Peel potatoes and place in large stockpot. Cover with salted water by 1 inch and bring to a boil. Reduce heat to low; cover and simmer 10 to 15 minutes or until potatoes are almost tender. Drain and cool until potatoes can be handled. Chop into ½-inch cubes and place in large mixing bowl.

Dice SPAM into ½-inch cubes and fry over medium-high heat in a large nonstick skillet until sides are seared (add a bit of nonstick spray if needed). Remove from skillet and toss with potatoes. Spoon into prepared pan.

Return skillet to medium-high heat and add butter, onion, and celery; cook until vegetables are just tender, stirring occasionally, about 3 minutes. Add flour and whisk to combine; cook an additional 3 minutes. Slowly add 1 cup of the milk, whisking continuously to remove any lumps. Add remaining milk and stir over medium-high heat until mixture begins to simmer and thicken. Lower heat and stir in cheese. When cheese is melted, remove pot from heat and season to taste with salt, pepper, and nutmeg. Pour sauce over potatoes and SPAM. Top hotdish evenly with breadcrumbs and bake for 30 minutes or until crumbs are golden and crispy.

Meatball Pinwheel Hotdish

SERVES 8 GENEROUSLY   FAY LEYDEN

The weeknights when my mom served her meatball hotdish were special. I gravitated toward meat and bread, and never missed vegetables when they failed to make an appearance on my plate. A good dollop of ketchup over the meatballs made this meal feel like a party.

For the meatballs

1 pound ground beef
½ pound pork sausage
½ cup dried breadcrumbs
½ cup evaporated milk
2 tablespoons minced white onion

1 tablespoon minced curly parsley
2 teaspoons chili powder
1 teaspoon salt
½ teaspoon pepper

Heat oven to 400 degrees. Grease a 2½- to 3-quart casserole dish; set aside.

Combine all ingredients and mix well. Shape into about 25 meatballs, about 2 tablespoons each. Add a tablespoon of vegetable oil to a large skillet and, working in batches so you do not crowd the skillet, sear all sides of meatballs. Return all seared meatballs to the skillet and add ⅓ cup of water. Cover and cook on medium-low heat for 10 minutes. Transfer meatballs to prepared dish and arrange in a single layer.

For the binder/gravy

1 (10.75-ounce) can condensed cream of mushroom soup
1 (10.75-ounce) can condensed cream of celery soup

1 cup evaporated milk
½ cup water

Combine all ingredients in a large pot and bring to a simmer over medium-high heat. Pour over meatballs.

For the biscuits

1⅓ cups all-purpose flour
1 tablespoon baking powder
½ teaspoon chili powder
¼ teaspoon salt
⅓ cup butter, cold, cut into
    1-teaspoon chunks

⅓ cup evaporated milk
1 large egg
1½ cups shredded Cheddar
1 tablespoon minced curly parsley

In a large mixing bowl, whisk together flour, baking powder, chili powder, and salt. Cut in butter until mixture looks mealy. Add milk and egg and stir until just combined. Knead on lightly floured surface 10 times. Roll out into a 12-inch square. Sprinkle with cheese and parsley. Roll up and cut into 8 slices.

Place biscuits evenly over meatballs. Bake for 25 minutes, or until biscuits are slightly golden and cooked through.

Diary of a Minnesota Congressional Delegation Hotdish Competition Judge

In DC it was as hot as August in Minnesota, but back home folks were bracing for a blizzard. We were an assortment of travelers standing in what we hoped was the Upper Level Door 3 of the Washington National Airport where our Lyfts, shuttles, and Uber apps directed us to meet our drivers to save us from the sweaty April heat and take us to our hotels and Airbnbs.

My driver reprimanded me for selecting the Upper Level because he'd circled for a few minutes below, but he was friendly enough as we sped past the National Mall where ten years earlier I was a grad student and peripheral member of the University of Minnesota ICON Solar House team at the US Department of Energy competition. Twenty little modular homes were set up right on the mall, and I was our team's cook. We had two dinner parties in the houses with team members from other houses as guests. It was surreal and amazing, and for a week I felt like I lived right there between the Lincoln Memorial and the Washington Monument, which I could see out the kitchen window as I washed up each night. How cool is that?

I returned to Washington to embark on another really cool adventure. I was in DC to judge the Minnesota Congressional Delegation Hotdish Competition. It was the ninth annual, having its roots with Senator Al Franken thanks to input from his press secretary, Maggie Rousseau. Maggie continues the tradition, which brings together both sides of the aisle in an increasingly combative political world. Minnesotans, showing everyone else what it takes to have a meaningful discussion, even if the topic is how best to showcase tater tots. The best conversations often begin in the kitchen.

That night, driving past the glowing monuments, the beauty of the Capitol made me breathless. For a moment I forgot the politics that continued to divide us.

In the morning my nephew Oliver found me, and we took the Metro from Dupont Circle to Dirksen Senate Office Building. Oliver went to college in DC and had acted as Minnesota senator Amy Klobuchar's intern the year prior. His good company and knowledge of the map made him an excellent companion. As we stood in the security line, a parade of assistants marched behind a man I didn't recognize. The man held a foil-covered hotdish with the reverence of Rafiki presenting Simba on Pride Rock. The ensemble left the building with much fanfare, and I wondered if they were non-midwesterners attempting to make casserole cook-offs a thing.

We made our way to the hotdish room, where dozens of reporters were already vying to be closest to the display table, jostling cameras of every shape and size and positioning furry microphones. Senator Tina Smith's press secretary Molly Morrissey greeted us and got me settled on the judge's side of the large hearing room. I familiarized myself with the judging sheet. Along the left column were boxes for Hotdish 1 through 10, and the top row designated the point scale: up to ten points for taste, five for originality, and five for presentation (meaning the inclusion of starch, dairy product, protein, and Minnesota ingredients). A disclaimer on the bottom of the sheet stated that in the event of a tie the master of ceremonies would cast the winning vote. Contrary to public perception, politicians can be proactive when it comes to making decisions.

We three judges introduced ourselves, and as the room continued to fill with reporters, the Minnesota congressional members and their interns arrived with hotdishes and varied components of flair: a Minnesota-shaped baking dish cradled something covered in foil, hotdish towels and a matching hot pad blinged out a tater tot number, while Representative Angie Craig and her interns added a basketball hoop, foam finger, and cheese ball "basketballs" to construct a hotdish basketball court honoring Minnesota's WNBA Champion Lynx. The packed room filled with conversation, laughter, and delicious smells. I heard a story about Minnesota governor Tim Walz's reign as hotdish champion: "He won three times, and he and his staff made quite a production. They'd form a parade with his trophies and the hotdish."

We judges sat at a table while, one by one, samples of hotdish were placed before us. We tasted, we assessed, we scored. Finally, we conferred and realized that we agreed on the top three dishes. "If the Lynx hotdish came with the cheese ball garnish, it would have been a contender," I offered. "And if the curry hotdish was a little spicier, it would be my winner." The other two judges nodded, and our tallied sheets were confirmed before the winner was announced.

Across America there was a rise in anti-immigrant sentiment and racist rhetoric, and it was not lost on me that our three favorite hotdishes represented the flavors of new immigrants: Representative Betty McCollum's Hotdish A-Hmong Friends, Representative Ilhan Omar's Little Moga-hot-dishu, and Representative Dean Phillips's From Monrovia with Love: Liberian Inspired Hotdish. Diversity doesn't only make us stronger; diversity also gives us amazing flavors. I was reminded of Chef Yia Vang, who introduced me to Hmong hotdish that tells his story of food, place, and belonging (see page 4).

You learn a lot about a person when you eat their hotdish. To sit down together at the table has always symbolized an understanding and even a certain intimacy. The food we serve represents our culture and values, our likes and dislikes, and our history. That means that I appreciate your tuna noodle regardless of whether your peas are canned or frozen (but if you really want to get my admiration, you'd better top it with a thick layer of potato chips before baking). The heart of hotdish is its humble wisdom. Hotdish is not grandiose. It is a good Minnesotan who refrains from discussing their disappointment in your voting record before you've finished dessert.

Minnesota is not a melting pot. We are a hotdish.

WINNER

Hotdish A-Among Friends

SERVES 14–16 REPRESENTATIVE BETTY MCCOLLUM

1 (16-ounce) bag tater tots
½ cup plus 1 tablespoon vegetable oil
4 cloves garlic, minced
1 large onion, finely chopped
2 cups grated carrot
1 small cabbage, quartered and sliced
2 pounds ground beef
½ cup umami seasoning
1½ teaspoons salt

1½ teaspoons pepper
1 (10.75-ounce) can cream of mushroom soup
½ cup whole milk
2 egg roll wrappers, cut into quarters
5 Thai chilis, diced

NOTE
To test this recipe I used Trader Joe's Umami seasoning and added only 3 tablespoons rather than ½ cup. I also used 6 egg roll wrappers because I love crunch. I added a tablespoon of oil to the recipe for sautéing the vegetables.

Heat oven to 350 degrees. Grease the bottoms and sides of a 13x9–inch (3-quart) casserole dish. Add tater tots to cover the bottom of the dish.

Add 1 tablespoon of the oil to a large skillet over medium heat. Add garlic and cook, stirring, for 1 minute. Add onion and cook until translucent, stirring frequently, about 3 minutes. Add carrots and cabbage and cook until cabbage wilts, stirring frequently, about 5 minutes. Transfer veggies to plate and set aside.

Add ground beef to skillet and cook over medium-high heat for about 10 minutes, using a wooden spoon or spatula to break up the meat as it cooks. Return veggies to the pan. Add umami seasoning, salt, and pepper, and stir to combine well. Transfer mixture to hotdish pan, covering tater tots.

In a large mixing bowl, whisk together cream of mushroom soup with milk and pour over meat and vegetables. Bake for 30 minutes.

While hotdish is baking, add remaining ½ cup oil to saucepan over medium-high heat. When temperature reaches 350 degrees, add egg roll wrapper pieces and fry 1 to 2 minutes, using a slotted spoon or spider to move them around for even cooking. Transfer pieces to paper towel–lined baking sheet to cool. Crumble wraps and sprinkle them and the chilis over hotdish 5 minutes before it's done cooking.

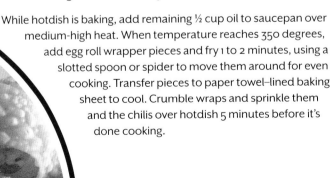

SECOND PLACE

Little Moga-hot-dishu

SERVES 12–14

REPRESENTATIVE ILHAN OMAR

Inspired by Worthy Pause Samosa Chaatdish (Indian Tater Tot Hotdish)

I woke up early on a Sunday morning to make Representative Omar's hotdish, and after the third onion I was crying so hard I had to take a break and mince the jalapeños. Soon my hands were perfumed with garlic and ginger, and my kitchen was fragrant with warm spices that reminded me of why I love cold weather and cozy homes. This hotdish takes time to prep, and it is worth every moment spent caramelizing onions and chopping vegetables. As I ate a first, then second plate, I thought about all of the ways I will riff on the original recipe—like using sweet potato tater tots instead of white potato and adding a good dose of cayenne to wake up eaters. A bonus to this hotdish is how healthy it is! I'd expect nothing less from former SNAP educator Omar (see note below).

4 medium yellow onions, minced fine
ghee or olive oil
salt
2 tablespoons seeded and minced jalapeño (approximately 2 medium chilis)
6 medium cloves garlic, minced
4 teaspoons minced fresh ginger
2 tablespoons garam masala
2 teaspoons ground cumin
2 teaspoons ground coriander
4 teaspoons turmeric
½ teaspoon ground cinnamon
2 pounds ground beef or lamb

pepper
6 Roma tomatoes, finely chopped
2 tablespoons tomato paste
1 (16-ounce) package frozen spinach
juice of 1 lemon (about 3 tablespoons)
1 cup chopped fresh cilantro (a large bunch or two)
1 cup frozen peas (optional)
1 (16-ounce) package tater tots
1 cup plain Greek yogurt (optional)
1 cup coriander chutney (recipe follows)

NOTE *SNAP stands for Supplemental Nutrition Assistance Program, the federal program that provides benefits to low-income families and individuals for purchasing food. Educators from SNAP-Ed provide participants with information on health and nutrition.*

Place a large stockpot or Dutch oven over medium heat. Add onions and cook, stirring frequently, until they start to caramelize, about 5 minutes. Add a tablespoon of ghee or oil to the pan and a pinch or two of salt. Reduce heat to low and cook until the onions are a medium golden color. Be patient: this step can take a little while, but it really lays the groundwork for all the layers of flavor in this dish.

Clear a space in the pan, and add an additional tablespoon of ghee or oil. Add the jalapeño, garlic, and ginger and fry for a minute or two, until fragrant. Then stir to combine. Add the garam masala, cumin, coriander, turmeric, and cinnamon and stir to coat everything. The mixture will be quite dry at this point.

Remove about half of the masala-onion mixture and set aside. Add half the ground meat to the pot, sprinkle with salt and pepper, and brown as you combine it thoroughly with the onion mixture. Remove and set aside. Repeat with remaining meat and masala-onions. When all the meat is browned, return first batch to the pot.

Stir in the tomatoes and tomato paste and sprinkle with a little more salt. Simmer on low, covered, stirring occasionally, about 15–20 minutes or until the tomatoes melt into the stew. Stir in the frozen spinach, lemon juice, and about half of the chopped cilantro. Remove from heat. Taste and adjust spices, salt, and pepper as needed. Stir in the frozen peas (if using).

Heat oven to 350 degrees. Transfer the mixture to a 13x9–inch (3-quart) casserole dish. Top with a single layer of tater tots. Bake for 40–50 minutes or until the tots are crispy and golden brown.

Serve with the remaining fresh cilantro, plain yogurt, coriander chutney, and bonus chaat toppings (see below).

Coriander Chutney

MAKES ABOUT 1½ CUPS

1 cup minced fresh cilantro	2 teaspoons lemon juice
¼ cup minced mint	½ teaspoon ground cumin
1 inch fresh ginger, grated	olive oil
1 green chili, minced	salt

In a medium mixing bowl, stir together cilantro, mint, ginger, chili, lemon juice, and cumin. Stir in enough olive oil to make a loose paste. Season with salt to taste.

Bonus chaat toppings: minced raw onions, sweet tamarind chutney, sev (crunchy Indian chickpea noodle snacks), a sprinkle of chaat masala, chana masala

THIRD PLACE

From Monrovia with Love: Liberian Inspired Hotdish

SERVES 20   REPRESENTATIVE DEAN PHILLIPS

2 medium sweet potatoes, peeled and finely chopped

2 medium yams, peeled and finely chopped

2 cubes chicken bouillon

2 pounds chicken, finely chopped

salt and pepper

¼ cup vegetable oil

1 large onion, finely chopped

1 orange bell pepper, finely chopped

1 habañero chili, seeds removed and flesh finely chopped

2 medium cassava (fresh or frozen, thawed), peeled and finely chopped

4 cups chicken broth

3 ripe plantains, sliced into thin rounds

3 cups red palm oil

1 pound shrimp, peeled, deveined, finely chopped

12 ounces Gouda, grated

2 cups packaged crispy fried onions (such as French's or Lars Own), crushed

3 cups plain cornflakes, crushed

Grease a 4-quart casserole dish. Place sweet potatoes and yams in salted water and set aside. Boil 4 cups water; dissolve bouillon cubes in hot water.

Season chicken with salt and pepper. Heat vegetable oil in large Dutch oven over medium heat and add chicken, cooking for 15 minutes, until browned. Add onion, bell pepper, habañero, bouillon, and cassava and cook for an additional 10 minutes. Drain potatoes from salted water and add to the pan. Add chicken broth and simmer for 20 minutes, until potatoes are tender.

Remove half of potato-meat mixture and 2 cups broth and set aside to cool. When cool, use a blender to puree until smooth.

Add sliced plantains to pot and cook for an additional 10 minutes. Add palm oil and continue to simmer on low until palm oil is completely melted. Add shrimp and stir.

Heat oven to 350 degrees. Add blended mixture to pot, stir to combine, then ladle mixture into prepared pan. Top with light layer of grated Gouda. Mix remaining cheese with crispy onions and cornflakes and spread evenly over hotdish mixture. Bake for 30 minutes, until mixture is bubbling and toppings are golden brown.

NOTE *Instead of bouillon cubes I used "Better than Bouillon," which comes in a jar. The original recipe calls for cooking the shrimp for 10 minutes before adding it to the hotdish. I added the shrimp raw and it cooked while the hotdish baked, but that step does not necessarily jibe with food safety. If you have concerns about adding raw shrimp to your cooked dish before baking, give the shrimp a quick sauté in a hot pan before adding to the mix. You will need very large pots (9 to 10 quarts) for preparation as this recipe feeds a crowd.*

Meat Raffle

It was a pink-flesh peep show: packages of chops, roasts, an eight-pack of kosher dogs, bacon, and chicken wings propped up in bins loaded with ice on top of a long folding table. Between the meat parade and the plexiglass-enclosed pull-tab booth, the afternoon hostess sorted cash in a till drawer and dumped numbered tickets into a red plastic fry basket.

Folding tables and chairs filled about two-thirds of the VFW in orderly rows. Patrons began wandering in, sitting in groups and ordering tap beer. Some pooled dollars in the center of the table. Coolers at the ready collected beneath tables; players were breathless with anticipation: the meat raffle was about to begin.

"Meat raffle?" you ask. "What the heck is a meat raffle?" You must not be from around here.

The VFW hostess called the start of the first round, and players lined up eight-deep to buy dollar tickets. Each raffle had thirty tickets per round, and they sold fast. The hostess sold tickets, prepared the next spin's tray, marched to a paddlewheel, spun the wheel, and called the winning number over the intercom at the bar.

The first few rounds were orderly, organized, and subdued. Before long a chorus of good-natured "Boos!" erupted as a petite blonde came running from the back room, à la a *Price Is Right* contestant, to claim her meat.

"She wins *every* week!" a woman at the bar told me. The blonde selected a package of beef and pork roasts, winked at the hecklers, and held the meat overhead like an Olympic-medal winner.

The raffle began to heat up, and so too did the jeering. Two guys seated near the paddlewheel won a second round and received genial hisses. They told me they'd cook up all their winnings to enjoy while watching the Vikings play the Bears the next day. The chairs around their table were stacked high with white plastic bags: they'd have plenty of bacon, steak, and chicken for game day.

When it was over, the winners left to stash their meat in cold cars, and the losers consoled themselves with games of pool and college football on the big-screen TVs. Useless spoils of war covered the bar and tables: towers of losing raffle tickets and pull-tabs, baskets of popcorn hulls, empty beer glasses.

We gather in places like the VFW to commune with regulars, to tear open pull-tabs while filling the gaps between raffle spins, and to hang out where no one bats an eye if you order a third beer before 1 PM. Meat raffles are so woven into the landscape that many of us never notice them. Across Minnesota and

Wisconsin meat raffles happen at VFWs, sports and dive bars, and hipster bowling alleys. They are common in inner-city neighborhoods, in the eastern Twin Cities suburbs, in farm communities, and across the Iron Range. Throughout the cold months of winter, meat raffling is a way of life. We even clamor to win plant-based jerky, ham roast, and Brie when local vegan deli Herbivorous Butcher holds their meat-free raffle each year.

In recent years a new generation adopted the tradition, as twenty- and thirty-somethings found their way to the joys of winning packages of strip steaks and chops. But make no mistake: meat raffles are to meat as bowling is to exercise. They are a great excuse to experience community. If you are lucky you might bring home a good roast, or an entire box of meat, as did my friend Danny Sussman. He bragged about winning the meat box on social media.

"There was a LOT of meat in the box," he told me. "It was the grand prize at the raffle. A hundred dollars' worth of meat." *What do you do with a hundred dollars' worth of meat?* I wondered. Danny gave me details that made me hungry and reminded me what an enthusiastic food guy he is. When he isn't gambling for meat, Danny shares his opinions on snack foods from around the world on the *Food Scientists Podcast*. Danny says that while he isn't an actual food scientist, he does know how to experiment with Dairy Queen Blizzards and all-you-can-eat buffets to maximize value in both cost and calories. He's also an excellent cook.

"The filet mignon got very simple treatment on the grill. The boneless pork roast was coated in garlic powder, salt, and pepper and smoked with some chunks of hickory for a couple of hours. As good as the pork roast was, the leftovers were even better. Slices became the center of a family favorite recipe—roast pork on garlic bread. What was left after that became the protein in pork fried rice. The sirloin was cut up and frozen in packs to become kebobs. So far I've done some with my own teriyaki sauce, but there will be more as time goes on. The pork chops will eventually get coated in Grill Happy Seasoning [available for purchase at the Minnesota State Fair Peterson's Charbroiled Chicken-n-Chops on a stick stand] and grilled. The country ribs will become pulled pork either smoked on the grill or in a Crock-Pot. The bacon is making appearances in my breakfasts, and half of the ground beef was made into my world-famous onion burger patties. I've always grilled those suckers but turned some into smashed burgers on a griddle on the stove, and holy cow is that amazing with a slice of sharp cheddar."

Danny's Awesome World-Famous Onion Burgers

MAKES 6–7 LARGE PATTIES   DANNY SUSSMAN

1 large yellow onion, finely chopped into ⅛-inch pieces
2½ pounds butcher ground beef
Cheddar slices and onion rolls for serving

In large bowl, work the onion into the beef. (The idea is to knead the onion into the beef so that it is holding as much onion as possible. You should end up with some onion pieces left in the bottom of the bowl.)

I like a big ol' burger, so I form the beef/onion mix into 6-ounce balls that then get flattened into a patty between 1 and 1½ inches thick (with a dimple in the center to keep it from blowing up).

You can take two paths with the patty. Option one is grilling. That's simple. You can also cook it on a griddle, over medium or medium-high heat, pressing it down with a spatula when you first put it on the grill, flipping it somewhat frequently, and pressing it with each flip so that you get a flat burger with caramelized beef and onion on the exterior. Top either one with aged Cheddar and serve on an onion roll with just a little bit of ketchup, and it is AMAZING.

NOTE *Danny uses only butcher ground beef, "not that weird tube stuff—and this is meat raffle beef, of course it's the good stuff with the right fat/beef ratio."*

Pot Roast with Parsnip and Potato Puree and Horseradish Sour Cream

SERVES 4–6

For the pot roast

2- to 3-pound chuck roast
onion salt
dried thyme
2 tablespoons olive oil
1 white or yellow onion,
    chopped coarsely
1 carrot, chopped coarsely

1 stalk celery, chopped coarsely
1 clove garlic, smashed
salt and pepper
1 cup good red wine
about 1 cup beef, chicken, or
    mushroom broth

Coat all sides of roast with a few teaspoons each of onion salt and thyme. Set aside for 1 to 1½ hours.

Heat oven to 300 degrees. Heat 1 tablespoon of the oil in a Dutch oven over medium-high heat, and brown roast all over, about 3 minutes each side. Remove meat from pot and side aside on plate.

Add remaining 1 tablespoon oil to pot and stir in onions, carrot, celery, and garlic. Season with salt and pepper. Reduce heat to medium, and cook vegetables until they just begin to take on color, about 5 minutes. Add wine to vegetables and bring to a simmer. Allow to reduce for about 5 minutes.

Nestle roast in center of pot, over vegetables and wine. Pour in enough broth to cover the roast halfway. Bake, covered, for 1 hour. (Do not allow oven temperature to go above 325 degrees.)

After 1 hour, carefully remove lid and use tongs to flip the roast. Return covered pot to oven, bake for 1 hour, then flip roast again. After the roast has cooked 3 hours, remove it from the oven. Place roast on a plate and cover with foil. Let vegetables cool slightly, then transfer to a food processor. Strain fat from remaining liquid and add strained liquid to processor; puree. Place wire mesh colander over Dutch oven and strain mixture. Discard solids. Bring liquid to a simmer and reduce by half. Season to taste with salt and pepper and serve with warm roast, parsnip and potato puree, and horseradish sour cream.

For the parsnip and potato puree

4 parsnips (about 12 ounces), peeled and sliced

2–3 small Yukon Gold potatoes (about 6 ounces), peeled and cubed

1 clove garlic, smashed

½–1 cup whole milk

½–1 cup half-and-half

4 tablespoons butter

salt and pepper

Add parsnips, potatoes, and garlic to a large stockpot and add enough milk and half-and-half to just cover. Bring to a simmer and cook, uncovered, until the vegetables are tender, about 15 minutes.

Place parsnips and potatoes in food processor with butter; reserve cooking liquid. Process, adding enough of the reserved cooking liquid to make a thick puree. Season to taste with salt and pepper if desired.

For the horseradish sour cream

½ cup sour cream

1–2 tablespoons grated horseradish

salt to taste

lemon juice to taste

Combine all ingredients and refrigerate before serving.

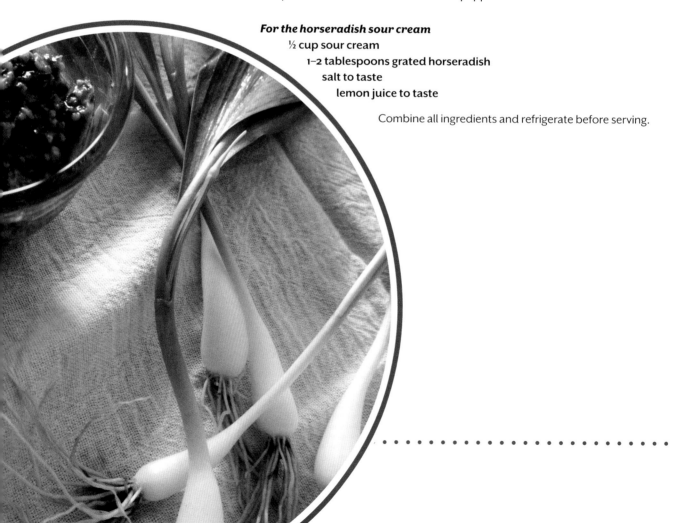

Beef Barley Stew

SERVES 6

2¼–2½ pounds stew meat, cut in
    1-inch pieces
¼ cup all-purpose flour
1½ teaspoons salt
pepper
olive oil
¼ cup dry red wine
4 cups beef broth
½ white onion, finely chopped
3 stalks celery, finely chopped
1 bay leaf
1 tablespoon cider vinegar

¼ teaspoon allspice
1 sprig rosemary
1 tablespoon butter
2 cups mushrooms, trimmed and cut
    into ½-inch pieces
salt
3 large carrots, cut into ½-inch pieces
3½ cups cooked barley (about
    1 cup uncooked)
1–2 tablespoons low-sodium soy
    sauce or tamari

In a very large mixing bowl, toss cubed meat in flour, salt, and pepper so that each cube is coated lightly.

Place a large stockpot or Dutch oven over medium-high heat. Add 1 tablespoon oil to pan and, working in batches, add a third of the meat at a time to sear. Do not crowd pot; add additional oil as necessary. Place seared meat on plate. Pour wine into pot and deglaze, using a flat wooden spoon or spatula to coax fond from bottom of pot. Stir in broth, onion, celery, bay leaf, vinegar, and allspice and bring to a simmer. Return meat to pot; place rosemary sprig on top. Reduce heat, cover, and simmer gently for 1 hour. Remove rosemary and bay leaf. Check tenderness of meat: if the meat is not quite tender, cover and let simmer an additional 30 minutes.

Place a skillet over medium-high heat, add butter and mushrooms, and cook until mushrooms are browned and release their liquid. Season with salt and pepper to taste and remove from heat.

Add mushrooms and carrots to soup and simmer, uncovered, until carrots are tender, about 30 minutes. Add cooked barley and simmer an additional 5 minutes. Season to taste with soy sauce.

Meatball Stroganoff

SERVES 8

For the meatballs

½ cup panko breadcrumbs
½ cup whole milk
1 large egg, beaten
1 clove garlic, minced
1 teaspoon mushroom umami
1 teaspoon onion salt

1 teaspoon dried thyme
1 teaspoon dried dill
½ teaspoon pepper
1 pound ground beef or turkey
vegetable oil and butter for frying

For the sauce

½ white onion, finely chopped
10–12 ounces mushrooms, sliced thin
½ teaspoon pepper
½ cup dry red wine

2 cups low-sodium chicken or beef
    broth, divided
1 tablespoon Worcestershire sauce
2 tablespoons all-purpose flour
1 cup sour cream

For serving

1 pound egg noodles, cooked
    according to package directions,
    then tossed in melted butter and
    fresh minced parsley and/or dill

additional minced fresh parsley
    and/or dill for garnish

TO MAKE MEATBALLS: In a small mixing bowl combine panko, milk, egg, garlic, umami, onion salt, thyme, dill, and pepper. Set aside for 5 minutes. Mixture should look like cooked oatmeal. Place ground meat in a very large mixing bowl, breaking it up into smaller clumps. Pour breadcrumb-milk mixture over meat and gently but thoroughly combine. Form mixture into 20 to 24 small meatballs.

Heat very large nonstick skillet over medium-high heat. Add 2 teaspoons vegetable oil and 1 teaspoon butter to the skillet and, working in batches, fry meatballs. Sear on all sides, keeping balls as round as possible. Place seared meatballs on plate and continue cooking meatballs in batches, adding additional oil and butter as needed.

TO MAKE SAUCE: Add 1 tablespoon butter and 1 tablespoon vegetable oil to same skillet over high heat. Add onions and cook about 5 minutes or until the onions are just golden, stirring frequently. Add mushrooms and pepper, and cook an additional 5 minutes. Pour wine into pan, scraping up any browned bits, and cook 5 minutes or until wine is nearly all reduced. Add 1½ cups of the broth and Worcestershire sauce. Bring to a simmer and then nestle seared meatballs into sauce. Combine remaining ½ cup broth with flour and whisk to make a slurry. Pour slurry into sauce and simmer for 10 minutes. Sauce should be bubbly and thickened.

Reduce heat to low and stir in sour cream. Heat thoroughly and season to taste with salt and pepper. Serve over buttered noodles and garnished with fresh parsley and/or dill.

A Swede in Minnesota Makes Sunday Gravy

Minnesota spaghetti sauce is a thing to be pitied. Similar to Minnesota chili, many local recipes are a thin sauce flavored with salt and ketchup, with random floating rafts of chopped celery and ground beef. It wasn't until I met a real Italian that I was introduced to Sunday gravy.

D. J. taught me the art of slow cooking the red sauce, adding spices along the way that brought the gravy to life. She added oregano, hand-minced garlic, a pinch of sugar, and ground Italian sausage to the tomatoes. Later she ladled a few cups of the sauce into a separate saucepan for simmering thick fennel-kissed sausage links.

Her lasagna was a work of art: layers of her tomato gravy, pasta, cheeses, and sliced links in an enormous pan. My favorite layer was the ricotta mixed with basil, Parmesan, egg, and nutmeg. A good lasagna teaches patience. Not only did we have to wait for the sauce to cook all day, but then the assembled lasagna cooked for an hour or more in a hot oven, and after that was an agonizing rest and cool before we could cut into it. That lasagna took center stage at every holiday we shared. At Easter there was ham and lasagna. We added lasagna to cookouts. There was turkey, stuffing, and lasagna for Thanksgiving. And at Christmas we celebrated with Swedish meatballs and lasagna.

There was no celery in D. J.'s Sunday gravy, but there was time and love. My riff on her sauce makes use of some of the good meats you can win at your favorite meat raffle, an event I believe D. J. would have enjoyed if she'd had an opportunity to attend.

Sunday Gravy

MAKES 3 QUARTS (12 CUPS)

1 tablespoon olive oil
1½ pounds bone-in beef short ribs
salt and pepper
1 large white or yellow onion,
    finely chopped
1 carrot, finely chopped
4 ounces pancetta, finely chopped
    into small cubes
½ cup dry red wine
2 tablespoons tomato paste
3–5 cloves garlic, minced

3 teaspoons Italian seasoning
pinch hot red pepper flakes
30–32 ounces crushed tomatoes
    (canned or boxed)
1 pound sweet Italian sausage,
    cooked and drained
1 tablespoon balsamic vinegar
1 teaspoon dried oregano
½ teaspoon garlic powder
pinch sugar

In a large Dutch oven, heat oil over high heat until it shimmers. Liberally season short ribs with salt and pepper and add them to the pot. Cook, turning after each side browns, for about 10 minutes. Transfer to a plate.

Pour fat from the pot and add onions, carrot, and pancetta to the pan. Cook, stirring, until vegetables are soft and ham is crisp. Pour wine into pan, scraping up browned bits, and cook for 3 to 5 minutes. Add tomato paste, garlic, 2 teaspoons of the Italian seasoning, and red pepper flakes and continue cooking while stirring constantly, about 2 minutes. Add crushed tomatoes and bring to a simmer. Nestle ribs and their juices into the tomatoes. Cover and place over low heat for 4 hours, turning ribs occasionally.

Sauce should be very thick and ribs cooked through. Transfer ribs to a plate. Use a ladle to remove any fat on the surface of the sauce. Discard beef bones and fat, shred meat, and return it to the sauce along with cooked sausage. Stir in vinegar, remaining 1 teaspoon Italian seasoning, oregano, garlic powder, and sugar. Heat thoroughly and season to taste with salt and pepper.

Serve sauce with your favorite pasta and lots of grated Parmesan cheese.

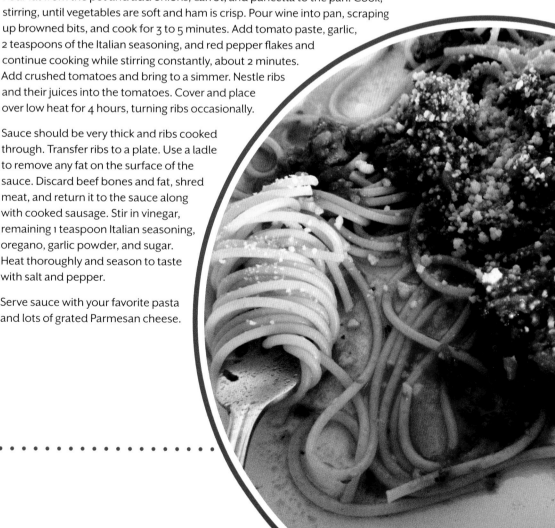

Slow Cooker Pulled Turkey

SERVES 6

One of the best vendors to hit at the Minnesota State Fair is Turkey To Go. The stand is run by the Minnesota Turkey Growers Association, and the menu not only advertises the best slow-roasted drumsticks around but the magnificent Giant and Half Pound Giant Juicy Turkey Sandwiches. Add bleu cheese and buffalo sauce or crispy bacon and sweet glaze if you must. That leaves more Brie and cranberry sauce to top my sandwich.

My only complaint about the ample number of Giant Juicy Turkey Sandwiches I consume each year is that I want them all year long. Happily, we Turkey To Go lovers devised ways to slow cook the pulled turkey at home.

2–3 pounds turkey breast
½ cup dry white wine
1 tablespoon Dijon-style mustard
1 teaspoon onion salt
1 teaspoon paprika

1 teaspoon garlic powder
2 teaspoons dried tarragon
1 bay leaf
soft buns
fennel apple slaw (recipe follows)

Place turkey in slow cooker. Add wine, mustard, onion salt, paprika, garlic powder, tarragon, and bay leaf and cook on high for 4 hours.

Remove turkey from slow cooker and set aside; discard bay leaf. Pour liquid into a small saucepan and bring to a simmer. Continue simmering to reduce by half, about 10 to 15 minutes.

While sauce reduces, remove skin and bones from turkey and discard. Use fork to shred meat and return meat to slow cooker set to warm. Pour reduced liquid over meat and keep warm until serving.

Serve meat on soft buns and top with slaw.

Fennel Apple Slaw

SERVES 4

2 cups red cabbage, sliced very thin
1 large fennel bulb, sliced very
    thin (reserve a tablespoon or
    two of frond)

1 large sweet-tart apple,
    finely chopped
¼ cup red onion,
    finely chopped

For the dressing
¼ cup mayonnaise
2 tablespoons cider vinegar
2 tablespoons pure maple syrup, or substitute
    1 tablespoon sugar or honey
2 teaspoons Dijon-style mustard
½ teaspoon salt
½ teaspoon pepper

In a medium mixing bowl, whisk together
dressing ingredients. Add cabbage, fennel,
apple, and onion, tossing to coat. Garnish
with frond.

Japanese Curry Rice Minnesota Style

SERVES 6

I lived in Japan as a young adult and suffered a miserable case of homesickness. On chilly days I wandered the streets of Tokyo and memorized the food smells that soothed me. There were roasted chestnuts during cold spells, yakitori and yakisoba fried in open street carts, and crepe shops where a hungry girl could spend hours drooling over the endless menu of both savory and sweet fillings.

When my nose detected the wafting scent of curry, I followed the smell to the local curry house, where I ordered fried chicken on rice with as much extra curry sauce as the cook would allow. Curry brought me home, back to my mom's curry dip (page 13) and the curried béchamel she served with salmon croquettes (page 72). Curry is warm comfort.

1 tablespoon vegetable oil
1 large white onion, sliced thin
3 ounces shiitake
    mushrooms, chopped
salt and pepper
2 cups chopped carrot
1 large potato, chopped
1 sweet potato, peeled and chopped
2 cloves garlic, minced

1-inch piece fresh ginger, peeled
    and grated
3 tablespoons curry powder
1 tablespoon tomato paste
½ cup dry red wine
4 cups low-sodium chicken broth
¼ cup minced sweet apple
3–4 tablespoons tamari or soy sauce
1½ tablespoons flour mixed with 1½
    tablespoons water

In a large stockpot, heat oil over high heat and add onion and mushrooms. Season with salt and pepper. Cook, stirring, until onion is translucent and soft and mushrooms are beginning to brown, about 5 minutes. Add carrots, potato, sweet potato, garlic, and ginger and stir well. Add curry powder and tomato paste and continue stirring to incorporate spice with vegetables, about 1 minute. Pour in wine and bring to a simmer; simmer 3 minutes. Add broth, apple, and tamari; simmer, uncovered, until vegetables are soft, about 30 minutes.

Whisk flour-water slurry into simmering curry and continue whisking as sauce thickens, about 3 to 5 minutes.

Serve over rice with chicken katsu (or tofu katsu if you win big at a meat-free raffle!).

Chicken Katsu

SERVES 4–6

1–1½ pounds boneless, skinless
    chicken breasts
salt and pepper
3 tablespoons all-purpose flour
1 teaspoon curry powder
1 large egg, beaten with 1 tablespoon water

1 cup panko
    breadcrumbs
vegetable oil
    for frying

NOTE *Most chicken katsu recipes call for pounding out the chicken breast. This helps the chicken to cook evenly. However, if cooked properly, chicken breast left intact is juicier and, in my opinion, prettier. Just be careful not to overcook the unforgiving chicken breast. Cook to an internal temperature of 160 degrees and the chicken will reach 165 degrees during rest time.*

Season chicken generously on both sides with salt and pepper.

Set up a dredging station by placing flour mixed with curry powder, egg, and panko in three separate shallow bowls. Coat chicken in flour, shaking off any excess. Dip into egg, and then press into panko until well coated on both sides.

Add at least 1 inch of oil to a large, heavy-bottomed skillet or Dutch oven and gradually heat over medium-high heat. When oil is 300–325 degrees, add chicken pieces and fry about 4 to 5 minutes each side, depending on size of piece, or until golden brown and internal temperature reads 160 degrees.

Tofu Katsu

SERVES 4

14 ounces extra-firm tofu
salt and pepper
3 tablespoons all-purpose flour
1 teaspoon curry powder

1 large egg, beaten with 1 tablespoon water
1 cup panko breadcrumbs
vegetable oil for frying

Cut the tofu into 6 to 10 rectangular slices (for crispier tofu, make thinner slices). Use a paper towel to pat slices dry. Season tofu generously on both sides with salt and pepper.

Set up a dredging station by placing flour mixed with curry powder, egg, and panko in three separate shallow bowls. Coat tofu in flour, shaking off any excess. Dip into egg, and then press into panko until well coated on both sides.

Add a few tablespoons of oil to a large, heavy-bottomed skillet or Dutch oven and gradually heat over medium-high heat. When oil is hot, add tofu and fry on each side for a few minutes, until golden brown. To fry the sides, use tongs to carefully flip the tofu onto its side until golden brown all over. Place on paper towels to soak up any excess oil.

Trautmueller Meat Pie

SERVES 8

Meat pie came from my French Canadian–German relatives, and it was one of my dad's favorites. I get my love of meat and pastry from him. Canadians eat Tourtière over the holidays, usually on Christmas Eve, and most recipes I've seen call for a variety of heady spices like thyme, rosemary, cloves, and nutmeg. My family's version is relatively spice-free, so I add a touch just to bring out the flavor of the pork. This is another one of those childhood favorites that I improved with a glop of ketchup, but as an adult I like to add anything from steak sauce to hot sauce.

NOTE
If your butcher can't grind the pork butt for you, use your food processor for a DIY fix. Chop pork into 1-inch cubes. Working in batches, add a portion of the chopped meat to a food processor fitted with the metal blade, and pulse 7 to 10 times, or until meat is coarsely ground.

1 pound pork butt, coarsely ground
¾–1 cup water
1 medium white onion, chopped fine
1 teaspoon salt
1 teaspoon pepper

1 teaspoon dried thyme
¼ teaspoon mace
pastry for double-crust pie
1 large egg beaten with
   1 tablespoon water

Crumble pork in a large, heavy skillet. Add enough water to just cover the meat, and bring to a simmer over medium-high heat. Stir in onion and salt, pepper, thyme, and mace. Cover skillet and cook over low heat for 30 minutes, stirring after 15 minutes. Check to see if meat is dry and add remaining water if needed; stir. Cover again and cook an additional 30 minutes, stirring after 15 minutes.

Meat should be thick like a pudding. If it isn't, stir in 1 tablespoon all-purpose flour.

Heat oven to 425 degrees. Press bottom pie pastry into a 9- or 10-inch pie pan. Spoon hot meat mixture into pastry and top with second pie pastry. Press the edges of the top and bottom pie pastries together, tucking the top edge under the bottom, and crimp. Cut slit in top of pastry to vent steam while it bakes. Brush top of pastry with egg wash.

Bake pie for 15 minutes. Reduce heat to 350 degrees and continue baking an additional 30 to 35 minutes, or until crust is golden brown and crisp.

Double Chip Bacon Cookies

MAKES 30 COOKIES

For a decade or two we were putting bacon in everything. Bacon wasn't just for breakfast and sandwiches. We started topping our donuts with crispy strips and serving candied bacon in cocktails. Americans proved that too much of a good thing isn't always great. It was overkill.

There are a few exceptions. Bacon obviously stands on its own as delicious, fatty, and crunchy. It is a fine garnish for salads and deviled eggs. It is also a surprise when added to cookies. Adding both bacon and potato chips to a chocolate chip cookie brings a salty-savory undertone that gives the chocolate a sweeter voice.

5 slices thick-cut bacon, fried crisp and chopped fine, ¼ cup fat reserved and cooled to room temperature

¾ cup (1½ sticks) butter, at room temperature

¾ cup granulated sugar

½ cup brown sugar

2 teaspoons vanilla extract

2 large eggs

2¼ cups all-purpose flour

2 teaspoons baking powder

½ teaspoon baking soda

½ teaspoon salt

2 cups crushed potato chips

¾ cup semisweet chocolate morsels

Heat oven to 375 degrees. In a large mixing bowl, beat together bacon fat, butter, granulated sugar, and brown sugar with mixer on high until fluffy, about 3 minutes; add vanilla and eggs and beat on medium until just combined. Add flour, baking powder, baking soda, and salt and beat on low until combined. Stir in half of the potato chips, the chocolate morsels, and the chopped bacon.

Roll dough into 1½–inch balls, and then push top of each ball into remaining crushed potato chips, pressing chips into dough as you gently flatten the balls. Place cookies 1 inch apart on nonstick or parchment-lined baking sheet. Bake 12 minutes or until cookies are just golden. Cool on wire rack.

Ice Fishing

I invited myself to a friend's annual ice fishing trip near Lake Superior, where every year thousands of ice houses sit miles from shore. Some ice houses are so elaborate that dwellers comfortably eat, drink, and sleep while they fish for pike, walleye, crappies, and trout through small holes drilled through ice twelve to fifteen inches thick. Some houses are hooked up with satellite dish TV, bunk beds, and portable bathrooms. It sounded luxurious, and I wanted to experience the real thing.

Then I heard that when driving across frozen lakes you buckle your seat belt *underneath* your body and keep windows rolled down in case the vehicle breaks through the ice and you need to escape. In fact, there are ice picks on the market made specifically for such an event, used by dunked drivers and passengers to pull themselves out of frigid lake waters onto solid ground (or stable ice) before hypothermia kicks in.

Then I heard that most ice houses don't come equipped with bathrooms (or televisions), and the options are, one might say, limited.

Then I heard that most fishers opt to stay in their ice houses for hours, soaking in the pleasure of the experience, and would be slightly put off if their guest wanted to drive back to shore because she'd finished reading both issues of *People* and the *Food Network Magazine* she'd brought to stave off boredom.

Then I remembered a story my old boss told about her husband, an esteemed ice fisherman so skilled that he had his own radio show on the subject, who brought his grandsons out and the ice started to break up and the family floated off like Rudolph looking for adventure, until at last, thankfully, they were rescued. (Traumatized, the boys never ice fished again.)

Seeing my panic, the friend didn't mention ice fishing again. I was gently uninvited.

• • •

We'd spent a few weeks inside our cozy homes peering out at the blizzards and snow, cuddling under blankets while binging the latest Netflix sensation. Our furnaces worked nonstop when temps stayed below zero for a month. The month turned into two, and we brave souls ventured outside only to realize it was too cold to ski or skate or walk for an afternoon, and we returned to our fireplaces and hot chocolate. When the annual St. Paul Winter Carnival outdoor festivities were canceled due to the weather, the irony was not lost on us. Minnesotans are used to weather-related cancellations, but the winter carnival closing due to winter was a new one.

Finally, the sun broke through and temperatures swelled to nearly thirty degrees one Saturday morning. I strapped on my Yaktrax ice walkers and headed to our neighborhood lake for an ice fishing contest. The high school boys' hockey team had drilled a few hundred holes in the ice earlier in the day, and competitors stood in line to get access to the holes furthest from the middle, where fishing would be less competitive and slightly quieter.

The lake was large and white, with patches of silver ice peeking through packed snow under an endless blue sky, the inside of a snow globe once it settled. Bare brown trees, long tan grasses, and trucks with trailers parked in rows framed the frozen shore, and orange cones guided me along a path to the event. Alongside me, competitors dragged their fishing supplies in huge rubber bins rigged with pulley ropes toward their holes of choice.

There were big rusty kettles surrounded by wood and filled with burning logs, presumably for warming the fisher people, but it was hot enough outside that no one even bothered with gloves. I was sweaty and removed layers one by one, first mittens, then scarf, then hat. The whole scene was a sensory collage: woodsmoke danced with the cool clean smell of lake; loud generators buzzed, muffling laughter and howls from the crowd. The lake was dotted with color: more orange cones, red buckets and mesh chairs, dark figures dressed in snow pants and parkas, an occasional dog, and blue outhouses.

Holes were claimed with mesh chairs and buckets with cloth seat covers in varying hues of camouflage. Clumps of buddies stood drinking canned beer, waiting for the horn to announce it was time to get lines into the water. A happy, friendly couple asked me to snap a photo of them and stood together smiling broadly with their Coors and Michelob.

The large warming house sat on the ice where the frozen lake was wide enough to accommodate it, and signs advertised booya for sale while supplies lasted. A good booya is something you need to arrive early for or there will be none left. An hour into the fishing event and the booya was sadly gone; I made note that this one must have been a particularly good batch. Inside the warming house burgers, hot dogs, walking tacos, and Jell-O shots were up for grabs, as were beer, booze shots, cocoa, and coffee (add Irish cream for a dollar!).

When the horn blew I heard a collective yelp as lines and hooks were dropped into holes, and when the first tiny fish was pulled from the lake, hoots and hollers followed the fisherman as he ran past the other fishers to the weighing station. The fish was only a few ounces, but the judges marked the score on a sheet where each catch was documented and tallied. The person with the heaviest cumulative count would be declared the winner and awarded the golden fish-topped trophy. Behind the weighing table was a stash of prizes to be awarded in drawings throughout the day. Augers, coolers, grills, and assorted fishing equipment I've got no names for drew a lot of excitement from pretty much everyone who stood at the foot of the treasure pile. When asked, competitors said the camaraderie and prizes were equal draws.

As I was leaving, I asked a somber dad why he enjoyed ice fishing. He was huddled over a hole, surrounded by his children, who played tag and laughed with delight. "I like the solitude," he told me.

Fish that swim in cold water are sweet and succulent. If I were an ice fisher, the draw for me would be the fish.

Oven-Roasted Butternut Hash with Pan-Fried Walleye and Dill Hollandaise

SERVES 4

For the hash

1 small butternut squash (about 1½ pounds), peeled and seeded, cut into ½-inch cubes (about 3–5 cups)

2 medium Yukon Gold potatoes, chopped into ½-inch cubes

olive oil

salt and pepper

2 teaspoons dried thyme

½ cup chopped red onion

½ cup chopped red bell pepper

1 sweet-tart apple, chopped

hot red pepper flakes

Heat oven to 400 degrees. Toss squash and potatoes in 1 tablespoon olive oil and place in single layer on 2 parchment-lined baking sheets. Season liberally with salt and pepper. Roast for 20 minutes. Remove from oven and move squash and potatoes to 1 sheet; season with thyme and return to oven. Toss onion and pepper in 1 teaspoon olive oil; place on empty parchment-lined baking sheet and season liberally with salt and pepper. Return sheet to oven and roast all vegetables for an additional 20 minutes. Add apples to the sheets and return to oven for additional 10 minutes.

Season with salt, pepper, and red pepper flakes.

For the walleye

1 cup all-purpose flour
2 teaspoons Old Bay Seasoning
2 teaspoons dried dill
2 teaspoons garlic powder
2 teaspoons onion powder

salt and pepper to taste
1½ pounds walleye, boned and skin
   removed, cut into 4 fillets
2 tablespoons olive oil
2 tablespoons butter

In a large dish with high sides, whisk together flour and seasonings (Old Bay through salt and pepper). Gently dredge each fillet in the mixture to lightly coat both sides; set aside.

Add oil and butter to a large skillet and place over medium-high heat. When butter is melted, stir oil and butter together to evenly coat bottom of skillet. Add fillets, one at a time, and fry about 3 to 4 minutes each side, or until fish is cooked through and flour-coated flesh is lightly crisp.

For the hollandaise

1 large egg yolk
1½ teaspoons fresh-squeezed
   lemon juice
¼ teaspoon cayenne (optional)

4 tablespoons butter, melted
2 tablespoons minced fresh dill
pinch salt

Add yolk, lemon juice, and cayenne (if using) to blender and puree. (Or use whisk attachment for immersion blender.) With blender running, slowly add melted butter until a sauce forms. If sauce is too thick or starts to break, add lukewarm water 1 tablespoon at a time. Blend in dill and salt to taste before serving.

To serve

Plate hash and walleye, and top with hollandaise. Add a poached or fried egg if desired, and garnish entire dish with fresh dill and chives.

Walleye Macaroni and Cheese

SERVES 6–8

I first tested walleye mac and cheese using the bones of an Ina Garten lobster macaroni and cheese recipe. The results were silky and succulent, and I bowed down to Ina for her superior macaroni and cheese skills. Then I realized I'd doubled the butter and that was likely the reason my mac and cheese was so ... silky.

½ pound cavatappi pasta
2 cups whole milk
1 cup half-and-half
6 tablespoons butter, divided
¼ cup all-purpose flour
½ teaspoon salt
½ teaspoon pepper
½ teaspoon Old Bay Seasoning
¼ teaspoon nutmeg, plus more for topping if desired

2 cups grated Gruyère (about 6–8 ounces)
1 cup grated extra-sharp white Cheddar (about 4 ounces)
12–16 ounces cooked and boned walleye, broken into bite-size pieces
1½ cups fresh white breadcrumbs (about 2 rolls or 3 slices)
fresh dill or parsley for garnish

Heat oven to 375 degrees. Spray a 13x9–inch casserole pan liberally with nonstick spray (or grease bottom and sides of pan generously). Cook pasta according to package directions in salted boiling water. Drain well and set aside.

Heat milk and half-and-half together in a saucepan, but do not boil. In a large saucepan or Dutch oven, melt 3 tablespoons of the butter over medium heat. Whisk in the flour, salt, pepper, Old Bay, and nutmeg and cook over medium-low heat for 2 minutes. Continue whisking while slowly adding the hot milk mixture. Cook and whisk an additional 2 minutes or until mixture begins to thicken. Remove from heat and stir in cheeses until they melt. Add the cooked pasta and stir to combine well. Gently fold in the walleye. Pour mixture into prepared pan.

In nonstick skillet, melt remaining 3 tablespoons butter. Add breadcrumbs and stir to coat crumbs well. Sprinkle butter crumbs over top of macaroni. Add a pinch of nutmeg if desired. Bake uncovered for 30 to 35 minutes, or until the sauce bubbles and the breadcrumbs are toasted brown. Garnish with fresh dill or parsley.

Vasaloppet

NOTE *Vasaloppet Nordic ski races honor Gustav Vasa, who in 1520 fled on skis from King Christian II's massacre of Swedish aristocracy, which included the murder of Gustav's parents. Eventually Gustav led a rebellion that defeated the Danish king, and Gustav was crowned king. Sweden's Vasaloppet is the oldest cross-country ski race in the world, having been around since 1922. Currently three countries outside of Sweden also host Vasaloppet races: the United States (in Mora, Minnesota), Japan, and China.*

We observed the adage "There is no such thing as bad weather, only bad clothing," and I bundled up in so many layers that I looked like Randy from *A Christmas Story* in the scene where his mom is swaddling him in an endless woolen scarf loop. I found it impossible not to giggle when repeating "I can't put my arms down!" to my equally shrouded husband.

Weather.com told us to prepare for a chilly day with windchills below zero. But the sun was shining and there wasn't even a hint of breeze, and we tromped through downtown Mora to inspect the Vasaloppet setup as the annual Nordic ski race got underway. The main street through the center of downtown was covered in a foot of packed clean, white snow, delivered from repositories throughout town where it had been collected from snowfalls earlier in the season, uniting the start and finish lines to the race route around Mora Lake. Due to recent warmer winters and inconsistent snowfalls, artificial snow is used during years with low snow accumulation and the course no longer meanders into the trails outside of Mora Lake.

My friend Alison Holland, a Mora native, acted as our tour guide. She introduced us to the volunteers at the finish line, where warm bilberry soup was offered to competitors and spectators alike. Blåbärssoppa is a Nordic racer's refreshment of choice, and a genial man told us to watch male skiers crossing the finish line for telltale frozen blue beards. He handed me a compostable paper cup filled with thin blue broth, and I drank it fast. The compost bin was framed with blue snow. A kranskulla (kranskullar are women who drape race winners with laurels as the skiers cross the finish line) told us they import the dehydrated blåbärssoppa from Ekströms in Sweden and add water before heating and serving to the multitudes.

At the start of the first race, hundreds of skiers decked out in colorful gear and helmets, faces covered in goggles and masks, pushed off in a pack while a recording of Roy and Dale singing "Happy Trails" played over a loudspeaker. Cowbells rang in the distance, rung by onlookers and jingling while fastened to the traditional Swedish folk costumes (red skirts and coats) of the kranskullar.

As the skiers disappeared down the street and beyond us toward the frozen lake, we visited the Vasaloppet staging area, a picturesque building bursting with tourists, Vasaloppet memorabilia for sale, and walls lined with photos displaying the history of Mora's races, skiers, founders, and kranskullar.

Years before, I interviewed Swedish Americans in our community for my master's thesis about Swedish food traditions. Daisy Samuelson invited me to her home in Minneapolis, and we spoke for nearly an hour before she warmed up enough to offer me coffee. I knew then that she thought I was okay. Daisy told me about growing up in Isanti County, marrying a Swede, and moving to Minneapolis to be close to Minnehaha Falls for the annual Swedish heritage celebration Svenskarnas Dag, raising two daughters, and cooking Swedish food for events at the American Swedish Institute. "In 2001, I was the Swedish Woman of the Year," she said, referring to the Minnesota title, awarded to notable members of the community during Svenskarnas Dag (also called Scandinavian Summer Fest) festivities each year. "I'll show you a picture." She paused with the kind of reverence one holds for Academy Award nominees or Pulitzer Prize winners before proudly revealing that she was the very first kranskulla at Minnesota's Vasaloppet. "And in 1976 I was the first wreath presenter at the ski race in Mora," she added.

Back then, I didn't know anything about Vasaloppet. I only understood from Daisy's deference that it was an important ski race and that the role of kranskullar was a high honor.

Blåbärssoppa (Bilberry Soup)

SERVES 4

Bilberries are a tart berry, blue in color and similar in flavor to blueberries. They are rich in nutrients and have long been used for their medicinal compounds. Bilberries are not as common in Minnesota as are blueberries. If you haven't got a supply of bilberries, substitute fresh or frozen blueberries and add a bit of lemon to mimic the tart bilberries.

While the reconstituted broth served at Mora's Vasaloppet is nutritious and warming, homemade recipes are thicker and more substantial.

2 cups frozen blueberries
2 cups water
¼–½ cup sugar, depending on how sweet you like your soup

1 tablespoon cornstarch dissolved in 1 tablespoon water
1 teaspoon fresh-squeezed lemon juice
whipped cream and mint for garnish (optional)

Combine blueberries, water, and sugar in a stockpot. Bring to a simmer over medium-high heat and simmer for 20 to 30 minutes, or until blueberries begin to break up a bit. If soup is thin, stir cornstarch mixture into simmering soup and stir until soup thickens, about 2 to 3 minutes. Stir in lemon juice.

Serve hot or cold, garnished with whipped cream and mint if desired.

Competitive Souping

I grew up eating an anemic Minnesota chili, a broth flecked with kidney beans and minced tomatoes. It was a pallid consommé of celery pontoons and hamburger floaties. Yet the stuff I have always craved is heroic and strong, built tough and meant to empower. When word got around the office that a coworker had won a chili competition, I immediately reached out to JoAnne asking if she was willing to share the recipe. She agreed and told me the following:

I created the chili on a dare. The Northern Clay Center has held a chili contest in February every year for the past eleven years. The contest is always divided into three categories: meat, chicken (or white) and vegetable. Usually, two celebrity judges pick a winner from each category and best in show. About a hundred people attend and they select a People's Choice winner.

My friend, neighbor and potter Kevin Caufield has won it a few times. He puts in a lot of effort, buying high-quality meat from the butcher, grilling it outside, even in sub-zero weather, and using special ingredients he keeps to himself.

I've entered a few times over the years with a five-bean vegan chili. I'm not vegan, I just like this chili, and thought my chances would be better in the vegetable category as there were fewer competitors. This past year [2019], I thought about entering a chicken, or white chili, because the vegetarian category was usually won by this one potter who makes a great sweet potato chili. But then Kevin told me he was going to be out of town and challenged me to enter with the vegan chili instead.

I'd added sweet potato or butternut squash to my chili in the past, but I always made the chili more bean-forward. This time, I decided to concentrate on the sweet potato and researched a few recipes. My son had just returned from a year in Chile and brought home a local spice, "merkén" (or merquen), a smoky ground chili pepper (aji cacho de cabra). I wanted to bring out the sweetness and complement with the smoke of the merkén and bitterness of the cacao.

I admit to being a spice wimp; not a fan of hot chili. This recipe has much more heat in it than I would normally add but I wanted to be competitive and hot chilis win! However, I think the sweetness downplays the heat profile pretty well and the gremolata also cools it off for me.

I was so surprised to win this contest, as there were so many tasty entries, and they did not award prizes to each category, just First through Third and the People's Choice. But the judges said they could taste Mexico in the chili, so I think the secret ingredient, merkén, was really the winner here. You can find merkén online but be sure to get one that is truly from Chile. I've heard the substitutes are not as good.

Ancho Mama's Chili

SERVES 20   JOANNE MAKELA

olive oil
1 large red onion, finely chopped
1 large yellow sweet onion,
    finely chopped
sea salt
2 large sweet potatoes, peeled and
    chopped into ½-inch cubes
1 green bell pepper, chopped
1 red bell pepper, chopped
1 yellow bell pepper, chopped
1 (12-ounce) jar roasted sweet
    peppers (or roast 2 more peppers
    on the grill and remove the skins)
3–5 cloves garlic, chopped fine
2 tablespoons chili powder
    (preferably Penzeys Hot)
2 tablespoons ancho chili powder
1 tablespoon merkén (Chilean chili
    powder), plus more for serving
1 tablespoon ground cinnamon
1 tablespoon unsweetened
    cocoa powder
1 teaspoon ground cumin

1 teaspoon ground coriander
½ teaspoon nutmeg
cracked pepper
1 (8-ounce) can tomato paste
8 ounces white button or cremini
    mushrooms, chopped into
    chunks (don't chop too finely)
2–3 dried ancho chilis, rehydrated in
    water overnight and chopped in
    large chunks
1 (32-ounce) can whole Roma
    tomatoes (organic or San
    Marzano; I used home canned),
    cut into large chunks
2 (15-ounce) cans black beans, rinsed
    and drained
2 (15-ounce) cans pinto beans, rinsed
    and drained
1 (15-ounce) can cannellini or
    great northern beans, rinsed
    and drained
cilantro gremolata (recipe follows)

In a Dutch oven add enough olive oil to cover the bottom of the pan and heat over medium heat until shimmering. Add onions and sprinkle with sea salt. Cook onions about 2–3 minutes. Add sweet potatoes and peppers. Season with salt and stir until all vegetables have touched the bottom of the pan. Add garlic and spices (chili powder through pepper). Stir until mixture is coated. Add tomato paste and stir in thoroughly. Add mushrooms and anchos, stirring gently to avoid crushing mushrooms. Stir in tomatoes and beans. Add sea salt and a light coating of ancho and/or merkén.

Cover and cook on medium to low heat until the sweet potatoes are cooked but still a little firm, about 15 to 20 minutes. Taste and add more salt or spice as needed.

Top with sprinkling of merkén and a little cilantro gremolata.

NOTE FROM JOANNE
This is the recipe for vegan sweet potato chili that won the 2019 Northern Clay Center Chili Cook-off. I use organic ingredients when possible, particularly canned beans. Rinse the beans from their canning juice either way. And be sure to soak the dried ancho chilis overnight.

Cilantro Gremolata

MAKES ABOUT 1½ CUPS

2 large bunches fresh cilantro,
    roughly chopped
1 bunch green onions,
    roughly chopped

2 cloves garlic, roughly chopped
zest and juice of 1 lime (about
    2 tablespoons juice)
sea salt

Toss together cilantro, onions, and garlic. Add lime zest and juice. Add salt to taste. Refrigerate until ready to serve.

• • •

While artists in St. Paul reveled in their spices, down in Sibley County, Minnesota, a milder cook-off was hosted by the Gaylord United Church of Christ. Elizabeth Reishus, a member of the planning committee (and, truth be told, my editor at the *Gaylord Hub*, where I contribute a weekly food column), provided insight about the origins of the 2019 Sibley County Heavenly Soup and Chili Cook-Off:

> In past years, Gaylord United Church of Christ hosted a soup and chili feed to raise money for the Sibley County Food Shelf. We held the event in March to take advantage of matching funds from Minnesota Food Share. In order to increase interest, the planning committee decided to challenge all Gaylord churches to cook-off. Members, American Lutheran Church, St. Paul's Lutheran Church, and Trinity Lutheran Church have accepted the challenge. In all, we had more than ten entries. People paid $5 to taste the entries and vote on a favorite. The winner received The Golden Ladle, which we hope will become a traveling trophy.
>
> When I filed for divorce, my four children were all under ten years old. Before I had an order for child support, I qualified for MAC, a federal food program for Mothers & Children. The food package pickup was at the Sibley County Food Shelf in Gaylord. The volunteers there saw me and four little folks walk in and immediately began filling a box for us. I explained we were just there for the MAC distribution, but they explained that we also qualified to use the food shelf.
>
> My then seven-year-old (now a student at St. Olaf) did not eat meat at that age. He could barely see over the counter, but he saw them putting a can of chicken noodle soup in the box. He sounded a little like Linus van Pelt when he spoke up and said, "Excuse me, do you have any tomato soup?"
>
> I don't remember today what the volunteers said.
>
> The next day, one of the volunteers came to me at work and asked if we could talk outside the office. She brought me a large container of tomato soup! My son had made quite the impression on her. (Who could resist? The kid was adorable!) This plastic bag of soup concentrate was too big for the food shelf to use because the facility was not set up to divide large packages into smaller ones.
>
> I was so grateful. I kept thanking her and blinking back tears.
>
> She just said, "There but for the grace of God go I."
>
> This cook-off was a chance to pay it forward for the next people who might need a gift of grace.

Easy Tomato Soup

SERVES 4–6

Elizabeth's story reminded me of a time in my own life when the pantry was bare and I had a child to feed. Soup is an inexpensive and healthy meal option. In the past I made this easy tomato soup using chicken stock, but in honor of Elizabeth's son I will make it vegetarian from here on out.

1 teaspoon butter
1 teaspoon olive oil
½ white or yellow onion,
  finely chopped
2 cloves garlic, smashed
4 cups vegetable broth
1 (15-ounce) can diced tomatoes

¼ cup tomato paste
¼ cup dry red wine
1 tablespoon sugar
1 teaspoon dried basil
1 teaspoon salt
½ teaspoon pepper

In a large stockpot, heat butter and oil and cook onions and garlic until onions are just transparent, stirring frequently. Add remaining ingredients and simmer for at least 15 minutes or up to an hour.

Serving options: For a chunky soup, serve as is. For a smooth soup, puree before serving. For a creamy soup, stir in ½ cup half-and-half before serving.

Susan's Cheese Crackers

MAKES 108–120 (1-INCH) CRACKERS   SUSAN JOHNSON SCHMIDT

A nice companion to Easy Tomato Soup (page 57). My sister Susan makes this dough with her granddaughter Sophia for cheesy noodles. They realized the dough makes a fine cracker as well.

8 ounces medium-hard cheese (such as Cheddar or Gruyère), shredded
1 cup all-purpose flour
½ teaspoon kosher salt
½ teaspoon seasoned salt
4 tablespoons butter, cold, cut into 8 pieces
3 tablespoons ice water
sea salt or flake salt

Place cheese, flour, and salts in a food processor fitted with a metal blade and process until combined, about 30 seconds. Add butter and process until mixture resembles wet sand, about 20 seconds. Add water and pulse until dough forms large clumps, about 10 pulses.

Transfer dough to a lightly floured surface and use your hands to pat into two large disks. If dough is dry, moisten fingers with a bit of cold water. Wrap dough in plastic and refrigerate at least 1 hour or up to 2 days.

Heat oven to 350 degrees. Roll out each dough disk into a 9x9–inch square, about the same thickness as pie crust. Cut into preferred 1-inch shapes, up to 60 from each square, and place in a single layer on parchment-lined baking sheets. Dot with wooden pick or skewer and lightly sprinkle with sea or flake salt. Bake for 20 minutes, rotating baking sheets halfway through baking time.

Store in a loosely covered container (a tight seal will result in less crunchy crackers) and serve at room temperature within a few days of baking.

Reuben Soup

SERVES 12   DAWN KRATZKE

Dawn says that she and her coworker Tara Sabako have been dubbed soup royalty at the office since 2013 when they started taking the office soup contest very seriously. "We both practice almost year-round to come up with a recipe that just might make it in the top three, only taking the summer off. The soup contest at our office was started in 1992, long before either of us started working in Sibley County. This recipe won second place at my office soup cook-off in 2016 and first place in 2019 at the soup cook-off hosted by the United Church of Christ in Gaylord. I doubled the recipe and made it in a roaster."

> **NOTE**
> *Dawn advises: Make the corned beef brisket ahead of time. Use the accompanying seasoning packet and slow cook it in a Crock-Pot with equal parts beer and water almost covering the brisket. If you're in a hurry, use deli corned beef. The soup will still taste great but will not be as robust.*

4 tablespoons unsalted butter
1 cup finely chopped celery
1 cup chicken broth
1 cup beef broth
1 teaspoon baking soda
5 tablespoons cornstarch
5 tablespoons water
2 cups sauerkraut (drained; do not rinse or you will lose flavor)

3 pounds corned beef brisket, cooked and shredded
4 cups half-and-half
3 cups shredded Swiss cheese
½ cup Thousand Island dressing
pepper
rye croutons (recipe follows)

In a large pot, melt the butter and cook the celery until tender, stirring frequently. Add chicken and beef broths and baking soda. In a small bowl, whisk together cornstarch and water (if you like thinner soup, use less of this mixture); stir into the pot and bring to a boil. Cook until thickened, stirring frequently.

Add sauerkraut, corned beef, and half-and-half. Simmer for 15 minutes, stirring frequently, being careful not to boil. Stir in cheese and Thousand Island dressing. Season with pepper to taste. Serve with rye croutons.

Rye Croutons

softened butter
rye bread
garlic salt

Heat oven to 350 degrees. Spread butter on bread and sprinkle with garlic salt. Cut into bite-size pieces, place on baking sheet, and bake until crispy, about 15–20 minutes. Allow to cool. The croutons can be made ahead of time and stored in a sealed container.

Four-Ingredient Tortellini Soup

SERVES 4–6   AMELIA KRATZKE

Amelia's mom, Dawn, explains:

This recipe won second place at the 2019 soup cook-off at UCC in Gaylord. My daughter, Amelia, doesn't like Reuben Soup and was complaining about what she would be able to eat at the cook-off. Amelia is my soup taste tester and has tasted and rated many of my practice soups throughout the years. She rates the soup as either: "it's good but not prize-winning good," or "this is the one."

I told Amelia she should make a soup so she had something to eat at the contest. Amelia has altered this recipe from a soup my friend and coworker, Tara, won first place with at the office soup cook-off. Our intent was to keep this one off to the side for children because most kids like this soup. It ended up being placed on the table and was a hit. At the end of the contest, Amelia and I were tied, with two people still eating, so the Reuben Soup won by only a small margin (I secretly was rooting for her).

When I make this recipe, I throw in a couple of handfuls of fresh spinach. Tara also did this as well as adding diced tomatoes. Amelia prefers it the way she made it.

1 (12-ounce) package turkey kielbasa
8 ounces cream cheese

1 (22-ounce) package frozen tortellini
4 cups reduced-sodium chicken broth

Add kielbasa, cream cheese, and tortellini to a slow cooker. Add enough chicken broth to cover. Cook on low until cream cheese has melted, about 4 to 6 hours, stirring occasionally.

Winning recipes from the 2019 Sibley County Heavenly Soup & Chili Cook-Off

Blonde Ale Cheese Soup

SERVES 4 GENEROUSLY

It wouldn't be the change of seasons in Wisconsin and Minnesota without a sturdy beer cheese soup. My springtime version came about because I always have a lone (one might say lonely) can of blonde ale in the fridge. I love the round, mild flavors of blonde ale.

2 tablespoons butter
½ yellow onion, finely chopped
1 stalk celery, finely chopped
1 carrot, finely chopped
¼ cup finely chopped red or yellow
    bell pepper
salt and pepper
2 cloves garlic, smashed
1 teaspoon prepared mustard
1 teaspoon paprika
1 teaspoon Worcestershire sauce
2 tablespoons flour
12 ounces blonde ale
2 cups chicken broth

1 potato, peeled and finely chopped
3 ounces cream cheese
¼ cup sour cream
1 cup shredded Jarlsberg or
    Swiss cheese
½ cup shredded Emmenthal or
    Gruyère cheese
½ cup cream or half-and-half
    (optional)
zest from 1 orange
¼ teaspoon nutmeg
lots of fresh dill, minced
croutons or popcorn for serving

In a large stockpot, melt butter and cook onion, celery, carrot, and peppers until soft, about 5 minutes, stirring frequently; season to taste with salt and pepper. Add garlic and whisk in mustard, paprika, Worcestershire sauce, and flour and continue whisking over medium heat about 1 minute. Increase heat and add ale, broth, and potato; bring to low simmer and cook, uncovered, 15 minutes.

Use an immersion blender or process in batches to puree vegetables. Over medium heat add cream cheese, sour cream, and shredded cheeses to soup and stir until cheeses are melted and well incorporated. Stir in cream if desired. Season soup with orange zest and nutmeg; garnish with dill and croutons or popcorn.

Consider the Radish,

& other signs of renewal

Spring arrives and I'm never sure what to wear. If I pull on winter boots and a parka, the sun comes out and heats us up to seventy degrees. If I wear sandals and a jean jacket, it snows. Pull out my rain boots, and you can bet the streets will be dry and the wind gusts will flip my umbrella inside out. In Minnesota we learn to dress in layers.

When I was little spring was muddy and damp and my nose was always dripping. Summer was too far out of reach to imagine. I hadn't made it to kindergarten yet, and my four older sisters left me behind every morning when they marched off to school. My days were long and sometimes lonely. I played with my friend Macaroni and her ally Alligator, who, although not everyone could see them, were as real to me as my human friends Shelly and Lila. Macaroni and I shared an improvised sit-upon under the big apple tree in our front yard on Main Street and read to each other from books we'd memorized. Sometimes my mom would set an extra place at the lunch table and Macaroni joined me for soup and sandwiches. Alligator was afraid of our Great Danes Khan and Trina, so he never came into the house.

Occasionally Mom needed to run errands, and she'd leave me with our neighbor Rueben. He set me up with his grown sons' old trains and cars, and I'd play until it was time for lunch. Unfamiliar but intriguing scents and a rumbling tummy always lured me into Rueben's kitchen. It was there that I learned to love seasonings outside of the Holy Midwestern Trinity of salt, pepper, and ketchup. Rueben always padded our sandwiches with liberal schmears of his homemade horseradish, and my life in food began with the first bite of that doctored bologna sandwich.

Even with my companions and the occasional devouring of horseradish sandwiches with my pal Rueben, I was restless. It felt like I'd never be old enough or wise enough to be a kindergartener. Just as the monotony of spring was about to swallow me, my mom presented me with a small envelope. "Radish seeds," she told me. The packet front was adorned with a picture of a shiny, bright red radish, and when I shook it the seeds inside rattled with promise.

Eventually the ground warmed and I took my radish seeds out to the side of the house, where my mom cleared a small area for my garden. I pressed the tiny seeds into the soil, watered the ground, and waited. For what felt like forever, I visited my radish patch every day, inspecting the ground for signs of life. Macaroni and I moved our reading activities to the sidewalk along the radish crèche. We watered the ground when it didn't rain, and we waited some more.

One glorious day the radishes finally pushed their green stems out of the soil. It was like watching a miracle. Every day the greens grew taller and unfolded, becoming leaves and reaching for the sun. Every day I asked my mom if they were ready to harvest. When it was time, I spent a morning pulling fat red orbs out of the soil and loaded the harvest on to my sister's Red Flyer armed with a homemade sign advertising "Radishes For Sale, 1 Cent Each." While other kids put up lemonade stands, I was drawn to produce. It was our town's first farmers market. Alas, I was not a successful vendor. My mother ended up purchasing the entire crop, which actually worked out pretty well for me.

Radishes, asparagus, and rhubarb are always the first signs in the market that spring has arrived, bringing fresh reasons for eating seasonally.

Bacon-Wrapped Roasted Radishes

MAKES 12 APPETIZERS

6 slices bacon, halved
12 round radishes (red, pink, or white)
barbecue sauce
flake salt
12 wooden picks or 3 bamboo skewers

Heat oven to 400 degrees. Put bacon strips on parchment-lined baking sheet; bake until just starting to brown but not yet crispy, about 10 to 15 minutes. When bacon is cool enough to handle, wrap each radish with one strip and secure with wooden pick or skewer. Brush all sides with barbecue sauce. Return to oven and bake until bacon is crisp and radishes are soft, an additional 15 to 20 minutes. Sprinkle with flake salt and serve while still hot, with additional barbecue sauce for dipping.

Radish Greens Pesto and Asparagus Pasta Salad

SERVES 4–6

If you can get your hands on radishes just pulled from the ground, this is the pesto for you.

For the pesto

⅓ cup walnuts

2 cups very fresh radish greens, rinsed well and patted dry

½ cup fresh basil leaves

¼ cup fresh chives or garlic chives

1 clove garlic

zest and juice of 1 lemon (about 3 tablespoons juice)

about ½ cup olive oil

¼–½ cup grated Parmesan cheese

salt, pepper, and nutmeg

Heat oven to 350 degrees. Arrange walnuts in a single layer on parchment-lined baking sheet. Toast for 6 minutes. Check to be sure the walnuts are not burning and return to oven for an additional 2 to 4 minutes or until lightly browned and fragrant. Set your timer so you don't forget about them. Set the walnuts aside to cool.

Pulse greens, herbs, garlic, nuts, zest, and juice in food processor or blender until well combined, scraping down sides as needed. With the motor running, drizzle in olive oil until pesto texture results. Fold in cheese. Season to taste with salt and pepper; add nutmeg if desired.

For the salad

1 big bunch asparagus, cut into ½-inch pieces; separate tops and set aside

1 bunch red radishes, sliced thin

7 ounces pasta (orzo, elbow, or rings), cooked in salted water according to package directions and drained

Prepare a medium bowl of ice water. Bring a small pot of salted water to a boil and add asparagus pieces, reserving the tops. Simmer for 2 minutes; add tops and cook 30 seconds longer. Drain asparagus and immediately set in iced water to stop cooking.

In a very large mixing bowl, combine asparagus, radishes, pasta, and enough pesto to coat everything. Toss well, adding additional olive oil if needed. Garnish with additional cheese and radishes. Serve at room temperature or refrigerate for later.

Save any leftover pesto to top steak, fish, or chicken.

Rhubarb Pudding

SERVES 8

I first read about vispipuuro (Finnish whipped porridge) in my old Time and Life *Cooking of Scandinavia*. My friend Leigh and I hosted a dinner party for college friends who were home for the holidays and decided to serve the porridge for dessert. The original recipe calls for cranberry juice, but I've updated it using rhubarb because in Minnesota we are always looking for new ways to use our abundance of the perennial that grows so prolifically in our climate.

3 cups rhubarb juice (recipe follows)
½ cup sugar
½ cup farina (such as Cream of Wheat)

1 teaspoon vanilla extract
whipped cream for serving
candied rhubarb for serving (recipe follows)

In a large saucepan, bring juice to a boil. Sprinkle juice with sugar and farina. Cook to a brisk boil while stirring with a wooden spoon. Reduce heat and simmer 6 to 8 minutes, stirring occasionally, until mixture becomes a thick puree.

Transfer puree to a large mixing bowl, add vanilla, and beat with a mixer on high for 10 to 15 minutes. Mixture will plump into a soft, lumpy pudding. Garnish with whipped cream and candied rhubarb.

Rhubarb Juice

MAKES 4½ CUPS

2 cups rhubarb, chopped
6 cups water
½ cup sugar

Add all ingredients to a large saucepan and bring to a boil. Reduce heat and simmer for 15 minutes. Remove from heat and allow to steep for 30 minutes. Use an immersion blender to puree mixture, then pour through fine-mesh strainer. Discard solids.

Candied Rhubarb

½ cup sugar
½ cup water
1 rhubarb stalk, cut into thin strips

Heat oven to 200 degrees. Add sugar and water to small saucepan and bring to a simmer, stirring often, until sugar is completely dissolved. Add the rhubarb to the warm simple syrup, then place in a single layer on a parchment-lined baking sheet.

Bake until rhubarb is no longer wet, about 35 to 40 minutes. Cool completely and use as garnish for pudding. If strips do not hold their shape, break them into rhubarb shards.

Fish Fry

Lenten fish frys were born from the Catholic tradition of eschewing meat every Friday, although the practice is even more common during Lent. In Minnesota, where Catholicism is the largest single religious denomination, Lenten fish frys are more predictable than conversations with strangers about the weather. Expect crowds, bring cash, and find a restaurant on Good Friday because most church kitchen are closed the weekend of Easter.

We are motivated to eat Friday night fish frys because of the dinner itself. Yet my best fish fry memories have lots to do with the food but much more to do with community. At a great fish fry, guests feel welcome. We don't return to forgettable dinners where we sit at a communal table with other diners who ignore us and each other, shoveling food into their gullets and periodically grunting. I don't care about all-you-can-eat because usually one serving is more than enough. But the sides? Oh yes, the sides are always a big draw.

In 2019 our Lenten fish frys were bookended by spring blizzards. We braved snowstorms and hidden potholes, determined to find parking, good fish, and some unique sides. Traditional fish fry sides are coleslaw and french fries, but the astute fish fry lover seeks menus that include pierogies, popovers, hush puppies, and pretzels alongside the usual fish suspects: battered or breaded cod, walleye, perch, and sunfish.

We hit a popular dive in St. Paul early, before 5 PM, when the famous line starts its expanse out the front door and down the block. We arrived with cash in our pockets because, as the posted warnings alert guests, this place takes cash and checks only. There is an ATM on-site, conveniently doling out tens and twenties for patrons who are new to the old ways of commerce. Years before the ATM appeared, a friend of mine dined without means to pay and was told, "Come back when you have cash, honey, and you can pay us then." She returned a few days later to pay her bill.

Once seated we chatted with our elderly neighbors. The couple next to us couldn't decide between the beer-battered cod and the breaded walleye. We had the same dilemma, so I ordered the fried cheese ravioli and a glass of white wine while we made our choices. "How is that ravioli?" the gentleman asked. I told him it was tasty and offered to share. He shook his head and pointed to my husband: "He looks hungry."

NOTE *There is dispute about whether the plural of fish fry is fish fries or fish frys. Avid grammar aficionados claim that fries is the proper plural. Fish fry enthusiasts contend that the term fries suggests a noun (such as french fries) rather than a cultural event. For them, frys is the proper term. Another group of fish fry fans argue that fish fry is the new plural. For our purposes we shall refer to the cultural event in plural as fish frys, because that's what my fine editor endorses.*

Our dinners arrived in a wave of precariously overfilled plates: side salads, soup, three monstrous pieces of golden cod, crisp breaded walleye, a baked potato, and mashed potatoes swathed in gravy. Finally, the reason I chose the place, beautiful outside-crisp/inside-eggy popovers were placed before us.

We continued to chat with our neighbors as we dug into our meal. Our server checked on us often to refill my husband's iced tea. Friends we hadn't seen in a few months walked in, and we greeted each other with glee and hugs. Fish frys are like that: you almost always run into old friends while making new ones.

Dayton's Popovers

MAKES 12 POPOVERS

Adapted from *The Marshall Field's Cookbook*

I've seen examples of what people from other places refer to as popovers or, if made with drippings from a roast, Yorkshire pudding. But too often the sad little puffy breads are flat topped and barely even reach the top of the popover pan. A Minnesota popover must pop out of the tin, reminiscent of those old Orville Redenbacher popcorn commercials: "It's blowing the top right off the popper!"

5 large eggs
1⅔ cups whole milk
5 tablespoons unsalted butter, melted
1⅔ cups flour
½ teaspoon salt
butter, sour cream, and caviar for serving

Heat oven to 400 degrees. Grease insides of popover pan (or deep muffin tin).

In a medium bowl, using an electric mixer on medium-high speed, beat eggs until frothy. Add milk and butter and mix well. Reduce speed to low, add flour and salt, and mix until just combined. Allow the batter to rest for 15 to 30 minutes; place popover pan in oven to preheat.

Divide batter among compartments, filling each cup just under half full (fill empty cups halfway with water). Bake for 30 to 40 minutes (do not open oven door), until popovers are puffy and well browned.

Remove from oven, transfer pans to a wire rack, and cool 2 minutes. Serve warm with room temperature butter or sour cream and caviar.

Salmon Croquettes with Dill and Peas Sauce

SERVES 4

Prep for the salmon croquettes began the night before they were to be served. I would watch my mom in the kitchen making a roux, then blending in canned salmon, bones and all. The salmon spent the night in the refrigerator, and I would have a hard time sleeping. Salmon croquettes for dinner was almost as exciting as Christmas.

An hour before dinner we would smell oil heating, and eventually we heard the crackle of croquettes hitting the hot grease and crisping into something miraculous. It felt like forever while Mom finished the white sauce with peas, but eventually we'd take our places at the dining room table and dine in luxury. Mom shaped the croquettes into cones, and each pyramid's crisp exterior cradled the plump, luscious salmon interior. Biting into salmon cartilage, I was triumphant.

I tried to pace myself, dragging each bite through the white gravy and willing myself to chew slowly. It was my first understanding of food and sensuality, as the entire plate was a balance of aromas, textures, flavors, and colors.

Today I make my mom's croquettes using the same recipe she passed along, carefully shaping each croquette into her special cone. The only differences are the addition of lemon zest and other seasoning, I typically reach for fresh salmon rather than canned, and I am no longer drawn to the bones.

For the croquettes

4 tablespoons butter
¼ cup all-purpose flour
1 teaspoon Old Bay Seasoning
1 teaspoon dried dill
½ teaspoon salt
⅛ teaspoon pepper

1 cup whole milk, warmed
1 pound skinless salmon,
 cooked and boned
zest of 1 lemon
1 cup breadcrumbs

In a large skillet, melt butter over medium heat. Whisk in flour, Old Bay, dill, salt, and pepper and cook for 3 minutes, whisking constantly. Slowly add milk and continue whisking until mixture thickens, 3 to 5 minutes. Remove roux from heat.

Use a fork to gently pull apart salmon. Blend salmon, zest, and crumbs into roux. Refrigerate for several hours.

To fry
1 cup all-purpose flour
3 large eggs, beaten

1½ cups breadcrumbs
3–4 cups vegetable oil

Prepare a dredging station by placing the flour, the eggs, and the breadcrumbs into separate dishes. Form chilled batter into desired shape. Coat with flour, then dip in egg, then breadcrumbs. Set aside and prepare each croquette in the same manner.

In large, heavy-bottomed pot or deep fryer, heat 3 inches vegetable oil to 365 degrees. Fry croquettes in batches until they are golden brown, turning at least once to cook evenly. (Alternatively, after rolling croquettes in breadcrumbs, place on a large parchment-lined baking sheet and bake in a 400-degree oven for 30 minutes.)

Serve warm with dill sauce.

For the dill and peas sauce
3 tablespoons butter
3 tablespoons all-purpose flour
½ teaspoon curry powder
¼ teaspoon salt
2 cups whole milk, warmed

1–2 tablespoons minced fresh dill
1 tablespoon lemon juice
1 cup frozen
        peas, thawed

In a medium saucepan, melt butter over medium heat. Whisk in flour, curry powder, and salt until smooth. Gradually whisk in milk and bring to a boil. Cook and stir for 2 to 3 minutes, or until thickened. Remove from heat and stir in dill, lemon juice, and peas.

Hush Puppies

MAKES 30 HUSH PUPPIES

A certain seafood restaurant franchise used to entice me because of the endless baskets of hush puppies that arrived at tables prior to the main meal. When said franchise replaced the hush puppies with Cheddar biscuits, I was crestfallen and refused to walk through the swinging doors into the aquarium-like lobby for years. To recover from my loss, I experimented with hush puppy recipes, frying my way through Betty Crocker, Cook's Country, and Epicurious, determined to find the quickest and tastiest recipe.

Eventually I discovered that using a cornbread mix adds a really nice texture to the interior. Normally I don't add baking powder to a self-rising product, but in this recipe it yields a soft interior that doesn't occur without the addition.

1 cup cornbread mix (such as
    Bob's Red Mill)
2 tablespoons sugar
1 tablespoon dried minced onion,
    reconstituted in a bit of water
2 teaspoons baking powder
1 teaspoon salt

1 large egg yolk
½ cup buttermilk
2 tablespoons melted butter
peanut oil for frying
tomato marmalade or cocktail sauce
    for serving

Whisk together cornbread mix, sugar, minced onion, baking powder, and salt. Combine yolk, buttermilk, and butter and add to dry ingredients; stir until mixed. Refrigerate at least 1 hour.

In a large saucepan, heat 2 inches of peanut oil to 350 degrees. Drop batter by tablespoons into hot oil about 6 at a time. Turn occasionally to brown all sides; fry 3 minutes to golden brown. Remove with slotted spoon to paper towels; season with salt.

Serve hot with tomato marmalade or cocktail sauce.

Colorful Coleslaw

SERVES 4–6

The coleslaws I grew up with are creamy and pale green. This recipe is neither, but the acidity cuts through any deep-fried attitude.

½ large or 1 small purple
    cabbage, shredded
1 red bell pepper, cut into matchsticks
1 carrot, shredded (optional)
½ red onion, sliced very thin
½ cup olive oil

¼ cup cider vinegar
¼ cup water
2 tablespoons sugar
1 teaspoon caraway seeds
1 teaspoon salt
1 teaspoon pepper

Place cabbage, pepper, carrot (if using), and onion in large, heat-resistant salad bowl.

In a saucepan, combine oil, vinegar, water, sugar, caraway seeds, salt, and pepper and bring to a boil. Whisk to dissolve sugar. Pour hot brine over vegetables and toss well. Refrigerate until ready to serve.

Rye Pretzel Bites with Caraway

MAKES 24 PRETZEL BITES

When one of my cooking class students took a bite into his rye pretzel, he closed his eyes, leaned back in his chair, and said with bliss, "Tastes like a shot of aquavit."

Aquavit is a distilled spirit that is best described in this way: caraway is to aquavit what juniper is to gin.

In recent years, Minnesota became a self-proclaimed Aquavit Capital of America, and it is true—we love our aquavit. More than a dozen local distilleries are churning out the spirit and distributing it to the thirsty.

Rye pretzel bites with caraway are delicious with or without a companion shot of aquavit.

½ cup baking soda

3 cups all-purpose flour

1 cup rye flour

1 packet instant yeast (about 2¼ teaspoons)

3 tablespoons brown sugar,
    plus 1½ tablespoons for bath

1 teaspoon caraway seeds

½ teaspoon salt

zest and juice from 1 orange

2 tablespoons butter, at room temperature

1 cup warm water

1 large egg yolk

2–3 teaspoons caraway seeds and
    2–3 teaspoons kosher salt, mixed together
    in small bowl

Heat oven to 250 degrees. Pour baking soda on parchment-lined baking sheet and bake for 30 minutes. Remove from oven and cool.

In a large mixing bowl, combine flours, yeast, 3 tablespoons of the brown sugar, 1 teaspoon caraway seeds, salt, and orange zest. Use hands to blend butter into flour as evenly as you can. Add water and stir until dough comes together. Remove from bowl and knead 10 to 15 minutes, or until smooth. Shape into a ball and return to bowl; cover with plastic wrap or clean kitchen towel and let rise in warm place until double, 1 to 2 hours.

Gently remove dough from bowl and divide into 24 pieces. Shape into bite-size twig or round. Place bites on well-oiled parchment-lined baking sheets. Cover sheets with clean kitchen towel and let rest 30 minutes.

Heat oven to 425 degrees; place racks on bottom and upper thirds of oven.

Bring 2½ quarts (10 cups) of water to a boil and add baking soda and remaining 1½ tablespoons brown sugar. Stir to dissolve; reduce heat to simmer. Gently place a few pretzel bites at a time in simmering bath. Turn after 30 seconds and simmer an additional 30 seconds. Remove bites with a slotted spoon or spider and return to prepared parchment. Continue simmering bites in batches.

In small mixing bowl, whisk together egg yolk and 1 to 2 tablespoons orange juice. Brush tops of pretzel bites with yolk mixture. Sprinkle with caraway-salt mixture. Bake 5 to 7 minutes, then switch rack positions and bake an additional 5 minutes, or until pretzels are dark and crisp on the outside. Serve hot.

Finding the Warmth

"I'm a little fished out," my husband admitted as I Google-mapped Our Lady of Guadalupe in St. Paul. Once inside the church, we were welcomed like dear friends. We bought our tickets and found two open seats at one of the dozens of communal tables. Around us people were laughing and talking, dipping tortilla chips into the best hot sauce I've ever tasted. Unlike some of the more solemn fish frys, this place felt like a celebration. The walls were painted in bright, happy colors, and in the center of the room was a trio of crosses draped in purple cloths. Dozens of volunteers of varying ages hustled in the kitchen, stirring refried beans and plating up enchiladas with plenty of rice. Tweens bused dirty dishes, and some ladies pushed dessert carts between tables, displaying cakes and cookies. A pair of teens sold takeout enchiladas at a stand next to the kitchen.

"Did you try the carrot cake?" a woman with movie star good looks asked us. "I made that." Delores "Lola" Franco introduced herself and sat with us to talk about the popularity of Our Lady of Guadalupe's Lenten lunches and dinners, where cheese enchiladas are served rather than the traditional fish fry.

"We serve enchiladas because it is everybody's favorite," she told us, referring to the mostly Mexican population among church members. When the Montez sisters began preparing enchiladas to serve during Lent, they had only one table yet served eight thousand enchiladas and made nearly eight hundred dollars. A decade later the event brings in hundreds of diners, more than half from outside the parish.

Before Lent begins volunteers have a chili cleaning party where they wash, clean, and dry four hundred pounds of hot chilis. Mondays during Lent, volunteers gather again and churn out six barrels of enchilada sauce each week. One of the parishioners creates the aforementioned hot sauce. The hot sauce used to be available in bottles for purchase, but the church had to stop sales when they ran out of sauce for the meals. The meals bring in tens of thousands of dollars, which is mainly used for church infrastructure and upkeep.

Perhaps more importantly, the dinners feed the community spiritually as well as physically. In a neighborhood that is too often associated with poverty, the church commits to this mission: never turn a hungry person away. Everyone is fed, regardless of their ability to pay.

When I asked Lola if she would be willing to share the enchilada recipe, she simply laughed and answered, "No." This recipe is my attempt at a decent enchilada, and it is pretty good. For the real thing, you'll want to get to Our Lady of Guadalupe next spring.

Cheese Enchiladas

SERVES 6–8

For the sauce

2 tablespoons vegetable oil

1 small or ½ large white or yellow onion, finely chopped (about 1 cup)

2 cloves garlic, minced

1½ tablespoons chili powder

1 teaspoon salt

1 teaspoon ground cumin

1 teaspoon ground coriander

½ teaspoon smoked paprika

½ teaspoon ground ancho chili

1 (14.5-ounce) can crushed tomatoes

1½ cups vegetable broth

3½ ounces canned chipotles in adobo sauce (about half a can)

2 tablespoons tomato paste

Heat a large saucepan over medium heat and add oil. Cook onions until just soft, about 3 minutes, stirring frequently. Stir in garlic and dry seasonings (chili powder through ancho chili). Cook an additional 2 minutes. Add remaining ingredients (tomatoes through paste), whisking together, and bring to a simmer. Reduce heat to low, and continue simmering for 10 to 15 minutes, stirring occasionally.

Puree mixture in blender or food processor.

For the enchiladas

8 ounces queso fresco, grated

8 ounces queso Cotija or Chihuahua, grated

8 ounces sharp white Cheddar, grated

12–14 (6-inch) corn tortillas

toppings: salsa, cilantro, sliced radishes, lime wedges, avocado slices, sour cream

Heat oven to 375 degrees. Coat a 13x9–inch (3-quart) casserole dish with nonstick spray. Add about ½ cup of the sauce to dish and spread to coat entire bottom. In large bowl, combine the cheeses.

Add about half of the remaining sauce to a large skillet over low heat. Dip tortillas one at a time in the warm sauce to make them pliable. (Note: this technique is messy but is less fattening than heating in oil.) Fill each tortilla with a handful of the cheese, roll tortilla around the cheese, and place seam-side down in a single layer in prepared dish. Cover tortillas with enough of the sauce to completely coat surface. Sprinkle remaining cheese over the sauce.

Bake 20 to 25 minutes or until the cheese is melted and bubbly. Serve immediately with toppings.

Chocolate Hazelnut Sheet Cake

SERVES 16

Hazelnuts are practically a perfect shrub. Their roots are robust, allowing the plant to thrive in a northern climate without need for plowing (which can result in erosion and polluted waterways). They redirect carbon from out of the air and into the ground, and in fact increase their carbon cleansing properties as they age. Pollinator-friendly, pest-resistant, self-regenerating permaculture: I've even discussed their skin healing properties with a local farmer who claims hazelnut oil can ease dry skin and psoriasis. And did I mention the nuts are delicious?

I frost my chocolate hazelnut cake with a seven-minute frosting. I love how the frosting glazes into a shiny spackle, like heavy snow in late spring.

1 cup unsweetened cocoa powder, plus a tablespoon or two to dust pan
1¾ cups all-purpose flour
1¾ cups sugar
1½ teaspoons baking powder
1½ teaspoons baking soda
1 teaspoon salt

2 large eggs
1 cup unsweetened coconut milk
½ cup hazelnuts
½ cup hazelnut oil
2 teaspoons vanilla extract
¾ cup boiling water

Heat oven to 350 degrees. Grease bottom and sides of a 13x9–inch cake pan. Use a small wire mesh strainer to dust pan evenly with 1–2 tablespoons cocoa.

In a large mixing bowl, whisk together flour, sugar, cocoa, baking powder, baking soda, and salt. Set aside.

Add eggs, coconut milk, hazelnuts, hazelnut oil, and vanilla to blender or food processer fitted with metal blade; puree. Add puree to the dry mixture, whisking to blend well. Slowly whisk in boiling water. Pour batter into prepared pan and bake for 30 minutes or until an inserted wooden pick comes out clean. Cool in pan before frosting.

Seven-Minute Frosting

MAKES ENOUGH TO COVER 13X9–INCH CAKE OR 2- OR 3-LAYER CAKE

1½ cups sugar
¼ teaspoon cream of tartar
¼ teaspoon salt
⅓ cup water

2 large egg whites (take care that absolutely no yolk is in the whites)
1 teaspoon vanilla extract

In bottom of a double boiler, bring water to boiling. In top of double boiler, whisk together sugar, cream of tartar, salt, water, and egg whites. Beat with handheld electric mixer for 1 minute. Place pan over boiling water (water should not touch the bottom of the top pan). Beat on high speed for 7 minutes. Frosting will increase in volume and become very white and shiny. Beat in vanilla. Use to frost cake immediately.

Maple

It is said that we don't know how we'd react in a crisis until we are in one. I disagree. I believe we should acknowledge our weaknesses so we can better face reality. When the zombie apocalypse happens, I know I will be the first to go. I'll be like Brad Pitt's kid in the movie *World War Z* and run out of asthma medicine. When we pilfer the local department store for supplies, I'll dillydally in the shoe section, teetering in four-inch heels while the real survivors pick sensible running shoes for the best escape. I'll insist on bringing a case of wine, and my husband will end up carrying the lot of it.

As for food, the strong among us will forage the wild for asparagus and mushrooms, while I go scouting for an open farmers market. I rely on farmers to grow my food, and would do poorly searching for maple trees, ramps, and honey-making bees.

Orange-Maple Vinaigrette

MAKES ABOUT 1 CUP

Getting a table at brunch on Sunday is nearly impossible in the city where I live. We usually end up asking to sit at the bar to circumvent a long wait. There is a pancake house near our neighborhood where the waitstaff is sassy and they keep your coffee mug full. One weekend when a metal condiment bowl containing gelatinous brown goop was placed next to my order of waffles, I asked for real maple syrup. "I don't mind paying extra," I told our server.

The server smiled and said, "Our maple syrup *is* real. We make it every morning with brown sugar."

I recalled a *Seinfeld* episode when Jerry and his girlfriend sneak a bottle of pure maple syrup with them whenever they eat out for breakfast. Now, I tuck a small bottle of the good stuff into my bag whenever brunch calls.

zest and juice from 1 orange (about ¼ cup juice)
3 tablespoons pure maple syrup
2 tablespoons lemon juice or white wine vinegar

1 small shallot, finely chopped (about 2 tablespoons)
1 teaspoon Dijon-style mustard
½ cup olive oil

Shake all ingredients together until maple and mustard are well blended; season to taste with salt and pepper. Serve over your favorite salad mix. This vinaigrette is especially good on roasted asparagus.

Maple Wings

SERVES 2–4

2 teaspoons ground ginger
1½ teaspoons garlic powder
1½ teaspoons chili powder
1 teaspoon ground cumin
1 teaspoon onion salt
1 teaspoon dry mustard
½ teaspoon salt

½ teaspoon pepper
1½–2 pounds chicken wings
⅓ cup pure maple syrup
⅓ cup sambal oelek (Indonesian chili paste)
3 tablespoons butter, cold

Combine spices (ginger through pepper) in a large mixing bowl. Add chicken and toss to coat well. Place in airtight container and store up to 12 hours in refrigerator.

Heat oven to 375 degrees. Place rubbed wings on parchment-lined baking sheet, skin-side down. Bake 20 minutes. Flip wings and cook an additional 20 minutes.

While wings cook, place maple and sambal oelek in a small saucepan over medium heat. Simmer for 5 minutes, remove from heat, and whisk in butter to blend.

Toss hot wings in sauce; return to sheet pan and bake an additional 10 minutes to caramelize sauce. Serve hot with remaining sauce on side.

> **NOTE** *You can also grill wings over indirect heat for 40 to 45 minutes, turning every 10 minutes. Toss wings in sauce, and place over direct heat for about 2 minutes on each side or until sauce caramelizes. Serve hot with remaining sauce on the side.*

Ramp Pesto

MAKES ABOUT 1½–1¾ CUPS

1 cup ramp tops (greens)
1 cup ramp stems and bulbs
2 tablespoons hazelnuts
2 tablespoons grated Parmesan or Asiago cheese
1 tablespoon cider vinegar

¼ cup olive oil
1½ teaspoons pure maple syrup
pinch salt
pinch pepper
pinch hot red pepper flakes

Bring a large pot of water to a boil. Prepare a large bowl of ice and water. Add ramp tops to boiling water and stir them down for 15 seconds. Drain and immediately move them to ice water. Drain again and squeeze out as much water as possible.

Place blanched greens, ramp stems and bulbs, hazelnuts, cheese, and vinegar in food processor fitted with metal blade. Process to a paste, then slowly drizzle in olive oil while processing. Stir in maple and seasonings.

Pickled Ramps

MAKES 1 PINT   **ERIN SWENSON-KLATT**

Erin is my boss at the American Swedish Institute, where I teach cooking classes a few times each month. Without batting an eye, she drops marvelous stories about foraging for spruce tips at a spot so secret no one else even knows it exists. She knows which mushrooms are poisonous and where to find the best wild ramps each spring. She spends solo summer afternoons picking several flats of strawberries for making jam and shares leftovers with the rest of us. I made Erin promise that if there is ever an apocalypse I can hang out with her.

About these pickled ramps Erin says, "My favorite pickle recipe ever. Do not substitute ground spices for the whole spices. I sauté the greens to serve with eggs, chop them up to add to biscuits, or make a zesty pesto for pasta."

8 ounces ramps, cleaned
1 cup rice wine vinegar (preferably unseasoned)
2 tablespoons sugar
1 tablespoon salt
2 teaspoons black peppercorns
1 teaspoon mustard seeds
½ teaspoon caraway seeds

½ teaspoon fennel seeds
½ teaspoon coriander seeds
½ teaspoon hot red pepper flakes (or to taste)
1 bay leaf
1 teaspoon cardamom pods (optional)

Sterilize a pint jar in boiling water.

Trim the root ends of ramps and discard, then trim the ramp stalks directly below where the leaves split from the stalk, or to fit in the jar with at least ½-inch head space. Reserve the green leaves for another use. Pack ramps tightly into the jar, leaving room at the top.

In a small saucepan, combine the vinegar, sugar, salt, and spices (peppercorns through cardamom, if using) and bring to a boil, stirring to dissolve the sugar and salt. Remove from heat and pour over the ramps.

At this point the jar can be cooled and refrigerated for up to 1 week or can be canned in a water bath for 5 minutes to remain shelf-stable for up to 1 year.

Jell-O Salad

The culinary history of gelatin is not unlike other foods that began with European nobility, migrated with the American elite, and eventually ended up in humble American kitchens (and church basements). Labor-intensive, rare, and expensive ingredients made way for science and technology to produce fast, economical, pre-packaged solutions for busy families.

Before its reign as the base for bejeweled salads, gelatin was made by boiling animal bones to release their gelatin properties. It took time and labor to serve up a plate of congealed wiggly jiggly. By the turn of the twentieth century, Jell-O and Knox were becoming popular in kitchens across America where housewives served aspics filled with chopped proteins, vegetables, and fruit. Manufacturers advertised that housewives could serve what the rich were eating for just ten cents a box.

Gelatin salad was thought of as the feminine balance to masculine meat and potatoes; thus, it became a perfect addition to light luncheons for ladies. Simply opening a can and plopping its contents onto a plate would have been frowned upon, so packaged gelatin was gussied up not only with spangles but with the decorative gelatin mold itself, as well as frostings made of mayonnaise and fancy garnishes.

By the 1980s anti-sugar and anti-processed food fads relegated gelatin in all its renditions to snack and dessert status. In my day kids devoured Jell-O Pudding Pops. As a young adult I consumed boxes upon boxes of sugar-free Jell-O Pops as part of every weight loss attempt. Yet, for years my mom continued to place lime Jell-O filled with floating shredded carrots on our Easter table. The salad, molded in a round Tupperware Jel-Ring, was complete with a mound of Miracle Whip in the center. Mom stopped making the salad years ago, and to this day I miss its presence.

• • •

Minnesotans proudly claim two phenomena that don't necessarily belong to us. One is "*Ope*, sorry." The word ope (rhymes with "hope") is a sort of substitute for "whoops." When combined with the word *sorry* it becomes a phrase used when accidentally bumping into someone, startling someone, or generally inconveniencing someone else. ("Ope, sorry" can also be self-applied. For example, when reaching for your credit card at checkout and fumbling with your wallet, you might exclaim, "Ope!" and possibly even use the entire phrase, "Ope, sorry." However, whether you are apologizing to yourself, the people behind you in line, or your wallet is debatable.)

The second phenomenon that Minnesotans love to claim is Jell-O salad. The final episode of the third season of the television show *Fargo* (based on the epic film of the same name, which was conceived of by Minnesota's own Coen brothers, Joel and Ethan) included a holiday feast during which one of the characters is asked to go to the kitchen to retrieve the salad. He opens the refrigerator and pulls out a beautiful molded (such a tragic word to use when describing something as lovely as Jell-O) salad. There was discussion in these parts about whether anyone other than a Minnesotan would have known that was a salad.

While both "ope" and Jell-O salad certainly play a role in most Minnesotans' vernacular, they don't belong solely to us. "Ope" has been identified as a midwestern word, yet I've heard tales of its existence as far west as California and Washington State and as far south as Texas. I don't know whether the phrase is ever uttered on the East Coast, as hardliners there might be too rushed for such verbal courtesies.

And Jell-O salad? That luxurious wonder is universally adored by retro dining connoisseurs, church basement ladies, and other culinary adventurers. You can find glorious recipes for Jell-O salad in church and community cookbooks, in *The Joy of Cooking*, and at least since the 1960s on everyday and holidays tables from Nebraska to Georgia. It is a misguided belief that only northern tables continue to herald jiggly fruit-, vegetable-, and meat-filled gelatins. Jell-O salad complements any meal, anytime, anywhere.

• • •

I first heard of the Anoka County Historical Society's Jell-O Salad Cook-Off and (Naked Thumb) Wrestling Tournament at a conference on Minnesota history. Over lunch I was chatting with friends about writing about hotdish competitions for this book when the women at the end of our table interjected, "What about Jell-O? Are you writing about any Jell-O cook-offs?" I admitted I hadn't even heard of such an occasion, and just like that I had the event on my calendar. Naked thumb wrestling and copious amounts of gelatin salads? Who can resist that?

The Anoka County Historical Society (ACHS) is remarkable for many reasons, and I admire the group because of their willingness to approach history with contemporary vision. ACHS markets the history of its region with unique and playful fundraisers because its team members understand that history is exciting when we can experience it with all of our senses. Their Jell-O Cook-Off was a fantastic example of this.

We walked into the event when it was already in full wiggle. Artist and historian Jill Johnson stood in the center of the hall, speaking about gelatin and Jell-O, past and present. Dozens of Jell-O cookbooks and molds lined a table where guests mingled, pointing to familiar recipes and reminiscing about family traditions. Tables pushed together created a U-shaped circle around the festivities, where a dozen Jell-O salads jiggled and teased, vying to earn titles in Best in Fluff, Best Fruit Suspension, and Best Family Story. I tasted each salad, made small talk with contestants, and voted for my favorite Jell-Os and stories. Soon, Johnson was guiding participants in making colorful art from dry Jell-O powder, a Jell-O Jiggler toss game broke out, and the thumb wrestling kicked off as two young women dipped their hands into an orange gelatinous ring.

One of the event organizers stood with me for a moment, and we listened to the conversations happening around us. "I love when people don't realize they are telling their oral history," she said. We were surrounded by people sharing their memories as Jell-O salad became the trigger to evoke family rituals.

Cheryl's Jell-O Salad

SERVES 12   CHERYL VOLKENANT

This Jell-O salad is a Linde family recipe passed down from Lillian Linde to Cheryl Volkenant. Cheryl said: "This was a recipe that my mom [Lillian Linde] used to make for all the holidays. [We had] orange Jell-O with mandarin oranges for Easter and Thanksgiving and red (strawberry, cherry, or raspberry) with corresponding fruit for Valentine's or Christmas. My husband Wes suggested trying other varieties, and we came up with lime Jell-O with pineapple. He started bringing that one to his office party potlucks and it was a hit."

2 cups water
3 ounces tapioca
1 (3-ounce) package orange Jell-O

1 (11-ounce) can mandarin
    oranges, drained
8 ounces nondairy topping (Cool
    Whip), thawed

In a saucepan over medium heat, whisk together water and tapioca. Cook until mixture comes to a rapid boil, stirring frequently. Whisk in Jell-O powder and continue whisking until gelatin is dissolved. Transfer to a clean mixing bowl and cool. Fold in orange slices, reserving a few for garnish, and nondairy topping. Transfer to serving bowl and refrigerate overnight. Garnish with reserved orange slices.

Winning recipe for Best in Fluff from the 2019 Anoka County Historical Society Jell-O Salad Cook-Off

Old-Fashioned Jell-O Shots

MAKES 14–16 SHOTS

Jell-O shots appear at ice fishing contests and keg parties across Minnesota. They are requisite on cold nights when you need to warm up, and on hot days when you want to feel like a kid again (except with alcohol).

In a wine store shopping with a Danish friend, I noticed a giant bucket filled with gelatin shots in plastic cups. Rita confessed she'd never heard of Jell-O shots, so we bought one in every color and flavor. They were on sale, after all: five for two dollars. We brought our gelatinous loot to dinner with friends, and we all watched in awe and delight as Rita tasted her first Jell-O shot. Of course, homemade Jell-O shots are preferable to manufactured.

1 (3-ounce) package cherry or orange Jell-O
1 cup boiling water
½ cup bottled ready-to-drink Old Fashioned (such as Tattersall)
½ cup cold water
14–16 long-stemmed cherries

In a large bowl, stir together Jell-O and boiling water and whisk until Jell-O is completely dissolved. Stir in whiskey and cold water and mix to thoroughly combine. Place a cherry into each shot cup and pour Jell-O mixture into shot cups until half to three-quarters full. Refrigerate for 2 to 4 hours, or until set.

Jell-Epilogue

When I was a teen there was never junk food in the house except for a steady rotation of three-gallon tubs of Baskin-Robbins tucked into our coffin-sized freezer in the garage. The tubs presumably came from my mother's second husband's ability to negotiate discount deals with clients, and were an effort to relieve my mother's daily scoop requirements. (My mom is known for her one and only weakness. Ice cream is her drug of choice.)

One summer a tub of Tin Roof Sundae took its place next to a pumpkin something-or-another. Pumpkin ice cream was a flavor so foul it didn't tempt anyone. But Tin Roof? Heaven. However, ice cream was off-limits, and I was reduced to sneaking a teaspoon here and there, keeping the declining level of ice cream unnoticeable. Somehow my friend Leigh and I got the convoluted idea to mix Tin Roof with lime Jell-O, concocting a new flavor profile and allowing us to extend afternoon treats to more than a bite. Leigh remembers, "It was summertime and we were not permitted to have your stepfather's ice cream. We made lime Jell-O and added just enough [ice cream], but not so much that he would notice, that we could taste with the Jell-O."

Years later Twin Cities ice cream purveyor Izzy's created an ode to Jell-O salad, mixing lime and cranberry sauce plumped with marshmallow. The flavor was first sold at the Hamline Church Dining Hall during the Minnesota State Fair. Leigh and I were convinced we were the only two humans to have enjoyed the combination, but lime Jell-O and ice cream are obviously a classic pairing.

To get the skinny on Izzy's Jell-O Salad ice cream, I spoke with Jeff Sommers about the origins of the legendary flavor and also got a lesson in how to run an ice cream dynasty. Jeff and his wife, Lara Hammel, own Izzy's and manage their business and staff with equal doses of love and discipline, just as good church basement denizens do. Jeff, a former middle school teacher, always loved the positive experiences with the kids he taught. "We do a lot of teaching at Izzy's," he said, then described how he speaks with the parents of every new hire under eighteen years old to talk about expectations, scheduling vacations, and Izzy's culture and training program. He and Lara think of their staff as a large family, and he wants parents to know when he has concerns about their kids: "Young people need to know that the adults in their lives are all on the same page."

Self-taught in ice cream and business, Jeff and Lara learned how to make ice cream from a book and from a two-and-a-half-day class Jeff took from gelato guru Luciano Ferrari, who said, "None of what I've been teaching you matters. What really matters in frozen dessert is that you smile and give free tastes of ice cream to visitors."

"I got really wound up about that. That's where the idea of the Izzy Scoop came from," Jeff told me, referring to the mini scoop customers can opt for either complimentary on top of a single or double or purchased on its own and, as the menu says, "great if you're in the mood for just a taste of Izzy's."

Just as Dairy Queen trademarked its iconic cone swirl, the Izzy Scoop is now part of business lexicon. Every business needs an Izzy Scoop, that little extra something to surprise and delight customers.

When Izzy's began partnering with the Hamline Church Dining Hall at the Minnesota State Fair, the collaboration was kismet. Jeff grew up working the fairgrounds when his family bought a hot dog stand that stood just west of the Grandstand, a block or two from Hamline's famed hall. Jeff and his sister began running the stand together when he was in tenth grade. "I watched Sweet Martha's open in a tent," he recalls, the humble beginning to a chocolate chip cookie empire. The state fair experience informed Jeff and Lara's approach to Izzy's.

Each year Izzy's supplies Hamline's dining hall with ice cream usually created especially for the fair: "The crew at the dining hall has embraced the opportunity and work hard to make it meaningful." That same crew starts sending in ideas for possible flavors and themes each winter, months before the fair opens for business.

Why Jell-O Salad? "Jell-O Salad *is* Minnesota."

Izzy's Jell-O Salad ice cream starts with a key lime base, mixed exclusively for Izzy's by Birchwood Cafe in Minneapolis, where great care is taken to produce fare with thoughtfully sourced ingredients. The lime is swirled in cranberry sauce and marshmallows. While the Izzy's team thought it would be fun to make the ice cream green, they quickly realized they'd need artificial ingredients to do so. Instead, Jell-O Salad ice cream is white with a red swirl.

I left my interview with Jeff armed with the recipe for Jell-O Salad ice cream. I carefully ran the numbers to make the 2½-gallon recipe into 2½ pints. I measured and weighed out limeade and marshmallow fluff. I made a sauce from organic cranberries and bought inverted sugar online. (Inverted sugar is made from heating two simple sugars—glucose and fructose—with water. The result is sweeter than, retains moisture better than, and doesn't crystalize as easily as table sugar. Inverted sugar is preferred for ice cream making. You can make inverted sugar at home, but I was feeling lazy.) I spent a morning tasting the mélange as it whirled in my ice cream maker, then froze it for a while, then added a few cups of half-and-half and whirled some more. You know what? It tasted pretty good. But it was Pepto-Bismol pink and came nothing close to the wonder that is Izzy's Jell-O Salad ice cream. For this taste, you need to make a trip to the Twin Cities and buy it straight from the source.

NOTE
Jell-O Salad ice cream is an Izzy's limited-edition flavor. Check with the store for availability. If you can't make it to Izzy's, give my mother-in-law's ice cream Jell-O (page 90) a try. Add some marshmallows for full frozen Jell-O salad experience.

Yummy Jell-O Mold, aka Ice Cream Jell-O

SERVES 6   MAUREEN ROONEY-WELSCH

My mother-in-law Maureen started making this salad years ago, but no one in the family agrees where the original recipe came from. A magazine, a neighbor, a relative? Once a recipe becomes part of a family tradition, the significance of its place on the table outweighs its origin story and family lore fills in the missing pieces.

Maureen selects Jell-O flavors (and colors) according to the time of year, and she uses a corresponding lid on her vintage fluted Tupperware mold to form a red, orange, or blue tulip; green pine tree; red heart; or yellow star.

1 cup boiling water
1 (3-ounce) box Jell-O, any flavor
4 cups vanilla ice cream, thawed slightly

In a mixing bowl, pour boiling water over Jell-O powder and whisk to dissolve gelatin. Add ice cream and stir together until ice cream is completely melted and incorporated with Jell-O. Pour into mold and refrigerate until firm, about 4 hours.

Field Day

Elementary school ended each year with a field day where we were bused to a park to explore nature and vie for ribbons in random athletic events like kicking a football farthest or running the fastest hundred-yard dash. I couldn't care less about nature or sports because my entire day was spent fantasizing about the brown bag lunch that awaited me. It was the one time each year I got to dictate my meal, and I always chose a bologna sandwich, bag of chips, can of pop (wrapped in tinfoil because we all believed foil kept things cold), and Hostess Twinkie, Cupcakes, or Ho Hos. On really lucky years I was allowed a banana flip: an enormous flat cake folded over creamy filling, like a Twinkie on banana steroids. My family did not indulge in store-bought treats, and field day was my only opportunity to enjoy those packaged delights all at once.

Bourbon Banana Flip

MAKES 12–14 CAKES

The irony of a recipe based on a favorite childhood taste being made with booze is not lost on me. That's why I was also inspired to use baby food: booze and baby food as a balance of age, or aging. If a Twinkie and banana bread had a baby and slathered it with marshmallowy cream and booze, it would be a bourbon banana flip.

1½ cups all-purpose flour
1½ teaspoons baking powder
½ teaspoon salt
¼ teaspoon fresh ground nutmeg
¾ cup whole milk or half-and-half
6 ounces (about ¾ cup) banana
    puree (or banana baby food)
¼ cup bourbon
6 tablespoons butter, softened
¾ cup sugar
2 teaspoons vanilla extract
2 large eggs
banana cream (recipe at right)

Heat oven to 350 degrees. Generously grease and flour muffin top pan; set aside. In a mixing bowl, sift together flour, baking powder, salt, and nutmeg. In a large measuring cup, whisk together milk, banana puree, and bourbon. In a large mixing bowl, beat butter for about 30 seconds. Add sugar, vanilla, and eggs and beat an additional minute. Continue beating and add dry ingredients and milk alternately in batches.

Add ¼ cup batter to each divot of prepared pan and bake in upper and lower thirds of oven, switching position of sheets halfway through baking, until tops are puffed and cakes spring back when touched, 10 to 12 minutes. Transfer with a spatula to a rack to cool completely. Fill with banana cream.

Banana Cream

MAKES ABOUT 2½ CUPS

¾ cup marshmallow crème
2 ounces (about ¼ cup)
    banana puree (or banana
    baby food)
1 teaspoon vanilla extract or
    good glug of bourbon
¾ cup heavy cream, whipped
    to stiff peaks

Beat marshmallow, banana puree, and vanilla together until well mixed. Fold in whipped cream.

Graduation

The year my oldest sister graduated from high school, I was devastated. Cheryl was my best sister. I shared a room with her, imitated her, and generally worshipped her. Losing her to adulthood was not something I was prepared for. To make the situation less traumatic for me, my mom sewed a new dress for me to wear for Cheryl's graduation party. It was a pink seersucker midi with white polka dots and short ruffled sleeves, and it was the prettiest thing I had ever owned.

In between stints at the sewing machine, Mom spent weeks preparing for the party. There were finger sandwiches stuffed with salty ham and creamy egg salads, and platters of bars in every color and flavor. The spread became my kid standard by which I have compared every other graduation party since.

I've been bar challenged my entire life. In fact, one of my first kitchen experiments was a batch of brownies baked at my friend Lorelei's house that was so dense we had to throw away the pan in order to hide the disaster from her mother. In later years I developed a reputation for destroying everything from Rice Krispie Treats to blondies, but I was determined to master my mom's recipe for graduation bars, and once having acquired that skill I moved on to two recipes worthy of any party.

Graduation Caramel Bars

MAKES 16 BARS

I asked my mom why these bars are called graduation bars, and she recalled she named them that because she made them for my sister's graduation. While I've always been bar challenged, the memory of these delicious bars spurred me into very careful replication of my mom's recipe. Bars success!

For the base
1 cup all-purpose flour
¼ teaspoon salt
½ teaspoon baking soda
½ cup packed brown sugar
¾ cup quick-cooking oats
8 tablespoons butter

Heat oven to 350 degrees. Grease an 8x8–inch baking pan; set aside. In a large mixing bowl, whisk together dry ingredients (flour through oats). Cut in butter until mixture is crumbly. Reserve 1 cup. Press remaining mixture into prepared pan and bake for 10 minutes.

For the caramel layer
24 vanilla caramels (about 11 ounces)
2 tablespoons cream
2 tablespoons all-purpose flour
½ cup semisweet chocolate morsels

In a saucepan over low heat, melt caramels with cream, stirring occasionally. When the caramels are completely smooth, blend in flour. Spread carefully over base. Sprinkle top evenly with chocolate morsels, then remaining oat mixture. Bake 12 to 15 minutes or until light brown. Cool before cutting into bars.

NOTE *Regarding doneness, Mom's recipe emphasizes the word* light *with an underline. Also in Mom's recipe, "I use a few more caramels."*

Erma's Special Lingonberry Bars

MAKES 16–20 BARS   ERMA COMSTOCK

Erma volunteers at the American Swedish Institute in Minneapolis. At the annual Kräftskiva (crayfish party; see page 126), Erma is always our table guide. She is enthusiastic and gleeful as she leads us singing Swedish drinking songs and makes sure we know how to crack open our crustaceans. Kräftskiva just isn't the same when she isn't there. I tease Erma that our group has never won the singing competition that decides which table gets first dibs at the buffet. One year, Erma wasn't at the event and my table still lost the singing competition. We joked that I was the common denominator of loss, not her.

Erma shared her lingonberry bar recipe for me to use in a Classic Cookies and Bars class. My students loved the bars, and I loved how they are not only pretty and delicious but also achievable for even a bar-challenged baker like me.

¾ cup (1½ sticks) butter, softened
½ cup granulated sugar
⅓ cup packed brown sugar
1 tablespoon lemon juice
2 cups all-purpose flour

¼ teaspoon baking soda
¼ teaspoon salt
1 cup preserved lingonberries
   (Felix brand)

Heat oven to 350 degrees. Grease a 9x9–inch baking pan; set aside. In a large mixing bowl, combine butter, sugars, and lemon juice and beat with an electric mixer until very well blended.

In a medium mixing bowl, whisk together flour, baking soda, and salt. Add to the butter mixture and work the dough with your hands until crumbly and well mixed. Reserve 1 cup. Press remaining dough into prepared pan. Spread lingonberries evenly over the crust. Sprinkle reserved crumb mixture evenly over lingonberries.

Bake for 40 minutes, or until lightly brown. Cool before cutting into bars.

Coffee Toffee Bars

MAKES 35–40 BARS   CAROL PETERSON, CIRCA LATE 1960S

Carol assists at our American Swedish Institute cooking classes. She keeps us organized and the kitchen clean, and is always ready with a smile and a hug. Carol's bars are a thin shortbread, and an exceptional taste combining coffee, chocolate, and nuts. The blended flavors become an addictive crunchy toffee pastry.

Carol says, "[These bars were] made often by my mother when company was coming. I often revise the original recipe and use a full bag of mini–chocolate chips and instant espresso. They are crunchy and good!"

2¼ cups all-purpose flour
½ teaspoon baking powder
¼ teaspoon salt
1 cup (2 sticks) butter
1 cup packed brown sugar

1 teaspoon almond extract
1½ tablespoons instant coffee
1 cup semisweet chocolate morsels
½ cup chopped nuts (almonds
    or walnuts)

Heat oven to 350 degrees. In a mixing bowl, sift together flour, baking powder, and salt; set aside. In a separate mixing bowl, mix together butter, brown sugar, almond extract, and instant coffee. Gradually beat in dry ingredients. Stir in chocolate morsels and nuts.

Press dough into an ungreased 15x10–inch jelly roll pan (or rimmed cookie sheet) and bake for 20 to 25 minutes. Bars should just start to turn golden, not brown. Cut into diamonds.

Lazy Heat

My Swedish language teacher spoke about summer's arrival as though it were a sacred time. She'd demonstrate how Swedes would wander out of their homes into the season's first warm sunshine and stop as though hypnotized, faces lifted toward the light.

The same is true for Minnesotans. As soon as temperatures creep up to fifty degrees or so we don shorts and flip-flops and stumble out of our homes, squinting as we turn faces toward the sun, soaking in enough vitamin D to bolster us into believing that summer has begun again. We treat the changing seasons with reverence, and no season is so holy as summer.

On evening walks through our neighborhood, summer always smells of fresh mowed lawns and grilling meats. My household uses a chimney charcoal starter, but nostalgia overtakes me when I get a whiff of lighter fluid. It reminds me of my dad, who used an entire can of the stuff to get a small grill lit. Every hot dog and burger tasted of the fuel.

Lake people disappear each weekend and leave the cities to the rest of us. In my youth I dated a boat guy for a few years and spent every waking hour floating on the lake. Now all that relaxation makes me nervous, like I'm missing something exciting happening closer to home. I find solace in farmers markets, dining alfresco, the occasional outdoor concert, and day trips for hiking through pine-scented state parks.

In Minnesota we are good at summer because we compare it to non-summer and we know our warm days are fleeting. We liberally dose ourselves with mosquito lotion and forget the SPF until our skin turns red. We frolic, clamoring to patios, decks, lakes, and parks to do outdoors for our three months of heat pretty much everything we do indoors for the other nine months of the year.

Until we don't.

Something happens in late July that lulls us into a passive calm. The humidity rises, and we retreat either indoors to the false cool of air conditioning or to our patios, where we channel our inner slugs and resist any urge to move. Heat and humidity cradle us, womb-like. It isn't until the panic of August kicks in with the countdown to the state fair that we shake ourselves out of the spell. Summer is a dream that we have to be awake to enjoy.

99

Taking 'er Easy for All Us Sinners

We kick off summer with an annual Memorial Day viewing of *The Big Lebowski*.

Not familiar with this fine flick and its Minnesota connections? *The Big Lebowski* debuted in 1998. Written, produced, and directed by Minnesota's favorite siblings-who-got-away, Joel and Ethan Coen. The Coen brothers grew up here, so we claim them as ours. (Although truth be told, even if you didn't grow up here but maybe spent summers at language camp up north like Chelsea Clinton or spent a few years making music in Minneapolis like Janet Jackson or Lizzo, we claim you as ours also. Whether you like it or not, you are one of us.)

Memorial Day Weekend is the perfect time for a viewing of *The Big Lebowski*, with its rainbow of fragile pacifists, conscientious objectors, veterans (or is he a draft dodger?), nihilists, and a rich, powerful white man with ties to Nancy and Ron. They remind us of the politics behind war and the characters who play their parts in America's history of drawing lines in the sand. For two hours we hang out in a smoky bowling alley drinking Caucasians (White Russians), macro-beers, and Sioux City Sarsaparilla with the likes of the Dude, Walter, Donny, Maude, Bunny, and the Stranger. *The Big Lebowski* is a mystery about mistaken identity, a kidnapping plot, bowling, and a soiled rug. Our conversations are sprinkled with quotes from the movie:

- The Dude abides.
- He's a good man, and thorough.
- Yeah, well, that's just, like, your opinion, man.
- Calmer than you are.
- Ever thus to deadbeats.

Every time we watch *The Big Lebowski* we notice more of the "ins and outs," the strands in the old Duder's head, and that the rug isn't the only thing that ties the room together. To me, *The Big Lebowski* is a perfect movie, although, as the Stranger once asked, "Do you have to use so many cuss words?" It is nearly impossible to quote from the flick without injecting a swear word here and there.

And there is the bowling. And the food.

Our Memorial Day weekend includes a Lebowski-themed menu of copycat In-N-Out Burgers, lingonberry pancakes, White Russians (Caucasians, as the Dude refers to them), and a dessert flavored with sarsaparilla.

Bison Lucy

MAKES 3–4 BURGERS

During a momentous adventure in the movie, our protagonists get takeout from the In-N-Out Burger. I've never eaten at In-N-Out, although it is on my short list for must-do-someday. In Minnesota the only opportunity we have to eat at the acclaimed fast food burger joint with its bible-versed wrappers is if we travel to a state where they reign. Instead, we make do with creating our own versions of In-N-Out.

Minnesota's most distinguished burger is called a Ju(i)cy Lucy. There is some argument about where she originated (and how her name is spelled). We all agree that she was born in south Minneapolis, but was her birthplace at Matt's or the 5-8 Club? While most of us in the Twin Cities have an opinion (usually due to which diner is our favorite), there are others who have spent time paying homage to the cheese-stuffed burger by developing our own versions.

My Bison Lucy is one part jucy/juicy and one part In-N-Out, with a nod to our beloved prairie-roaming bison. The trick in cooking the burger is getting the lean meat to temp while simultaneously getting the cheese inside to melt.

1 pound ground bison (or any ground meat you prefer; I've even had luck with turkey)
3–4 squares American cheese, each folded into a 1½x½–inch cube
salt and pepper

3–4 buns
butter or mayonnaise
pickles
fried onions (recipe follows)
special sauce spread (recipe follows)

Divide meat into 3 or 4 equal portions (3 if you prefer a larger burger; 4 if you prefer a smaller one). Divide each portion into two equal pieces and shape them into two flat patties. Lay a cube of cheese in the center of one patty, then top with the other patty. Press together to form one patty. Repeat with remaining portions. Season generously with salt and pepper.

Heat a cast-iron skillet over medium-high heat. Cook the burgers 4 to 5 minutes each side, flipping only once.

Slather buns with butter or mayonnaise and lightly toast on a hot skillet. Serve burgers in buns and top with pickles, fried onions, and special sauce spread.

Fried Onions

MAKES ABOUT 2 CUPS

Adapted from Stig Hansen's crisp onions recipe in *Cooking Danish*.

I met Danish chef Stig Hansen years ago when I first started traveling to Minot, North Dakota, to cook Nordic food for guests at Norsk Høstfest, a four-day Scandinavian festival. Chef Stig's smørrebrød (open-face sandwiches) are magic, and his demos are standing room only. Chef Stig tops his beef smørrebrød with delectable crisp onions, which I often copy when I'm teaching Scandinavian sandwich classes. My copycat version here swaps out buttermilk for milk and yogurt because I usually have those ingredients in my kitchen. For a more delicate topping, use shallots rather than onions.

1 cup half-and-half or whole milk
1 cup plain yogurt
1 yellow onion or 2 large shallots, very thinly sliced

3–4 cups vegetable oil for frying
2 cups all-purpose flour
salt

In a medium bowl, whisk together half-and-half and yogurt. Add onions to yogurt mixture, stirring gently to separate the slices. Let stand 8 minutes or longer. Drain onions and discard the yogurt mixture.

Add oil to a deep, heavy saucepan or deep fat fryer, and heat to 375 degrees. Place flour in a shallow bowl. Add onion rings, a few at a time, to coat well. Shake off excess flour. Working in batches to not crowd the pot, deep-fry in heated oil for 3 minutes or until golden, using a slotted spoon to turn at least once. Remove cooked onions and drain on paper towels. Repeat process with remaining onion rings. Season with salt while still hot.

Special Sauce Spread

MAKES ABOUT ½ CUP

This is my version of In-N-Out's special spread. Layer it on burgers and serve it alongside fries.

Whisk together ¼ cup mayonnaise, 2 tablespoons ketchup, and 1 tablespoon sweet pickle relish.

Lingonberry Pancakes

MAKES ABOUT 16 (4- TO 5-INCH) PANCAKES

When we meet the entire group of nihilists in *The Big Lebowski*, they are dining out, ordering up one "three pigs in blanket" and a few rounds of "lingonberry pancake." These crepe-like pancakes get all of their leavening from the air beaten into the eggs, sugar, and half-and-half before the dry ingredients are added.

3 large eggs
2 tablespoons sugar
1½ cups half-and-half
1½ cups all-purpose flour
¼ teaspoon salt
zest of 1 lemon
½ cup whole milk ricotta cheese
4 tablespoons butter, melted

1 teaspoon
   vanilla extract
pinch salt
nonstick spray
lingonberry
   maple syrup
   (recipe follows)

Add eggs, sugar, and ½ cup of the half-and-half to large bowl of standing mixer. Use whisk attachment to beat on medium for about 3 minutes or until foamy batter forms. Add flour, salt, and zest all at once and continue beating. Add remaining 1 cup half-and-half, ricotta, melted butter, vanilla, and salt and beat 2 to 3 additional minutes. Batter will be quite wet. Rest batter for 30 minutes.

Heat oven to 250 degrees. Place nonstick skillet or griddle over medium-high heat. Coat with nonstick spray. Spoon 3 to 4 tablespoons of batter onto pan for each 4- to 5-inch pancake. Work in batches so that the pan is not crowded, coating pan with nonstick spray as needed. Cook pancakes until bubbles form on surface, 1 to 2 minutes. Use flat spatula to gently flip pancake and cook an additional 1 minute or until underside is golden. Keep warm in very low (200-degree) oven. Serve with lingonberry maple syrup.

Lingonberry Maple Syrup

MAKES ABOUT 1 CUP

½ cup lingonberry preserves
½ cup pure maple syrup
1 tablespoon butter

Combine lingonberry preserves with maple syrup in a small saucepan. Heat over medium-low, whisking in butter just before serving.

White Russian Float

SERVES 2

The Dude drinks a steady flow of White Russians, aka Caucasians, throughout the movie. So do we, although this dessert version is even better than the cocktail.

2 cups vanilla ice cream
3 ounces Kahlúa or similar
   coffee-flavored liqueur

1 ounce vodka
white chocolate shavings and whole
   hazelnuts for garnish

Place 1 cup ice cream in each of 2 large tumblers. Divide coffee liqueur and vodka between glasses and garnish with chocolate and nuts.

Sarsaparilla Snaps

MAKES 42 (2-INCH) COOKIES

A critical character in *The Big Lebowski* is the Stranger, who not only interacts with the Dude when he orders drinks at the bowling alley bar but also acts as our narrator. He loves a good sarsaparilla, and in particular a Sioux City Sarsaparilla. These snaps honor him and his drink of choice.

6 tablespoons butter
1 cup packed brown sugar
1 large egg
12 ounces sarsaparilla or root beer,
   reduced to ¼ cup and cooled
2 teaspoons balsamic vinegar

1 teaspoon vanilla extract
2 cups all-purpose flour
1½ teaspoons baking soda
1 teaspoon ground anise
½ teaspoon salt
½ cup granulated sugar

NOTE *The sarsaparilla reduction will be quite gooey.*

Heat oven to 325 degrees. In a large mixing bowl, combine butter and brown sugar, mixing well. Add egg, reduced sarsaparilla, vinegar, and vanilla. In a separate bowl, sift together flour, baking soda, anise, and salt. Add dry ingredients to wet and mix to form dough. Roll into balls, about 1 tablespoon each. Place granulated sugar in a mixing bowl. Toss balls in sugar and place 1 inch apart on parchment-lined baking sheet. Gently press tops of each cookie with tines of a fork. Bake about 12 minutes. Cool on rack.

Rainy Days & Front Stoop Food

In my youth, summer days were spent at the Gaylord swimming pool. A typical day meant morning swimming lessons, running home for a quick lunch, then back to the pool to swim the afternoon away. Some days there were a few cents tucked into my shorts pocket to spend on a treat. If I had a nickel, I'd persuade my buddies to walk with me to the corner store, where the big ice cream freezer with the sliding glass lid contained a colorful assortment of giant Mr. Freezes, and I'd rifle through the ice pops to find orange. In a pinch cherry might suffice. Occasionally I'd grab an orange push-up, and on really flush days I'd buy an expensive single-serve bag of Cheetos or a can of Orange Crush from the pool snack counter. Orange was my favorite food color.

A well-fed kid works up quite an appetite when she swims all day, every day. I came home for dinner so famished that I couldn't stand up straight. On really hot nights Mom might make shrimp and carrot salad topped with potato sticks. She got the recipe from her friend and our neighbor Jan, and over the years I've seen copycat recipes in church cookbooks, usually replacing the shrimp with canned tuna. Mom always served the salad with sweet baked beans (I didn't care about the beans, but I loved the fancy decanter with vinegar that I was allowed to pour over them), snappy dill pickles, thick rounds of Colby cheese, and biscuits so hot the butter melted into every delicate crevice. Dinner wasn't complete until we had our ice cream (my mom's one addiction), and when cantaloupe came into season Mom placed an entire half melon on each dessert plate, replacing the center seeds with a big scoop of vanilla.

Forty years later I still re-create that menu on the hottest days of summer. Orange carrots, pinkish orange shrimps, orange cheese, orange melon: I guess orange is still my favorite food color.

· · ·

When thunderstorms kept me away from the pool, I'd set up a Barbie town on our front porch. The screen windows were open to the sound of rain, and there was a whiff of mildew from ancient Barbie clothes that my mom sewed before I was born for a Christmas gift to my older sisters. The entire world was right there where I needed it to be. Barbie, Skipper, and Malibu PJ (we had the same initials and hair color!) played dress-up, and our lounging Great Danes became grassy hills for picnics and dune buggy rides.

If my sister Susan wasn't home, I'd sneak into her Dawn doll mansion, a beautiful, spacious cardboard palace decorated with vibrant painted walls, carpeting, chandeliers, and store-bought furniture, with walk-in closets and fashion dolls so tiny and posh they made Barbie seem like a frumpy clod. There was even a garage for Dawn's yellow scooter.

If the storms continued into the afternoon, I'd break out the Lite-Brite with so many missing pegs I had to substitute pinks for whites. When that got dull, I'd beg Mom for a few pieces of paper and ask one of my sisters to remove the Lite-Brite light bulb and screw it into the old electric drawing set. I'd carefully trace the mod Francie and Barbie stencils, but the bulb made the set so hot that my fingers burned before I finished a single drawing. I'd move the entire project from the floor near the outlet to the dining room table. Eventually I'd switch to Spirograph, with only black and blue pen colors to choose from, the best colors having dried up from too much use.

If my sister Susan still wasn't home, I'd sneak into her Hot Wheels loop-to-loop set, set up the tracks from the dining room table to the living room, and race the forbidden cars over and over until it was nearly dinnertime and I knew Susan would return home soon. (Funny how Susan always knew I'd trespassed Dawn Drive and committed tiny auto theft when I took such pains to put everything back *exactly* as I'd found it. I feared her wrath, but not as much as I loved her toys.)

Once the storms passed, I'd be sent to the front stoop with my popcorn bowl filled with sugar or salt and a handful of whatever had been pulled out of the garden that day. I'd sit on the steps, watching the semitrucks parading Main Street, dipping radishes into salt and rhubarb stalks or whole tomatoes into sugar (the tomatoes eaten like an apple). Decades later I sent my own daughter to the front stoop to eat her snacks, and the neighbor kids came around and had their first bites of raw rhubarb and artichokes.

Minnesota summers are endless in their abundance. We soak it all in with our indulgences.

Sort-of Jan Doerr's Shrimp and Carrot Salad

SERVES 6 (UNLESS I AM INVITED)

¾ cup mayonnaise
3 tablespoons sugar
3 tablespoons lemon juice
1 tablespoon prepared mustard
1 teaspoon Old Bay Seasoning
pepper

4 cups shredded carrots
2 large green onions, finely chopped
  (3–4 tablespoons)
2 cups cooked shrimp
1 cup potato sticks

Whisk together mayo, sugar, lemon juice, mustard, and Old Bay and season to taste with pepper. Combine with carrots, onions, and shrimp. Refrigerate until ready to serve. Garnish with potato sticks.

Orange Push-Up Jell-O Shots

MAKES 44 SHOTS

This is a grown-up version of a childhood treat.

1 (6-ounce) package orange Jell-O
2 cups boiling water
1½ cups vodka
½ cup cold water
1 teaspoon vanilla extract

8 ounces nondairy topping (Cool Whip), thawed
4–5 tablespoons orange-flavored liqueur (such as Tattersall Orange Crema)

Empty Jell-O packet in a mixing bowl. Add boiling water and whisk until gelatin dissolves. Add vodka, cold water, and vanilla and whisk to combine. Pour into plastic Jell-O shot cups or shot glasses, filling about three-quarters of the way to the top. Cover and refrigerate 2 to 3 hours or until firm.

In a mixing bowl, whisk together nondairy topping and orange liqueur. Spoon over each Jell-O shot. Refrigerate before serving.

The Fourth of July

Though I never received an allowance, my parents gave generously on July 4. My pockets jingled with cash when we spilled into the city park. There were vendors and games, and adults drinking beer and eating burgers along the shores of Lake Titlow. I spent the bulk of my budget on the ponies. About half a dozen shaggy Shetlands circled a post in a corral set up in the park. I handed a fistful of coins to a tall cowgirl and found myself swept up by a roadie and placed on the Western saddle of a real pony. I always asked the names of each horse, and after a few rides I'd strategize my place in line so I could ride my favorite Silver or Dusty. The ride never lasted long enough, but after four or five trysts in a day, I was convinced that I would soon be discovered and the rodeo people would beg me to appear on the circuit.

We were allowed pop twice a year in my house, three if there was a family reunion, and the Fourth of July was a soda pop free-for-all, especially if you could figure out the ring toss. As a result, the ring toss was my best game. One year I took home both a bottle of Orange Crush and a root beer.

The Fourth of July is also my big sister Susan's birthday. She believed, as we all did, that the festivities in our little town were in her honor. From the kiddie parade to the party in the park and nighttime fireworks: it was all for Susan's birthday. Why wouldn't it be? She was a phenomenon.

While I was a kid who craved instant gratification, Susan was the calculating sort. She'd spend months patiently collecting Kool-Aid and bubble gum points to redeem for really cool stuff like a Kool-Aid pop-up tent, a Kool-Aid Man pitcher, and an odd assortment of Bazooka Joe swag. A budding Tony Soprano, she organized the neighborhood kids, always took on the banker role when we played Monopoly, and was legendary for the themes she created for the Fourth of July Kiddie Parade. We neighbors marched as one unit, and Susan pulled costumes and enthusiasm out of the air. She knew kids two blocks over who owned props we could use, and she'd invite them to join our group. She spent so much time organizing that she never actually marched in the parade. Instead, she ran to the finish line to see if we won any prizes. We never did.

Susan was constantly scouting the neighborhood to find some kid who had a talent so she could manage their career and send them to the Fourth of July talent show. The promise of cash prizes made her eyes shine with anticipation.

One year, for reasons none of us can guess, Susan decided I had talent. After another tough loss in the kiddie parade, Susan marched me up to the talent show sign-up table. We missed the deadline for the kids' division, so she made the decision to send me onstage to battle the adults. She gathered her associates (the older neighborhood kids) and collected the financing she needed for the entrance fee. Funding secured (something like five bucks, which was big money in those days), Susan looked me in the eyes and demanded, "Be sure you hit that high note."

The details flood back in a collage of visuals peppered with the recall of friends and family who witnessed the spectacle. The stage: the flatbed of a truck. The microphone: too tall for a six-year-old, even if she was tallest in first grade. A clown stepped in to hold the microphone toward me, but I was (and still am) terrified of clowns. Later my sister said, with some pride, "It was a move to try and intimidate you. A kid competing against adults has to be a ringer."

Down by the lake, our parents were with their friends. The loudspeakers screeched and an announcer barked, "Next up, Patti Johnson will sing."

"Isn't that your youngest daughter?" the friends asked.

"Oh, no," my mom answered in true modest Minnesota honesty. "Our daughters don't have any talent."

Up on stage, er ... the flatbed, I grabbed the bulb of the microphone with my chubby hands, eyed the clown with trepidation, and began singing my favorite song from school.

"Blue bird blue bird in and out the window blue bird blue bird in and out the window," YOU ARE RUSHING THE LYRICS SLOW DOWN. "Blue bird blue bird in and out the window." DEEP BREATH OH MY GOSH THAT SCARY CLOWN IS WATCHING ME HE MIGHT KILL ME. HIT THE HIGH NOTE HIT THE HIGH NOTE. "Oh, Johnny," I HIT THE HIGH NOTE AUDIBLE GASP AND GULP, "are you sleeping?"

I don't know whether I sang all the verses or just the chorus. Probably no one does. I do know that when it was over a tepid applause greeted me and some guy in overalls lifted me off the flatbed, where my sister Susan was waiting for me. She stood there, expressionless. Likely she realized her mistake blowing her friends' money on my entrance fee. I had no talent. Wincing, I waited for her wrath.

"That was pretty good. You hit the high note." She put her arm around me to pat my shoulder in a brief and rare moment of solidarity and added, "You did okay, kid." With that, Susan looked up toward the stage to hear the results.

When your big sister believes in you, it changes everything.

The day ended with fireworks, best viewed from the baseball field bleachers while holding my dad's strong hand: looking up at the sky in wonder, smelling the sulfur, and covering my ears when the explosions got too close. We giggled when the old ladies cooed a collective "Oooh" and "Ahhh." Afterward, somehow I beat a soda-induced sugar rush and fell asleep as soon as I was dropped into bed, where I dreamed of ponies and pop.

I still wake on July 4 convinced that I'll win the parade, or at least get an honorable mention. I remain convinced that the rodeo will discover me, that I will win the talent show, that nothing beats an ice-cold Orange Crush. And the fireworks? I've accepted that they are in honor of my sister's birthday.

Orange Crush BBQ Sauce

MAKES 1½ CUPS

1 teaspoon olive oil
1 teaspoon sesame oil
⅓ cup minced shallot
¼ cup sambal oelek (or your favorite hot pepper sauce)
1 tablespoon grated fresh ginger
1 clove garlic, grated
2 teaspoons ground cumin

20 ounces Orange Crush (or other orange soda pop)
⅓ cup ketchup
⅓ cup rice vinegar
3 tablespoons prepared mustard
soy sauce or tamari to taste
1 teaspoon pepper

Add oils to saucepan; stir in shallots, hot pepper sauce, and ginger. Cook over medium heat about 5 minutes, stirring frequently. Add garlic and cumin and cook an additional 30 seconds. Add remaining ingredients (soda through pepper) and continue to cook, stirring frequently, until reduced to 1½ cups, about 30 minutes.

Fried Chicken

SERVES 6

I love the outside of fried chicken even more than the inside, and this recipe is for people like me. I use skyr, a drinkable Icelandic dairy product similar to yogurt, rather than buttermilk for the brine because I almost always have skyr in the refrigerator.

3 cups plain skyr
2 tablespoons honey
1 tablespoon whole-grain mustard
1 tablespoon Dijon-style mustard
1 large sprig dill
2 teaspoons paprika
2½- to 3-pound whole chicken, cut into 8 pieces
vegetable oil for frying

For the seasoned flour
2½ cups all-purpose flour
1½ tablespoons baking powder
1½ teaspoons salt
1 teaspoon pepper
1 teaspoon celery salt
1 teaspoon onion salt
1 teaspoon dried dill
1 teaspoon paprika
1 teaspoon dry mustard

In a large mixing bowl, combine skyr, honey, mustards, dill, and paprika. Add chicken to a large, sealable freezer bag. Pour marinade over chicken, seal bag, and place chicken in refrigerator for 2 to 6 hours.

Add 1 inch of vegetable oil to a large Dutch oven or cast-iron skillet with a tight-fitting lid. Gently heat oil to 350 degrees. Place a wire rack over a rimmed baking sheet.

In a shallow dish, whisk together ingredients for seasoned flour. Remove chicken from marinade, leaving as much marinade intact as possible. Dredge through the flour so that both sides of chicken are coated well. Working in batches so that chicken is not crowded, place chicken skin-side down in hot oil. The oil should nearly come over the top of the chicken. Cover pot with lid, reduce heat to medium or medium-low, and cook for 10 minutes. Remove lid and increase heat to high. Continue cooking chicken, turning once, until internal temperature reaches 170 degrees, about 5 to 10 minutes, depending on cut (check temperature on breasts after 5 minutes). Chicken should be deeply browned and crisp. Place cooked chicken on rack to cool. (Chicken can be kept warm for an hour in a 170-degree oven.)

Potato Salad

SERVES 6

Japanese potato salad, with its mashed potatoes and sweet crunchy additions of apple and cucumber, is my favorite, but those flavors don't necessarily speak to my childhood potato salad experiences. This recipe takes a page from Japanese salad by slightly mashing the potatoes before adding them hot to the dressing, but the flavor is all about my Minnesota childhood.

2½ pounds Yukon Gold potatoes, peeled and quartered
1 tablespoon salt
¾ cup mayonnaise
¼ cup sour cream
2 tablespoons sweet pickle relish
2 tablespoons sugar
1 tablespoon coarse-ground mustard
1 tablespoon cider vinegar
1 teaspoon celery salt, plus more for garnish

½ teaspoon paprika, plus more for garnish
4 hard-boiled eggs
¼ cup finely chopped onion
¼ cup finely chopped red radish
1 stalk celery, finely chopped
1 tablespoon minced fresh dill, plus more for garnish
pepper

Place potatoes in a large stockpot and fill with cold water to cover potatoes by 1 inch. Bring to a boil and add salt. Cook potatoes until fork tender, about 13 to 15 minutes.

In a large mixing bowl, whisk together mayonnaise, sour cream, pickle relish, sugar, mustard, vinegar, celery salt, and paprika. Drain potatoes and, while still hot, place potatoes on a clean kitchen towel and chop fine. Add to dressing. Chop 3 of the eggs and cut the other into thin slices. Fold in chopped eggs, onion, radish, celery, and minced dill and refrigerate before serving. Season with salt and pepper. Garnish with egg slices and top with additional celery salt, paprika, and dill.

Strawberry-Cherry Pretzel Jell-O Salad

SERVES 12

We didn't go to a lot of family reunions, but I remember well the summer we attended one on my mom's side. It was a warm summer day on a city lake. I ran wild with cousins I did not know well (did I mention how rare our reunion participation was?) to the other side of the tree-lined shore, where we climbed as high as we dared without adults telling us we couldn't. From across the lake we could hear the rumblings of our family reunited, and above the hum was the distinct sound of my mother's laughter. All of the cousins looked at me with revulsion. "Your mom is so loud!" They mocked her laughter, and I, dejected, climbed down the tree and walked back to the reunion. I was proud of our mom, who was known for her beauty and exhilaration. It never occurred to me that anyone would find fault in someone expressing joy.

A half dozen picnic tables were packed with hot dog buns, salads, and chips. My mother, concerned about the lack of hygiene in other people's homes, had warned earlier that I shouldn't eat anything that hadn't come from our house. But I was feeling wicked after the tree incident when I eyed, amid the three-bean salads and Shasta pop, a salad (à la dessert, aka bars) commonly associated with Minnesota Lutherans. I reached for a plate, and an auntie whose name I couldn't remember scooped up a colossal portion for me.

My paper plate wobbled dangerously from the weight of the pretzel-butter crust topped with cream cheese and strawberry-laced Jell-O. I added a fistful of potato chips and pickles to be sure all of the basic food groups were represented, then washed the entire meal down with as many cans of Shasta as I could manage. With the first bite of sweet, salty, creamy, crunchy, all of my hurt feelings mended, and I had a new appreciation for Baptists who dabbled in Lutheran cookery. Anyone who lives in Minnesota understands the legacy of Lutheran food, and that strawberry pretzel Jell-O salad sealed my reverence for Church Basement Cuisine.

As soon as the first Minnesota strawberries hit the market in early June, I make this salad. Each bite reinforces my gratitude toward a mom whose laughter is so joyful it reaches above loud conversations and across any landscape, where it resonates with those of us who love deeply.

2 cups crushed pretzel sticks

¾ cup (1½ sticks) butter, melted

¾ cup plus 3 tablespoons sugar

8 ounces cream cheese, softened

8 ounces whipped cream (most recipes call for Cool Whip)

1 (0.3-ounce) package sugar-free strawberry Jell-O (or 3-ounce package of regular)

1 (0.3-ounce) package sugar-free cherry Jell-O (or 3-ounce package of regular)

2 cups boiling water

1½–2 cups fresh-picked strawberries, halved or quartered

1½–2 cups sweet cherries, pitted and halved

Heat oven to 325 degrees. Mix together crushed pretzels, melted butter, and 3 tablespoons of the sugar and press in bottom of a 13x9–inch cake pan. Bake for 8 to 10 minutes, until crust is set and begins to smell quite fragrant. Cool completely.

Use electric mixer or food processor to combine remaining ¾ cup sugar and cream cheese. Fold in whipped cream and spread over pretzel crust. Refrigerate.

Whisk together Jell-O and boiling water until gelatin is dissolved. Cool about 30 minutes, then stir in fruit. Set aside for 10 minutes. Pour over cheese mixture. Refrigerate. Cut into bars.

Up North, aka To the Lake

When my mom married her second husband, we five sisters gained four step-brothers, who brought an unfamiliar whiff of testosterone into our home. There were volleyball games in the backyard and hikes out in nature. Those first few years we attempted to create a mishmash family, like if Mike and Carol had met and married when the kids (except for Cindy) were already in college. No matter how much you love *The Brady Bunch*, reality isn't always as functional and witty.

In the early years, the older siblings met my mom, me, and the new husband for extended weekends at a campground. We rented the large main cabin and the adjoining guesthouse for raucous afternoons of … well, more volleyball probably. This place wasn't anything like Kellerman's Resort, but it isn't possible to force young adults to bond as family even if the setting is remarkable. There are only three details about that time that I remember vividly: the ponies, "Dancing Queen," and scrambled eggs.

I hung out at the stables, which were along the dirt path directly in front of our cabin, and once or twice a day I was allowed to take a pony on a group trail ride. It was one of those setups where the ponies were bored and smart and tested their riders by refusing to stay on the trail and instead would wander into the woods to snack on tall grasses. When I wasn't riding, I'd sit atop the fence that framed the corral, trying to lure my favorite shaggy mare with a fistful of hay.

The teen camp workers gathered at the rec center, situated kitty-corner from both our cabin and the stables, and the year that "Dancing Queen" came out ABBA played in an endless loop that became the backdrop of my entire summer. One of the pretty camp counselors was especially fond of the song, and when she ran out of dancing partners, she'd jump up on the picnic table and put on her own show.

And then there were the eggs. In my memory it was my sister Steffie who made them, although no one remembers now whether it was her or someone else. Those scrambled eggs were so soft and so tender that I actually ate my entire plate without complaint. All these years later I remember those exquisite eggs almost as well as the ponies and "Dancing Queen," but I have not ever been able to duplicate them. Instead, we rely on egg bakes.

Egg bakes are technically a breakfast hotdish and are highly adaptable because you can prep them ahead of time and use ingredients that your guests prefer. I've even seen recipes that allow for making egg bakes in a slow cooker, beginning the night before breakfast service.

Egg Bake

SERVES 12

STEPHANIE MCCAULEY AND CHERYL MESSNER

My sister Steffie, the one who I think made those delectable scrambled eggs, contributed her mother-in-law Dot's egg bake recipe. This is the first egg bake I ever tasted, and it's still a classic. My sister Cheryl also contributed her family's egg bake. I combined the two recipes for one that includes the ingredients I really like.

9 large eggs
2 cups whole milk
1 cup heavy cream
1½ teaspoons salt
1½ teaspoons dry mustard
1 teaspoon pepper
3 slices bread, cubed

16 ounces sausage
5 ounces mushrooms, chopped
½ white onion, finely chopped
½ green bell pepper, seeded and
  finely chopped
2 cups shredded cheese

Heat oven to 350 degrees. Grease a 13x9–inch (3-quart) casserole dish; set aside. In a large bowl, whisk together eggs, milk, cream, salt, dry mustard, and pepper. Be sure that eggs are completely combined with other ingredients. Stir in bread cubes. Set aside.

In a large nonstick skillet, brown sausage over medium heat, breaking it up as it cooks. When sausage is cooked, remove it from skillet and drain, reserving 1 tablespoon of fat to add back into skillet. Add fat and mushrooms to skillet and cook until mushrooms release their liquid, about 5 minutes. Add in onion and green pepper and cook, stirring occasionally, an additional 3 minutes. Remove from heat and cool 5 to 10 minutes.

Stir cheese and cooked ingredients into egg mixture. Pour into prepared pan. Bake for 35 to 40 minutes. Let stand 5 minutes before cutting.

Egg Bake with Hash Browns

SERVES 12　　　　　　　　　　　　　　　　　　　　**LORI O'DONNELL**

My daughter Stephanie's stepmom Lori makes an egg bake with hash browns instead of bread. Stephanie raves about this dish, and after preparing it I understand why. The hash browns make this egg bake feel like a complete brunch.

Lori won't take full credit for the recipe because she got it from an ex's mom. She's changed a few things over the years and makes Stephanie a vegetarian version. Lori says, "For Steph's special little egg bake I sauté whatever veggies we have and make a pie tin with 3 eggs, some almond milk, and her [vegan] cheese." That seems to be the overwhelming opinion about egg bakes: they are flexible and always tasty. "This is a basic recipe, but I have added peppers and mushrooms. Just gave them a quick sauté (not even sure you need to). I think you could put whatever you want in it and it'll be delicious." Lori adds, "I like a little spice, so I do a combination of Colby-Jack and whatever spicy cheese I can find. I always look for some habañero/jalapeño mix. Adjust the [spice] ratios to your liking."

1 pound hot Italian sausage (such as Jimmy Dean)
1 pound shredded hash browns
4 cups shredded Colby-Jack cheese
1 medium onion, finely chopped
1–1½ cups whole milk
6 large eggs, slightly beaten
salt and pepper
1 teaspoon dried oregano

Grease a 13x9–inch (3-quart) casserole dish. In a large skillet, brown meat over medium heat, breaking it up as it cooks. Remove from heat and cool for 5 to 10 minutes.

In a large mixing bowl, whisk together meat, hash browns, 3 cups of the cheese, onion, milk, and eggs. Season with salt and pepper. Pour mixture into prepared pan. Sprinkle top with oregano, cover, and refrigerate overnight.

Heat oven to 350 degrees. Bake uncovered for 45 minutes. Sprinkle the remaining 1 cup cheese evenly over the top of the bake and continue cooking an additional 5 to 10 minutes, until cheese is melted. Dish is done when inserted knife comes out clean.

Gary's Famous Fish and Chips

SERVES 2–4   GARY REUTER

I asked a dozen fishing authorities about their favorite ways to fry fresh-caught fish. Nearly every one of them told me "I use Shore Lunch," referring to the popular breading and batter mixes. Happily, my friend Gary's approach was unique and yet familiar.

For the fish

¼ cup all-purpose flour
2 large eggs, well beaten
20 crackers, crumbled with rolling pin
     or food processor
salt and pepper (optional)

oil for frying
1¼–1½ pounds catch of the day
     (walleye, perch, cisco), boned
     and skin removed, sliced
     into 4 fillets

Set up dredging station with three shallow dishes filled with flour, eggs, and crumbs. Season eggs and flour with salt and pepper if desired.

Heat deep fryer filled with oil. Pat fish dry and dredge in flour, then egg, then crumbs. Place in deep fryer and cook until golden, about 5 minutes. Work in batches and do not crowd the fryer. Remove cooked fish, place on paper towel on baking sheet, and put in low (200-degree) oven to keep warm.

For the chips

Slice potatoes as thin as possible. Place slices in deep fryer, one slice at a time, and fry until golden, about 3 to 4 minutes, stirring frequently.

For the tartar sauce

½ dill pickle
1 cup Miracle Whip

Dice dill pickle into small chunks, about 1⁄16-inch cubes. DO NOT use a food processor. The trick to good tartar sauce is to keep the juice in the pickle and not spread through the sauce. In a small mixing bowl, stir pickle into Miracle Whip but do not overmix.

Farmers Market

In Minnesota farmers markets plump and mature according to the season, and our market bags get heavier as summer progresses into fall. First come radish, rhubarb, spring greens, and asparagus. Strawberries, blueberries, herbs, and cucumbers signal July is near. When at last we welcome tomatoes, corn, and peppers, we know we are in the thick of it. Melons, eggplant, and apples warn us that the end is near, and soon it is time for pumpkins and winter squash. Parsnips, turnips, beets, and carrots are sweetest after the first frost, and the entire farmers market calendar is decorated liberally with zucchini. Lots and lots of zucchini.

On a warm spring day too many decades ago to politely number, we picked up a few supplies at the farmers market and returned to our friend Kathryn's house for lunch. I do not know whether she had a plan or was simply inspired by what we found that day, including bread still warm from the oven when we bought it. The simple but special meal she created for us remains one of those taste memories I am always reaching back for.

Many of my best meals have been in Kathryn's company. On another occasion she served us cheesy, creamy, savory pudding topped with roasted cherry tomatoes and a splash of balsamic vinegar (see page 122).

Farmers Market Bread Pudding

SERVES 8   KATHRYN O'BRIEN

About the bread pudding Kathryn said, "Well, really, it should simply be a grand foraging and return with whatever strikes your fancy, but ours was built around tomatoes, zucchini, and corn: the holy trinity of midwestern summer bounty. I suppose if we'd been fancy, we might have thrown some herbs in, and that would have been all for the better."

NOTE *When I make Kathryn's Farmers Market Bread Pudding, I alternate the vegetables according to what I find at the market. My favorite combination includes mushrooms and red peppers.*

3 tablespoons olive oil
1 pound tomatoes, cored, seeded, coarsely chopped
3 fat ears sweet corn, kernels cut from the cob; reserve cobs to make a corn soup
½ pound zucchini, finely chopped
fresh herbs (dill, basil, parsley, etc.)

½ teaspoon kosher salt
¼ teaspoon pepper
6 large eggs
2 cups whole milk
1 loaf good, sturdy bread, torn or cut into 1-inch chunks
fresh grated Parmesan cheese

Heat oven to 350 degrees. Generously grease bottom and sides of a 13x9–inch (3-quart) baking or cake pan.

Heat the olive oil in a large skillet. Add the tomatoes, corn, and zucchini and cook, stirring, for 2 to 3 minutes. Stir in fresh herbs and salt and pepper; set aside.

In a large mixing bowl, whisk together the eggs and milk.

Scatter the bread cubes into the prepared baking dish, then spread the vegetable mixture into the bread cubes. When all is well combined, pour the egg mixture over everything.

Bake for about 40 minutes or so, until the pudding is puffed up a bit and you can poke in a knife (or some other implement) and have it come out clean. Scatter the Parmesan over the top for the last 10 minutes of baking.

Savory Pudding with Roasted Cherry Tomatoes and Radishes
AKA OMG CAN I CALL IT A FLAN?

SERVES 6

This recipe is a composite of my re-creation and Kathryn's recollection.

For the pudding

1½ cups heavy cream

2 slices dense white bread, crusts removed, pulsed into crumbs in a food processor or chopped fine

3 large eggs plus 1 yolk

½ cup grated smoked Gouda

½ cup grated Gruyère

1 teaspoon prepared horseradish

pinch pepper

nutmeg to taste

roasted cherry tomatoes and radishes (recipe follows)

olive oil

balsamic vinegar

basil or other herbs

Heat oven to 350 degrees. Generously grease bottoms and sides of 6 (5-ounce) ramekins. Place in a 13x9–inch cake pan. Set a kettle of water over heat and bring to boiling, then set aside.

Pour cream into a saucepan and place over medium-high heat. Watch closely for skin to form on top of cream and for the cream to just start steaming.

In a large mixing bowl, whisk together breadcrumbs, eggs plus yolk, cheeses, horseradish, pepper, and nutmeg so that mixture is completely blended.

Slowly pour thin stream of hot cream into egg mixture while whisking continuously, pouring just enough of the cream to blend with but not cook eggs. Fill each prepared ramekin with equal amounts of the mixture. Carefully add hot water to pan so that it comes up an inch around ramekins. Bake for 30 minutes or until pudding is set and an inserted knife comes out clean.

Cool for 15 minutes. Run a small spreader along sides of each ramekin to loosen pudding, place plate over top of ramekin, then flip so that pudding releases from ramekin onto plate.

Serve pudding warm or at room temperature garnished with roasted tomatoes and radishes, adding olive oil, balsamic vinegar, and herbs as desired.

For the roasted cherry tomatoes and radishes

1 pint cherry or other small tomatoes, halved

1 cup red radishes, sliced

salt and pepper

Heat oven to 275 degrees. Scatter the tomatoes and radishes on a parchment-lined baking sheet and season with salt and pepper. Roast for about 25 to 30 minutes, or until desired level of tenderness.

Pasty

MAKES 6 LARGE PASTIES JENNIFER WAGNER-HARKONEN

Meat and vegetable pasties are best when root vegetables come into season, making this warm hand pie a proper meal from fall until spring, although pasty lovers savor the hand pies year-round. The Cornish receive credit for pasties' American origins in the mid-nineteenth through the early twentieth centuries, when immigrants in Michigan's Upper Peninsula and Minnesota's Iron Range brought these portable pies to eat while working in the mines. However, other immigrant groups later brought similar pies to the table, including the Finns, who added rutabagas to theirs. Many historians claim Finnish immigrants adopted, then adapted the Cornish pasty. Yet, there are multiple versions of meat and root vegetable hand pies across Finland.

Jennifer says, "Many people enjoy using a pie crust recipe, but a few years ago I learned that the boiled crust recipe yielded a tender pie crust that would also hold together better, which the miners likely appreciated more than flakiness when eating their handheld pie down in the dark, dank mine shaft. I found the boiled crust recipe much easier to make, so I've been using it since, but my mom's crust is flaky and delicious.

"It has been said that the Italians put a little ground Italian sausage in their pasties, and that Swedes like more rutabaga, and that the Finnish pasty is heavier on the carrot, but I am not sure about that. All the old muumuus [Finnish grandmothers] that I knew used their clean hands to squish the meat and potato mixture together. I like to add a beaten egg to the mixture as a binder. There is also a debate about gravy or ketchup as a condiment, and to me, that is undebatable: ketchup! Don't worry if your pasty doesn't look dainty, as it wasn't meant to be served at a tea party."

Jennifer's recipe is a Lake Superior region miners' pasty, and the crust is not only tasty but very forgiving regardless of your pastry prowess.

For the crust

1 cup butter or lard or a mixture
    of the two
1 teaspoon salt

1 cup boiling water
3 cups all-purpose flour

Place the butter or lard in a large mixing bowl with the salt. Pour boiling water into the bowl and stir until the fat melts and the salt dissolves. Stir in the flour, forming a ball. Wrap the ball in plastic and let it rest in the refrigerator while making the filling ingredients. Note: do not chill pastry for more than 20 minutes. This is not a make-ahead crust.

For the filling

1 pound ground beef
½ pound ground pork, or mild Italian
    sausage for a slight kick
3–4 medium Yukon Gold potatoes,
    peeled and finely chopped into
    ¼- to ⅓-inch pieces
1 small rutabaga, peeled and finely
    chopped into ¼- to ⅓-inch pieces

1–2 carrots, peeled and finely
    chopped into ¼- to ⅓-inch pieces
1 medium yellow onion,
    finely chopped
1 large egg, beaten
salt and pepper
4 tablespoons butter, divided
    in 6 pieces
cream or milk for brushing

Heat oven to 350 degrees. In a large bowl, stir together meats, potatoes, rutabaga, carrots, onion, and beaten egg. Season with salt and pepper.

Divide dough into 6 pieces and roll out each piece on a lightly floured surface into about an 8-inch circle. Divide filling equally, placing in the center of each pasty, and top with a butter pat. Fold over the crust until the ends meet and it forms a half circle. Roll up the edges of the crust, pressing to seal. (The miners liked to have a heavy end piece of crust to hold onto with their dirty hands and discarded that piece.)

Place the pasties on a large baking sheet and prick several holes on the top of each. Bake for 1 hour. Brush pastry tops with cream or milk after removing from the oven.

Parsnip Almond Cake

SERVES 10

Adapted from Alaska Carrot Cake as
it appears in *Always on Sunday*

I am not a lover of carrot cake. I don't get what all the fuss is about.
When I read about Alaska Carrot Cake in Eleanor Ostman's *Always on Sunday*, the recipe's surprise ingredients — shredded coconut and Rice Krispies—were intriguing. My ode to Ostman's cake swaps out the carrots for parsnips (because I love parsnips), decreases the sugar slightly, and replaces pineapple and walnuts with orange and almonds.

A note about Eleanor Ostman: Eleanor wrote a food column in the *St. Paul Pioneer Press* for thirty years, and her book is a collection of those columns. I am only slightly biased because I am such a fan, but I believe *Always on Sunday* belongs on every cook's bookshelf.

1¾ cups sugar
¾ cup vegetable oil
3 large eggs
2 cups all-purpose flour
2 teaspoons baking soda
2 teaspoons ground cinnamon
1 teaspoon ground cardamom
¼ teaspoon nutmeg
½ teaspoon salt
¾ cup buttermilk

2 teaspoons vanilla extract
1 teaspoon almond extract
2 cups grated parsnips
zest and juice from ½ orange
2 cups coconut flakes
1 cup crisped rice cereal
1 cup blanched sliced almonds
cream cheese frosting
(recipe follows)

Heat oven to 350 degrees. Grease and flour 2 (9-inch) round cake pans, and line bottoms with parchment; set aside. In a large mixing bowl, blend together sugar and oil. Add eggs, one at a time, beating well after each addition.

In a medium mixing bowl, whisk together flour, baking soda, cinnamon, cardamom, nutmeg, and salt.

While beating continuously, alternately add flour mix and buttermilk to sugar-oil mixture. Mix until smooth. Add vanilla and almond extracts. Fold in parsnips, orange zest and juice, coconut, rice cereal, and almonds. Batter will be thick and gooey.

Divide batter between prepared pans; bake for 30 minutes or until inserted wooden pick comes out clean. Cool in pans; invert and remove cooled cakes. Remove parchment. Layer and top the cake with cream cheese frosting.

Cream Cheese Frosting

**MAKES ENOUGH TO FILL IN
LAYERS AND TOP 1 CAKE**

4 ounces cream cheese
6 tablespoons butter
4 cups confectioners' sugar
zest and juice from ½ orange
1 teaspoon vanilla extract
¼ teaspoon almond extract

Using electric mixer, blend all
ingredients until smooth.

Crayfish Boils

In Minnesota there is a long tradition of fishing native and, more recently, invasive species of crayfish. Our lakes, streams, wetlands, and rivers provide the freshwater habitat where crayfish live. Throughout the Twin Cities hipster eateries throw summer parties to celebrate the shellfish, many utilizing the southern style of crawdad boil. The boils commonly include Cajun seasonings and a variety of vegetables and occasionally sausage.

I associate crayfish with a Swedish kräftskiva. In Sweden crayfish was considered a delicacy during the sixteenth century, and a food limited to the aristocracy. By the mid-nineteenth century crayfish parties became a tradition among the middle class. Families gathered on beaches to harvest crayfish under the light of the moon. Overfishing and parasites wiped out local crayfish populations, and for a time harvest was limited to three days in August.

The crayfish party marks the end of summer and the beginning of a new school year. Today crayfish are available year-round, but eating them on a warm summer evening is my idea of heaven. We gather in the courtyard at the American Swedish Institute (weather permitting), sitting at long, communal tables and wearing funny paper hats and plastic bibs. We sing Swedish drinking songs and learn the proper way to skål with shots of aquavit. The meal is extravagant and leisurely, centered around platters overflowing with beautiful red crustaceans that are soaked and boiled in a brine of beer and dill. We pull off the heads, suck out the juices, then tuck into the meat. There is about half a bite of meat in each tiny creature, which means we fill up on sides: salads, cheeses, rye breads, savory *paj* (pie), and desserts.

Swedish Cheese Tart
(VÄSTERBOTTENSOSTPAJ)

SERVES 8

Adapted from Trina Hahnemann's
The Scandinavian Cookbook

In Sweden is it traditional to serve Västerbottensostpaj (Västerbotten cheese pie) at crayfish parties, but Västerbotten cheese is at the moment unavailable in Minnesota. Buttery, nutty cheese like Gruyère, Comté, or unaged Cheddar combined with a salty Parmesan makes an acceptable substitute.

1 puff pastry, thawed
4 large eggs
⅔ cup whole milk
10 ounces Cheddar or Gruyère, grated

2 ounces Parmesan cheese, grated
½ teaspoon salt
pepper
chives or dill for garnish (optional)

Heat oven to 350 degrees. Grease an 8- or 9-inch pie plate. Roll out pastry on floured work surface until thin, then use it to line pie plate.

In a large mixing bowl, beat together the eggs and milk. Stir in grated cheeses, salt, and lots of pepper. Pour into tart shell. Bake 45 minutes. Garnish with fresh chives or dill if desired.

Tomato Pie (TOMAT PAJ)

SERVES 8

A tomato pie in August honors tomatoes at their peak.

For this recipe use commercial mayonnaise rather than homemade, as the processed mayo helps to set the custard. Substitute any of your favorite soft vegetables for the tomatoes, everything from kale and mushrooms to asparagus and onions. Add a good garnish of fresh basil to your tomato pie, and in cooler months reach for dill, parsley, or fried sage leaves.

pastry for single 9-inch pie
1 tablespoon Dijon-style mustard
½ cup plus 2–3 tablespoons grated
    Parmesan cheese
2 large ripe tomatoes, sliced into ¼- to
    ½-inch-thick pieces
salt and pepper

8 ounces crème fraîche
    (recipe follows)
¾ cup shredded unaged white
    Cheddar or Gruyère
2 tablespoons store-bought
    mayonnaise
¼ cup minced fresh basil, plus more
    for garnish

Heat oven to 350 degrees. Arrange pastry in pie plate, crimping edges around top. Use a fork to prick the bottom of the pastry; spread mustard across bottom and cover with ½ cup of the Parmesan. Bake for 5 to 10 minutes, until cheese is melted.

Generously season tomato slices with salt and pepper and place on paper towel to absorb some of the liquid. In a large mixing bowl, whisk together crème fraîche, shredded cheese, remaining 2 to 3 tablespoons Parmesan, and mayo. Season generously with pepper.

Place a layer of the tomatoes over the cheese-filled pie crust. Spread the crème fraîche custard mixture over the tomatoes, sprinkle basil evenly over custard, then layer remaining tomatoes over the basil. Return pie to oven and cook an additional 35 minutes or until the custard is set and golden where it peeks through the tomatoes.

Cool pie at least 10 minutes. Cut into wedges and garnish with additional basil.

Crème Fraîche

MAKES ABOUT 1¼ CUPS

For an inexpensive homemade crème fraîche, combine 1 cup heavy cream with 2 tablespoons buttermilk and 1–2 tablespoons full-fat unflavored yogurt in a glass Mason jar. Use a rubber band to secure a paper towel around the opening of the jar and let sit on the kitchen counter for 18 to 24 hours. After that, secure the jar with a lid and shake the mixture well. Store unused crème fraîche in refrigerator for up to 2 weeks.

Crayfish with Dill
(KRÄFTOR MED DILL)

SERVES 2–4

5 pounds frozen crayfish
1 large bunch dill including crowns
1 onion, chopped
1½ gallons water
12 ounces dark beer (porter or English stout)

1 teaspoon anise seeds
½ cup salt
1 tablespoon sugar
lemon wedges

Thaw crayfish overnight in fridge or place in large pot and cover with cold water, keeping a stream of cold water running while crayfish thaws. Separate any fish that are stuck together and discard any small claws that have cracked off.

Set aside some of the best-looking dill crowns to use as a garnish.

In a large pot, combine dill, onion, water, beer, anise seeds, salt, and sugar. Bring to a boil. Drop the crayfish into the boiling water. Bring back to boiling, then immediately remove from heat, cover, and allow to soak at least 1 hour.

Drain crayfish and arrange on a large serving platter. Garnish with dill and squeeze lemon juice over. Enjoy while singing Swedish drinking songs.

NOTE *Most recipes call for 3 pounds of crayfish per person. I have not found this to be the case, possibly because at the parties I attend we are filling up on pie. There are approximately 15 to 20 crayfish in a pound, depending on the size of the fish. In my house, 5 pounds of crayfish easily serves 2 to 4.*

The Main

We Gen Xers are collectively wincing as we purchase our first reading glasses and receive offensive AARP materials in the mail. Aging often causes nostalgic urges to kick in, and we look back on yesteryear with the kind of passion normally reserved for old men yelling at the kids to get off the lawn. My go-to moment on the nostalgic timetable is freshman year in college when I worked at St. Anthony Main's Pizzeria in Minneapolis. We wore orange T-shirts with an American Pie logo, and by quitting time there was a line of grease across my stomach where I rubbed against the prep board. Every night for the first week I worked there I dreamed of sinking into deep tubs filled with pepperoni. I always smelled like olive oil. It was the best job I ever had.

We served Chicago-style: heavy and loaded. After a few weeks of working there, I could easily distinguish which employee made which crust: everyone's personality came out in the shape of the dough, how high the outer walls rose over the lower crust, and how the sausage crumbles stuck closely or coarsely into the melted cheese after par-baking.

Back then I didn't see the job as a pinnacle of career accomplishments, but back then I didn't know what I do now about chasing success. My boss Robert (I was the only one allowed to call him "Noonie," a nickname he earned as a child when he refused to wear clothes and ran around his house nude) taught me work ethic, quality food service, and taking pride in what you do. Serve up your best, at all times.

Staff were allowed one pizza slice for every four hours worked, and we could trade our slices for food from other vendors. One slice could get you a full meal from Dino's Greek, a small dish of fried rice from Thieves Market, or a burger from Prince Street Bar. Häagen-Dazs wasn't allowed to trade. That staff operated under a boss with strict rules about employee benefits, but early on Sunday mornings before the mall awoke one of the Häagen-Dazsers might sneak out an illicit vanilla shake in exchange for a slice of extra cheese. Still, that transaction was rare even if you knew someone on the highest rung of the authority ladder. I called them the ice cream mafia.

We who love food are often drawn to the memories of food moments that changed our assumptions and eating habits. That year, 1985, delivered the most unique and surprising flavors I had, up to that moment, ever experienced. That was the summer of the pesto and clam pizza special. I'd never even heard of basil, much less tasted it fresh and raw, blended with garlic, lemon, pignoli (I delighted in repeating the Italian word for pine nuts, as if saying the word made me fluent in another language), and good, long glugs of extra-virgin olive oil. It tasted alive.

Senses overloaded, I slouched over my free slice in the back of the kitchen, scarfing down the pungent pesto and briny clams, and keeping a watch on the front of the shop in case a customer approached. More than once I greeted a hungry patron with a green basil-toothed smile. It is no coincidence that this book includes not one but three pesto recipes. Pesto and clam pizza changed everything.

Pizzeria's owner, Mike, beamed with pride the day the case of Torani flavored syrups arrived. It was decades before Starbucks and Caribou, eons before every corner had a specialty coffee shop complete with flavor syrups to add to your latte. We had never seen or tasted anything like it: guava, hazelnut, orgeat?! Exotic flavors with intoxicating possibilities. Italian cream soda was a new kid in town, and we were the only show. We charged nearly three dollars per small cup, almost as much as a slice (that calculates to just over seven dollars in 2020).

We could drink all the soda pop we wanted, and I survived each eight-hour shift on buckets of diet cola. It was understood that no one was allowed to drink the Italian cream sodas, which of course meant that on slow days when Noonie was gone we'd experiment in the back of the shop. How would passion fruit taste with a splash of orange? With or without cream? How about adding 7UP instead of soda water? My favorite combination was cherry and orgeat. It was a smooth pairing to a slice of pesto and clam.

Ode to St. Anthony Main American Pie Pizza Dough

MAKES 2 PIZZAS / EACH PIZZA SERVES 6

1 packet active dry yeast (2¼ teaspoons)
1 tablespoon honey
1 ⅛ cups warm water
3½–4 cups all-purpose flour
½ cup olive oil

1½ teaspoons salt
1½ teaspoons Italian seasoning
12 deli mozzarella or provolone rounds (or 3 cups shredded cheese)
preferred pizza toppings

In large bowl for standing mixer fitted with dough hook, whisk together yeast, honey, and water. Set aside to bloom for 5 minutes. When the yeast mixture is foamy, mix in 3 cups flour, oil, salt, and Italian seasoning. Knead for 5 minutes, adding enough of the remaining flour to form a soft, pliable dough. (Alternatively, use a wooden spoon to stir yeast, honey, and water together to proof. Use hands to knead in 3 cups flour, oil, salt, and Italian seasoning. Move dough to a well-floured surface and knead in enough of the remaining flour to form a soft, pliable dough.) Form the dough into a ball, place in oiled bowl, cover with plastic wrap or a clean kitchen towel, and set aside to rise until double, about 1½ hours.

Divide dough in half and reshape into 2 balls. Place in greased 8- or 9-inch round cake pans (or springform pans), cover with plastic wrap or clean kitchen towel, and set aside to rise until double, about 30 minutes.

Heat oven to 425 degrees. Use your fingers to press the dough evenly into the bottom and up the sides of the pan. Cut 2 slices of the cheese into quarters. Press 5 rounds evenly into bottom of crust, using 4 quarters to fill in corners (or evenly spread 1½ cups shredded cheese over bottom of pie). Repeat with second pizza. Par-bake until cheese is melted, about 15 minutes. Top with preferred ingredients, return to oven, and bake for an additional 15 to 20 minutes. Cool for 5 minutes before removing from pan and cutting into 6 slices.

The Main (Sausage, Pepperoni, Green Pepper, and Onion Pizza)

SERVES 6

The Main was named for St. Anthony Main, the mall that used to run along Main Street, across the Mississippi River and north of downtown Minneapolis along St. Anthony Falls. Some of the oldest buildings in the city remain attached to the mostly depleted mall space, now converted into condos, lofts, and offices.

This spot along the river is part of my history. It is the neighborhood where my grandmother lived when she met my grandpa, and it houses the church she grew up in and where they married. The Main is where I spent my formative youth shopping, playing, and hoofing pizza. I walk the wooden halls whenever we grab a beer at Pracna or go to the movies at St. Anthony Main Theatre. The ghosts of St. Anthony Main Pizzeria compel me to return home and pay homage to the past with a pie.

4–5 ounces Italian sausage
1 American Pie pizza crust (page 132), bottom covered in cheese but not yet baked
3½ ounces pepperoni slices

½ cup tomato sauce (recipe follows)
¼ cup chopped white or yellow onion
¼ cup chopped green bell pepper
½–1 cup shredded mozzarella cheese
Parmesan cheese, grated

Heat oven to 425 degrees. Push bits of sausage into the cheese layer of the pizza crust, evenly distributing the sausage in small chunks. Par-bake until cheese is melted and sausage is cooked, 15 minutes.

Distribute pepperoni slices evenly over sausage and cheese layer. Spread tomato sauce evenly over pepperoni. Top with onion and green pepper. Top with mozzarella, return to oven, and bake for an additional 15 to 20 minutes. Cool for 5 minutes before removing from pan and cutting into 6 slices. Garnish with Parmesan.

Tomato Sauce

MAKES ENOUGH FOR 2 PIZZAS

1 (8-ounce) can tomato sauce
1½ teaspoons Italian seasoning
½ teaspoon garlic powder

1 teaspoon balsamic vinegar
salt and pepper

In a small mixing bowl, whisk together tomato sauce, Italian seasoning, garlic powder, and vinegar. Season to taste with salt and pepper.

Pesto and Shrimp Pizza

SERVES 6

While pesto and clams were my first taste of basil meets the sea, shrimp replaces clams in this recipe. The lemon peels are inspired by a pizza named Pearl that was served at Mucci's restaurant in St. Paul when it opened in 2016. Mucci's deep-fried Montanara-style pies topped with fresh oysters, cured chilis, and candied lemon peel lulled me into believing I was dining oceanside.

½ cup pesto (recipe follows)
1 American Pie pizza crust (page 132), bottom covered in cheese and par-baked

¼ pound shrimp, cleaned and shelled
½ red bell pepper, sliced thin
candied lemon peel (recipe follows)
Parmesan cheese, grated

Heat oven to 425 degrees. Spread pesto evenly over cheese layer of pizza. Dot evenly with shrimp, red pepper, and lemon peel, return to oven, and bake for an additional 15 to 20 minutes. Cool for 5 minutes before removing from pan and cutting into 6 slices. Garnish with Parmesan.

Pesto

MAKES ABOUT 1 CUP

2 cups fresh basil
⅓ cup grated Romano or Parmesan cheese
¼ cup toasted pine nuts, plus more for garnish
2 cloves garlic
juice from ½ lemon
⅓–½ cup olive oil
¼ teaspoon salt, or to taste
pinch hot red pepper flakes
pepper

Add basil, cheese, nuts, garlic, and lemon juice to blender or food processor fitted with metal blade, and blend to a paste, using rubber spatula to scrape down sides of bowl as needed. With processor running, slowly pour olive oil into the mix so that a smooth sauce forms. Season with salt, red pepper flakes, and pepper.

Candied Lemon Peel

1 organic lemon

1 cup sugar, plus more for finishing

Use a vegetable peeler to peel thin strips of zest from lemon, removing as much pith as possible. Place peels in a small saucepan with 2 cups water. Bring to a boil, drain, add 2 more cups cold water, bring to a boil, and drain. Repeat a third time, then drain and set peels aside. (The boiling process gets rid of any bitterness in the peel.)

Add sugar to pan along with 1 cup water. Whisk over medium heat until sugar dissolves. Add peels and bring to a boil. Reduce heat and simmer 10 minutes. Peels should be tender and sweet. Drain, reserving simple syrup for other recipes. Toss peels in a few tablespoons of sugar, then place peels in a wire mesh strainer and shake to remove excess sugar. Store peels in an airtight container for up to 1 week.

St. Anthony Main's American Pie Italian Cream Soda

SERVES 1

1 jigger flavored syrup
½ jigger heavy cream

ice
8–10 ounces soda water

In a large drinking glass, stir together the syrup and cream; add ice. Gently stir while pouring soda into glass. Serve immediately.

Pizza Farms: Which Came First, the Pizza or the Farm?

"Are you sure we are on the right road?" my husband asked. I consulted Google Maps on my mobile again and assured him we appeared to be headed in the right direction. The laminated cardboard Minnesota map we've kept in our car for the past twenty years probably isn't accurate in our ever-changing, constantly under-construction state. How did we ever leave the house before Google?

We drove south from the Twin Cities to Waseca on a mild summer afternoon. Turning off the highway onto a county road, we passed through a pristine little town with pastoral homes and freshly manicured lawns, then onto a two-lane road flanked by cornfields and ditches filled with budding clover. We turned again, this time along a gravel road that seemed to have no end, and we passed farms and more corn, until finally there was a simple sign that announced, "PIZZA!" Arriving at Pleasant Grove Pizza Farm is like waking up after a wonderful dream and realizing it is actually happening.

A few dozen cars lined a makeshift parking lot that led to an open field dotted with small groups of people lounging on picnic blankets, sitting on unfolded mesh chairs, and gathered around wooden picnic tables. Kids played tag and chased a wandering goat. Between the lot, a small enclosed pasture holding a donkey and alpaca, and the field, a barn sheltered a short line of guests waiting to order.

A tight, intriguing menu of specialty pizzas, the toppings painstakingly tested by owners Emily Knudsen and Bill Bartz, was posted on the barn wall. On the afternoon we visited, there were seasonal pies like the Lola (basil-infused olive oil, tomato, basil, kalamata olives, and mozzarella), as well as a charcuterie plate and pizza fries (baked pizza dough covered in cheese and served with a side of Bill's famous red sauce). Customers placed orders at a foldout table in front of the tidy white kitchen where two wood-burning pizza ovens perfectly char around forty pizzas on Thursday evenings and a hundred-plus pizzas on busy Sundays.

I wandered onto the lawn of picnickers, and a woman waved at me, "Patrice!" Emily Knudsen's sharp eyes found me, a stranger, instantly among her regulars. In fact, she kept an eagle eye out and greeted every guest, usually by name, as they entered the farm.

We sat down at an open picnic table and discovered we both learned about and fell in love with pizza farms outside of Stockholm, Wisconsin, at A to Z, where the midwestern pizza farm mythos was born. Emily refers to A to Z as the mother ship: "I remember sitting there thinking, 'This is so great! I wish I owned one of these. Bring your own alcohol! Bring other food!' And the entire time I was eating amazing pizza."

Emily grew up on a hobby farm with beef cattle, horse boarding, and rented pastures for corn and hay: "It was a wonderful childhood. I was never *not* going to live on a hobby farm." When Emily and Bill first met, he owned the land where Pleasant Grove now resides, but it wasn't a working farm when he bought it. "Eight months into our relationship I brought up pizza farms," Emily said.

Bill, who had joined us at the table, interjected, "What's a pizza farm?" and we all laughed. Bill became intrigued with the idea of doing something unique on the property and started researching. "I always wanted to do something here," he said. Bill pitched ideas to Emily, from using the land for dog training, to growing hops, to hosting outdoor weddings: "Outdoor weddings are so popular, but she said, 'No way.'"

"I'd been working weddings for many years," Emily told him. "But this place would be perfect for a pizza farm. That next Tuesday we went to A to Z. 'I can do this,' I remember his words and his hand in the air, 'I can do this.'"

The couple sat down and imagined how they would make a pizza farm work. They cleared the brush, and their vision slowly took shape over many months and countless hours of work. "We started to see the potential in the space. Now it is about improving the property. We started the process on June 4, 2013, and we opened August 2014," Emily said. Now, Pleasant Grove Pizza Farm hosts a few pizza afternoons and nights each week while the weather allows.

Bill and his dad are the primary carpenters, and with Emily's background in hobby farming and catering, the process is "very serendipitous for us." Bill continues to do winter construction, and Emily works banquets. But their true passions are on the pizza farm.

Bill developed the pizza dough and sauces by trial and error. Impressed by the quality of the crust, I asked about his experience, and he quipped about learning by doing. "I take pride in flavor, flavor explosion in your mouth that you feel in your bones."

The pizza farm is developing into a place for workshops and retreats. There is live music every Sunday. "They find me," Emily said of the talented musicians who perform each week. Musicians sign their names across the walls of the covered stage, built by Bill and his dad, leaving a musical legacy behind like a pizza farm First Avenue. There are walking trails through prairie and oak groves. A donkey, goat, and alpaca call the farm home. Local handmade products and produce are sold in a makeshift farmers market. "This was part of the plan and dream from the beginning," Emily told me. Autumn brings festivals aimed at families and kids with wagon rides, pumpkin carving, face painting, and games. Popcorn, apple cider, and of course pizza round out the events.

Pizza farms aren't like a traditional restaurant, where doors are open most days of the week. Typically, they are a way for a farm to diversify products and income. At pizza farms guests bring their own tables, picnic blankets, snacks, desserts, and beverages. After dining, customers take everything with them, including garbage.

"Bill and I are two passionate and creative people who recognize potential in farms especially for families." Emily looked around and gestured toward some children running and laughing as they chased each other across the open field. "No phones, no video games. This makes my heart very happy." Around us families played board games and cards. A jumbo Jenga game occupied two boys behind us. Half a dozen kids lined the fence to pet the donkey. "All of our animals are free range. We should all be free, right?"

Lola

SERVES 4–6

PLEASANT GROVE PIZZA FARM, EMILY KNUDSEN AND BILL BARTZ

Emily says, "This simple yet tasty vegetarian pizza is packed full of my two favorite summer vegetables and tons of flavor. I love eating it when the tomatoes in the garden are plump and ripe and the fresh harvest aroma of basil is strong with sweetness. The kalamata olives bring forth a distinctive rich, smoky, and fruity flavor. Combining all of these ingredients, along with the seasonings, will not disappoint and creates a vibrant artisan pizza."

NOTE *If you don't have a wood-fired oven, cook 10 to 12 minutes in a preheated 500-degree oven on a hot pizza stone that has been preheated at least 30 minutes.*

3 tablespoons basil-infused olive oil
   (recipe follows)
dough for 1 (16-inch) pizza
¼ teaspoon minced garlic
¼ teaspoon Italian seasoning
2 fresh Roma tomatoes, thinly sliced

¼ cup sliced kalamata olives
3 tablespoons fresh basil
1 cup shredded
   mozzarella cheese
2 slices fresh mozzarella cheese

Brush basil-infused olive oil over top of the dough with the back of a spoon. Sprinkle garlic and Italian seasoning evenly over oil. Evenly spread sliced tomatoes over top; add olives and 2 tablespoons of the fresh basil. Add the shredded mozzarella. Tear the fresh mozzarella into little chunks and place them on top of the shredded mozzarella. Cook in a wood-fired pizza oven at 550 degrees for 4 to 6 minutes or until the bottom of the crust is light brown and spotted and the cheese is melted on top. Garnish with reserved 1 tablespoon basil.

Basil-Infused Olive Oil

MAKES ENOUGH FOR 2 PIZZAS

½ cup tightly packed basil
3 tablespoons olive oil
salt

Prepare a medium bowl with water and ice; set aside. In a saucepan, bring 2 cups salted water to a boil. Add basil and blanch for 10 seconds. Drain immediately and plunge into ice water. Remove from water and pat very dry with paper towels.

Add basil and oil to blender or small food processor fitted with metal blade. Puree, and season with salt. Pour through a fine-mesh strainer and discard solids. Refrigerate and use within 1 week.

House Salad

SERVES 4

Some of my favorite pizza and burger joints in the Twin Cities serve a house salad that I could live on. In fact, last summer I ate this salad every day for a week and still wasn't tired of it. It travels well, making it an ideal salad to bring next time you visit a pizza farm. While most dressings call for a ratio of 3:1 oil and acid, I prefer a lighter version. If you want more oil, tweak the recipe to suit your tastes.

For the dressing

3 tablespoons lemon juice
1 tablespoon whole-grain mustard
1 tablespoon honey
½ teaspoon dried tarragon

2–3 teaspoons balsamic vinegar
¼ cup olive oil
salt and pepper

Add all ingredients except salt and pepper to a Mason jar or other airtight container. Cover, shake well, and season to taste with salt and pepper. If dressing is too thick, add a little water to thin it.

For the crispy prosciutto

Heat oven to 400 degrees. Place 2 ounces thinly sliced prosciutto on a parchment-lined baking sheet so that the slices do not overlap. Cover prosciutto with another parchment sheet and place another baking sheet over the parchment. Bake for 8 to 10 minutes. Remove from oven and cool on baking rack. The prosciutto will crisp as it cools.

For the pine nuts

Roast ¼ cup pine nuts in a saucepan over low heat until toasted. Watch carefully; they burn easily.

To assemble

8 cups arugula or other dark greens
1 shallot, sliced thin
Asiago or Parmesan cheese

In a large bowl, toss arugula, shallot, cheese, crispy prosciutto, and pine nuts so that ingredients are evenly combined. Drizzle with a few tablespoons of the dressing. Leftover dressing will keep in the refrigerator for up to 1 week.

Corn Creeping

The best corn I ever ate was ill-gotten. It was a hot summer night spent with my brother-in-law and his friends in some guy's garage. Rather late into the evening, someone decided that food was a necessity. My normally stoic brother-in-law became as giddy as a schoolgirl when he made the suggestion: "Let's go Corn Creeping!"

(The actual phrase used for the practice of stealing cobs of corn from an unsuspecting farmer's field may actually be Corn Stealing, or Field Theft, or Misdemeanor. But that bygone night is now family lore and the details long since tainted. Therefore, Corn Creeping suffices as both description and act. Admittedly, an endless supply of Miller High Life is typically involved in any decision to Corn Creep.)

My sister informed me later that her husband's corn appropriation always followed a phone call to the farmer whose field was to be violated. The call had a twofold purpose. First, obtain permission from the farmer so that participants wouldn't be shot or attacked by watchdogs (or arrested). Second, get directions to the field that contained sweet rather than field corn.

A few guys who hadn't over-imbibed became our designated drivers, and we caravanned into the black night. My brother-in-law held a flashlight over a scrap of paper and barked directions to our driver: "He said go to the south field, closest to the road." His voice pitched with excitement: "Corn Creeping!"

We parked on the edge of the field as my brother-in-law commanded in loud whispers for car lights to be dimmed. The group became a well-trained reconnaissance team, wandering into the stalks, swatting at mosquitoes, and side-stepping on dirt mounds. We pulled fat ears off the stalks and stuffed them into grocery bags, not leaving the field until my brother-in-law was satisfied with our plunder. Our raid was swift and thorough.

Less than an hour later we were back in the garage. Garage Guy and his wife removed tools from a shelf and set up a vat of boiling water. I inhaled corn off the cob so fast I hardly tasted the salted butter slathered over it.

There are many champions in this story: my brother-in-law, Garage Guy, and the generous farmer. And in Minnesota during late summer, corn is always a hero.

Sweet Corn Ice Cream

MAKES ABOUT 5 CUPS

Sweet corn season is fleeting, and I often bring home more corn than we can eat in a day or two. Leftover corn often gets the ice cream treatment.

4 ears sweet corn, shucked
2 cups heavy cream
1 (14-ounce) can coconut cream
⅔ cup sugar, divided
1 vanilla pod
6 large egg yolks
nutmeg
salt

Slice kernels from corn and place in a large pot. Add cream, coconut cream, and ⅓ cup of the sugar. Split vanilla pod and use tip of knife to scrape out the seeds. Add the seeds to the pot; set aside pod. Bring mixture to a simmer and then remove from heat. Use an immersion blender to puree mixture. Add the split vanilla pod and steep for 1 hour.

Whisk together yolks and remaining ⅓ cup sugar. Bring cream and corn mixture to a simmer and slowly whisk 1 cup of the hot cream into the eggs. Add the egg-cream mixture back into the pot and cook over medium-low heat until a thick custard forms, about 5 to 10 minutes. Pass the custard through a fine-mesh strainer; discard solids. Add nutmeg to taste and a pinch of salt.

Cool the custard, then refrigerate for at least 4 hours. Freeze in an ice cream maker according to the manufacturer's directions.

It Ain't
Over Til the
State Fair

Dad smoked Winstons, and on hot days when he wore his T-shirt to wash the Pinto, he rolled a pack up in his shirtsleeve. That day he took me to my first Minnesota State Fair, he had a pack tucked into his shirt pocket, a nicotine pocket protector. He had two rules for going to the fair that I obeyed with reverence. First, I was not to complain when we began our day meandering through Machinery Hill so he could inspect every combine and tractor that littered the grass and lined the crowded sidewalks. (Dad had never been and would never be a farmer. Perhaps it was his way of showing respect.) Second, I was allowed one and only one food item. Again, this rule hinged on the no-complaint addendum. Outside of those two rules, the day was a free-for-all. I spent hours admiring horses and dragging Dad from the barns to the coliseum for the barrel racing. He patiently doled out cash for the pony paraphernalia I begged for (buttons, stickers, patches, jewelry).

Dad lit a final cigarette as we climbed into the Skyride, the enclosed gondola of brightly colored cars that soar above the fairgrounds, for a lift back toward the parking lot. When the teenage worker opened the door for us to disembark, a plume of smoke preceded us.

My love for the Minnesota State Fair began later in life, but it was love at first sight. I must have been about ten years old for that first Skyride that felt like magic, floating over the fairgrounds, with its beautiful buildings and all of the people who gathered to celebrate Minnesota. For a state fair lover, attending the fair for the first time at such a late age is considered a delayed experience, but in the following years I more than made up for the deferment.

Now my relationship with the fair is best described as an addiction. And I am okay with that. I've held state fair trivia contests for coworkers (complete with state fair–themed trophies for the top three winners), acted as an unofficial state fair tour guide, and facilitated an annual state fair bingo/beer garden–hopping group (we always meet up at the Perfect Pickle and share a few baskets of deep-fried Cajuns and pose for our group photo calendar at the Minnesota Department of Education). I've volunteered at every booth that would have me, from appearing as Smokey Bear at the Minnesota Department of Natural Resources Building (although the time I tag teamed as Smokey with my mom, she broke the rules about not approaching kids and chased down teenagers for hugs; we were never asked back); handed out endless cups of white, chocolate, and half each at the All-You-Can-Drink Milk Stand (where for years I'd meet up with high school friends and their children for our annual milk drinking contest); policed parents as their kids attempted to play games at the Alphabet Forest; and clumsily fielded questions about the University of Minnesota on the stage outside of the Driven to Discover Building. My annual duties now include working in the Eco Experience building for Renewing the Countryside (honestly, I'm there to meet cool local chefs who cook onstage and talk about sustainability) and teaching knife skills to 4-Hers before judging them in a cooking contest. I attend nearly every day, finding strength in the traditions and always discovering amazing new stuff.

There are two kinds of people in Minnesota: those who love the fair, and those who complain ad nauseam about how awful it is. If you are still reading this essay, you just might be a Fair Person. Fair People are my people. We understand how the Minnesota State Fair is the one place on earth where, regardless of politics, cultural differences, religion, and our other wildly divergent views on just about everything, we hang out together with acceptance and shared love of and pride in our state.

We meet up at the fish pond, search for our deceased loved one's bench, gawk at the spinning butter heads as Linda Christensen sculpts the dairy princesses, admire the largest boar, decide which new foods are worth the half-hour wait in line, listen to great music at the free stages, giggle nervously as we sail through the mildewed tunnels of Ye Old Mill, cheer the high school marching bands in the daily parade, ask 4-Hers about their alpaca's cute outfit after the Llama Costume Contest, and argue whether the garden photo in the Fine Arts Center was worthier of display than your friend's corgi watercolor. We check the Agriculture Horticulture Building hoping that our sister's or neighbor's (or editor's) cookies ribboned in Bee & Honey and to see if our coworker's pears collected the blue in Fruit & Wine yet again. We shake hands with our favorite politicians, try to identify the famous figures painted along the upper deck at the Ball Park Cafe while sipping Mini Donut Beer, wander through the Midway and realize we aren't kids anymore, wave at Giggles when we see him tending to walleye cakes, and then take a break inside the Lee & Rose Warner Coliseum and are thrilled to the core when an eight-horse draft hitch team stomps into view. We watch romance blossoming among the sweaty teens working at Fresh French Fries, Sweet Martha's, and the corn roast stand. We nod our heads in agreement with the political statements made with Crop Art & Scarecrows, and we *tsk-tsk* when our favorite church cafeteria closes.

And then we take a deep collective breath as summer fades.

Of all these phenomenal experiences, nothing beats the four years I entered the Creative Activities contests. A week before the fair begins, competitors gather in a line hundreds deep that sometimes extends past the Education Building. Hopeful contenders wait with rubber containers, coolers, wagons, duct-taped boxes, and childless strollers brimming sometimes perilously with chocolate Bundts and rye loaves and sugar cookies shaped like Minnesota. You get to learn a lot about a stranger when they confess how many hours of sleep were lost prepping for the early-morning drop-off or that this year will be their fifteenth even though they've never won a ribbon.

Occasionally you'll overhear someone grumbling about past winners possibly being affiliated with the University of Minnesota's now bygone Department of Home Economics, but mostly people are just happy to be there. One year, "Blue Ribbon Baker" and celebrity Marjorie Johnson entered the fairgrounds while I was in drop-off, and the crowd parted and swarmed her as if touching her hand could anoint us with what it takes to win best coffee cake or apple pie.

I wrote an article for a weekly alternative paper titled "Ribbon Junkies: Behind the Scenes at the State Fair Food Competitions." In it I described the camaraderie of competition and interviewed some repeat winners. A few months after publication, a Hollywood reality television producer contacted me. He was all excited about coming to Minnesota and meeting cutthroat bakers and canners who would stop at nothing for a ribbon. "Have you ever heard of someone sabotaging another contestant's entries?" he asked me. I could hear him drooling with anticipation. I laughed and explained that we want to win ribbons because we *earn* them, and it is an honor to compete with the best of the best. We don't step on other people to lift ourselves up. The state fair is about lifting everyone up. There isn't room here for the inflated drama of "Real Canners of Cottage Grove."

At the Minnesota State Fair we connect. We celebrate community. During these past few decades of political disconnect, we find humanity and companionship in the drop-off line and wonder at the possibilities of all the good things that happen at the Minnesota State Fair.

Friends describe the fair as if it is a persona they have a relationship with … something changes in the air between day one and Labor Day, when fall announces itself regardless of temperatures.

. . .

In 2018 I was honored to be invited to spend an entire day in the Creative Activities Building's brand-new Cambria kitchen. We billed it "Nordic Food Geek Goes to the Fair," and I combined my two favorite things (the Minnesota State Fair and Nordic food) to demo for the crowds. Guests sampled lefse pizza topped with SPAM and caviar, cheese curd–filled æbleskiver, deep-fried pickled herring. The best compliment I received came from a woman who asked for a second sampling of Not-So-Mini Ginger Pinchy Donuts: "This is the best thing I've ever eaten at the fair," she told me.

SPAM Lefse Pizza

SERVES 2–4

Potato lefse is a thin, soft round bread made of potatoes, cream, butter, and flour. Lefse is a Norwegian creation that became a Christmas tradition in many Nordic American homes. Think of it as potato tortillas. And I know what you are dying to ask me. Yes, SPAM and caviar form a delicious alliance.

1 large lefse round
nonstick spray
6 ounces SPAM, patted dry and cut into
    ¼-inch cubes
¼ cup sour cream

garnishes: minced chives and dill,
    lingonberry preserves, inexpensive
    caviar or roe, pickled mustard
    seeds (recipe follows), thinly
    sliced red onion

Heat oven to 325 degrees. Coat each side of lefse round with nonstick spray. Place lefse on parchment-lined baking sheet and bake 5 minutes, then flip. Keep an eye on the lefse so it does not burn. Remove from oven when lefse is just crisp and very light brown, an additional 10 minutes.

While lefse bakes, coat a nonstick skillet with nonstick spray and place over medium-high heat. Add SPAM cubes and fry; shake pan or use a spatula to sear all sides so that they are golden and caramelized, about 3 minutes.

Spread top of lefse with sour cream. Dot with fried SPAM cubes. Garish evenly with herbs, lingonberries, caviar, pickled mustard seeds, and red onion. Serve immediately.

Pickled Mustard Seeds

MAKES 2 CUPS

1 cup mustard seeds
1 cup white wine vinegar
2 cups sugar

3 cups water
salt and pepper
other spices as desired

NOTE *Add these to a cheese or charcuterie plate. Spread over sandwiches; use as a vegan substitute for caviar. Also delicious over deviled eggs or added to cranberry sauce.*

Bring a pot of water to boiling over medium-high heat. Drop in mustard seeds and continue to boil for at least 15 minutes. Drain through a wire colander.

Prepare vinegar pickling sauce by combining vinegar, sugar, 3 cups water, salt and pepper to taste, and any other spices you wish. Bring to a simmer. When sugar is completely dissolved, add seeds. Simmer 10 to 15 minutes. Cool and place in a quart jar. Store in the refrigerator for up to 1 month.

Cheese Curd Æbleskiver

MAKES ABOUT 26 BALLS

Æbleskiver are round pancakes, traditionally filled with apple slices, thus the name (æbleskiver means "apple slices" in Danish). Batter is poured into a griddle with curved divots, and any manner of utensil is used to flip the pancakes as they cook so that the spheres are uniformly golden.

While æbleskiver are usually a sweet dessert, this savory version is my spin.

1½ cups all-purpose flour
½ teaspoon baking powder
1 teaspoon baking soda
¼ teaspoon salt
1 cup buttermilk
2 large eggs, beaten
1 cup plain whole-fat
    Greek-style yogurt

zest from 1 orange
⅓ cup minced fresh herbs (such as
    chives, cilantro, dill)
2 tablespoons plus 1 teaspoon butter,
    cold, cut into ¼-teaspoon cubes
26 cheese curds (a little more than
    ½ teaspoon each)

Sift flour, baking powder, baking soda, and salt together. In a separate bowl, whisk together buttermilk, eggs, yogurt, orange zest, and herbs. Add wet ingredients to dry and combine well. Set batter aside 5 to 10 minutes.

Heat æbleskiver pan over medium-high heat. Add ¼ teaspoon butter to each pancake well. Fill wells two-thirds full with batter. When cakes are golden brown on the bottom and centers begin to bubble, loosen top edges using fork, skewer, or chopstick. Use tool to gently pull each cake so that the outer shell is perpendicular to the well and uncooked batter spreads into bottom of the well. Tuck cheese curd into center of each cake. As bottom becomes golden, use tool to pull orb closed over the cheese. Rotate cake to seal all edges, turning several times, until golden orb forms and inside of pancake is cooked thoroughly. Use tool to lift balls from pan.

Tempura-Fried Pickled Herring with Lingonberry Hot Sauce

SERVES 4

Tempura-fried pickled herring is the vehicle I use to persuade people who think they don't like pickled herring that they actually do.

For the fried herring

1½ cups all-purpose flour, plus ¾ cup for dusting
1 tablespoon baking powder
1 cup club soda
2 large eggs, beaten
2 tablespoons aquavit or vodka (optional)

1 pound pickled herring
1 quart (4 cups) peanut or vegetable oil
salt

Whisk together 1½ cups of the flour and baking powder in a deep bowl. Gently stir in club soda, eggs, and aquavit (if using) until loose batter forms (do not overmix; batter should be lumpy). Refrigerate or put bowl over ice until ready to use.

Rinse herring pieces well in cold water, remove onions and other pickling bits, and pat dry with paper towels. Pour remaining ¾ cup flour into a separate shallow dish and dredge herring in the flour. Dip the herring pieces into the batter so that they are well coated.

In a heavy-bottomed pot, bring oil to 350 degrees over medium-high heat. (Alternatively, use a deep fryer to heat the oil for frying the herring.) Deep-fry the herring, about 8 pieces at a time, for about 1 to 2 minutes. Use a metal slotted spoon or spider to remove the herring from the oil and place on a paper towel–lined plate; season with salt.

For the lingonberry hot sauce

Combine 1 part hot pepper sauce (use your favorite) to 1 part lingonberry preserves.

Serve fish hot with lingonberry hot sauce.

Not-So-Mini Ginger Pinchy Donuts

MAKES 32 DONUTS

A cookie named for my generously proportioned ginger cat Orson (nicknamed Pinchy) won the blue ribbon in the 2015 Minnesota State Fair Gold Medal Flour Cookie Contest. I love the flavors so much that I created a donut that mimics the cookie, honoring both Orson and those tasty mini donuts we all scarf down at the fair.

For the ginger dough

½ packet active dry yeast (about 1¼ teaspoons)
2 tablespoons brown sugar
1½ tablespoons warm water
½ cup whole milk
1 large egg yolk
1 tablespoon molasses
1 teaspoon ground ginger
1 teaspoon ground cinnamon
¼ teaspoon ground cloves
¼ teaspoon ground allspice
1¾–2 cups all-purpose flour
½ teaspoon salt
2 tablespoons butter, melted

For the citrus dough

½ packet active dry yeast (about 1¼ teaspoons)
2 tablespoons granulated sugar
2 tablespoons warm water
½ cup whole milk
1 large egg yolk
1 teaspoon vanilla extract
zest from 1 orange and 1 lemon
1¾–2 cups all-purpose flour
½ teaspoon salt
2 tablespoons butter, melted

For each batch, in a medium mixing bowl, dissolve yeast and sugar in water and let stand 5 minutes, until foamy. Add milk, yolk, seasonings, 1 cup of the flour, salt, and butter and beat by hand or with dough hook in standing mixer until smooth and satiny. Stir in remaining flour to form a stiff dough. Cover and let rise in a warm place until doubled, about 1 hour.

Dust work surface with flour. Turn ginger dough onto the surface and halve. With floured hands, pat half dough out until smooth, shaping into a 6x12–inch rectangle and to about ½ inch thick. Set aside on parchment and repeat with second half. Roll out the citrus dough in same manner. Carefully place one citrus dough over one ginger dough and roll into a long spiral. Pinch crease together and gently roll each log to about 14 inches long. Cover and let rest 30 minutes. Cut each log into 16 circles.

In a skillet or fryer, heat 3 inches of vegetable oil to 375 degrees. Work in batches to lift donuts into oil and fry about 1 to 2 minutes each side or until golden brown. Drain on paper towels; while still warm, toss in ½ cup granulated sugar mixed with 1 teaspoon ground ginger and 1 teaspoon cinnamon.

Chicken-Fried SPAM-n-Waffle Bites

MAKES 24 APPETIZERS

Hormel, maker of SPAM, sponsored The Great American SPAM® Championship Contest at state fairs across America for years, abruptly ending the event after 2018. I entered at the Minnesota State Fair a few times, but never came close to winning. My recipe for chicken-fried SPAM and waffles was disqualified because the judges believed it contained more than the ten ingredients allowed. I coulda been a contender.

For the chicken-fried SPAM
vegetable oil for frying
1½ cups all-purpose baking mix (such as Bisquick)
1 tablespoon sugar
¼ teaspoon cayenne
1 large egg
1 cup buttermilk
1 (12-ounce) can SPAM Classic, sliced into 24 triangles

In a heavy-bottomed pot, bring oil to 350 degrees over medium-high heat. (Alternatively, use a deep fryer to heat the oil.) Set a wire rack over a paper towel–lined baking sheet.

In a large shallow dish, whisk together baking mix, sugar, and cayenne. In a second large shallow dish, whisk together egg and buttermilk until thoroughly combined.

Working in batches, coat SPAM triangle bites in flour mixture, dip in egg-buttermilk, and again into flour mixture so that each bite is coated evenly. Shake off any excess batter. Working in batches, gently drop SPAM into hot oil and fry until golden brown, using slotted spoon or spider to flip SPAM for even cooking, about 2 minutes each side. Transfer cooked SPAM bites to the wire rack. (Keep warm by placing rack of SPAM bites in oven set at 200 degrees.)

For the waffles
2 cups all-purpose baking mix (such as Bisquick)
1 cup shredded Cheddar
1⅓ cups buttermilk
1 large egg
2 tablespoons butter, melted

Heat waffle iron; coat with nonstick cooking spray. Stir together baking mix, Cheddar, buttermilk, egg, and melted butter. Pour portion of batter onto center of hot waffle iron. Close lid and bake about 5 minutes or until steaming stops. Carefully remove waffle. Repeat with remaining batter. Cut waffles into 24 triangles.

For the maple "gravy"
1 cup pure maple syrup
½ cup hot pepper sauce
3 tablespoons butter

In a small saucepan, heat maple syrup, hot pepper sauce, and butter, whisking together until butter melts. Keep warm until ready to serve.

To assemble
Place one SPAM bite on each waffle section. Serve with maple gravy dipping sauce.

Deep-Fried Pickles

SERVES 4–6

I meet a group of friends every year at our designated state fair venue of choice, the Perfect Pickle. We share a few baskets of Perfects (deep-fried pickles), Cajuns (spicy Cajun pickles), and Gourmets (deep-fried and filled with cream cheese). We add hot sauce to our ranch dip and begin another year wandering the fairgrounds together, with periodic pit stops at the beer gardens. In the off-season, these are my pickles of choice.

2 cups kosher dill pickle
    sandwich slices
½ cup all-purpose flour
1 teaspoon Old Bay Seasoning
½ teaspoon dried dill

½ cup of your favorite beer
vegetable oil for frying
mayonnaise dressing
    (recipe follows)

Drain the pickles and pat dry on paper towels. In a large mixing bowl, whisk together flour and seasonings. Whisk in beer until just combined.

In a heavy-bottomed pot, bring oil to 375 degrees over medium-high heat. (Alternatively, use a deep fryer to heat the oil.) Set a wire rack over a paper towel–lined baking sheet.

Working in small batches, dredge individual pickle slices through batter to coat evenly, and gently drop into hot oil. Fry until golden brown, turning at least once for even cooking, about 1 minute each side. Drain on cooling rack; serve hot with mayonnaise dressing.

Mayonnaise Dressing

MAKES ABOUT ¾ CUP

½ cup mayonnaise
2 tablespoons Dijon-style mustard

2 tablespoons honey
1 teaspoon Old Bay Seasoning

Whisk ingredients together in small bowl.

Butter Head

I tend to romanticize farming, especially dairy farming, which is a disservice to the people who actually farm. Their hard work, dedication, and perseverance is on a level I cannot imagine. Long days, rare vacations, seemingly impossible odds at making a living. In 2019 across the Midwest dairy belt, our nation's best are in trouble. When I was a kid, we drank a glass of milk at every meal. Today the average person doesn't reach for cow's milk.

We visit the Minnesota State Fair with the understanding that our trip isn't complete without a stop in the Dairy Building, where we stand in long lines at the Dairy Goodness Bar to purchase the annual shake special flavor voted on by the public (Birthday Batter Bash! That's S'more Like it! Pie'n the Sky!).

Awkwardly cupping our cones, sundaes, and shakes to keep from jostling against other fairgoers, we shuffle with the crowds over to the spinning, glass-encased refrigerator where artist Linda Christensen has been sculpting the likenesses of each dairy princess from ninety-pound bricks of Grade A salted butter since 1972. It is mesmerizing to watch the princesses and artist rotate slowly, allowing for a 360-degree view of the circle of butter blocks that Christensen methodically morphs into smiling (possibly shivering) Princess Kay and her fellow dairy princesses. Day after day, the butter heads are revealed, until Labor Day weekend, when all of the heads are complete. But what happens to the butter heads (and the princesses!) when the fair is over?

. . .

On a perfect summer day in July, we drove north from the Twin Cities to just outside of Brooten and met with Alise Sjostrom at her family's farm and Redhead Creamery.

A long drive through our state reminds me of its beauty. Soybean fields and ditch flowers lined the two-lane highway. Corn as high as an elephant's eye melded with vast solar and wind farms, iconic water towers and silos and huge red barns, and towns occasionally named for the places people came from before we were Americans and Minnesotans, like Cologne, New Prague, Upsala, New Ulm, Vasa, and Nerstrand. We drove beneath green trees that I will probably never be able to identify, and plenty of pine, power lines, and billboards advertising area dentists. We drove over rivers that all meander to the great Mississippi, and we spoke their names out loud to each other with reverence, because any friend of the Mississippi is a friend of ours. Those who live along the Mississippi River feel a sense of pride and responsibility for her well-being, and it is good to view the streams and rivers that sustain her. When we eventually lost public radio, we scrolled through an endless chain of country western channels and admired the endless blue cloudless sky.

To get to Redhead Creamery, you've got to exit the highway, take a quick jaunt through a small town, then turn onto a rambling gravel road that tunnels through green fields of corn, wildflowers, and cows. The farm appears as bucolic as my romantic farm dreams, belying the hard work it takes to wrangle nature into something so clean and pretty. Past the pictorial farmhouse are small buildings that house cows and milking operations, and the Redhead Creamery, which doubles as a cheese making facility and restaurant/sales/catering.

A few dozen cows lined a pasture and munched on the hay on the other side of the fence, their large, gentle, white and black faces pushing toward us to get a better look at some new humans. Dairy cows are very accustomed to people, and the Redhead Creamery cows are known to affably greet the guests who come to tour the farm all summer. Two hundred cows live on the farm, which is average for a family farm, but large enough that there are a number of both full- and part-time employees outside of family.

Alise met us at the front door of the creamery. Alise is passionate about dairy farming and the award-winning cheese she produces. She and her three sisters (all redheads, hence the creamery name) grew up on the same land where Alise and her husband, Lucas, executive director at Minnesota Milk Producers Association, are raising their children. Her parents live in a house just a driveway away. Close family bonds are her favorite part of a farming lifestyle; even as a child she thought "it was weird that my friends didn't have parents at home all the time."

We talked about 4-H and how it shaped Alise's passion for farming, as her projects were focused mainly on dairy and baking. In fact, 4-H was also responsible for uniting Alise's parents, who met while showing cows. While Alise knew that a lifetime of milking wasn't in her future, she still wanted to be part of an agricultural lifestyle. When she worked at a neighbor's creamery, she was intrigued with a milk pipeline that brought milk from another farm to the creamery.

Alise's oldest sister, Tammy, was a Princess Kay finalist in 2000, and Alise followed when she participated in 2006. She was a food marketing major at the University of Minnesota, honing communications and media skills that are vital for a dairy princess who must speak to the public about the importance of dairy.

As we talked, one of Alise's cheese makers joined us. Rachel won dairy princess at the county level and was excited to be going to the Minnesota State Fair, which was only a month away. When Rachel won the county title, her cousin, a former dairy princess, reminded her that she was about to be a butter head, and she immediately began making plans for the butter bust. Both Alise and Rachel emphasized that the Princess Kay competition is not a pageant. The contestants participate in hours of training, interviews, and speeches, all meant to help prepare them to be goodwill ambassadors for Minnesota's dairy industry. Alise recalled her time as a dairy princess with pride: "We had credibility and the opportunity to share it with the right people. We are the ones with the knowledge. Let's have a discussion about that." With more experience, especially as a mom and a business owner, Alise earned a powerful new perspective, relatability, and confidence.

Alise's butter head was celebrated at a corn feed the summer following her princess year. "But my mom put out other butter so no one would use it," she told me. When I asked what happened to the butter head, Alise said, "It's in my parents' freezer. I can call and ask if we can look at it if you want." Of course, I wanted!

We walked to Alise's parents' home, where in the garage her dad was busy pulling frozen hamburger packages off a massive lump enclosed in a plastic garbage bag. He hefted the thing out of the freezer and estimated its current weight at around seventy pounds. "I bet it has some freezer burn," Alise said as she arranged the butter head on a crate in the back of a pickup truck. Yet, when the bag was pulled away from the head, we noted that the only damage was a bruised nose. Other than that, the head looked very much like the Alise who stood next to it.

I asked what happened to Tammy's butter head, and Alise's dad noted that Tammy wasn't as sentimental as Alise. In fact, Alise looks forward to the day her own daughter can compete for the Princess Kay dairy crown and their butter heads can live together in the freezer, perhaps pulled out for special occasions and the odd visit from a cookbook writer.

I was curious about Alise's take on the dairy crisis. To her it came down to supply and demand. Because dairy farmers are so efficient, "We have too much. We are really good at what we do." To combat this abundance, Alise believes in diversifying, using the skills and resources a farm already has to produce a new product or service.

I asked Alise what the most commonly misunderstood thing about farming is, and she answered, "Animal care. If you didn't care for your animals, they wouldn't produce: they wouldn't eat, grow, produce milk." She went on to describe the general care farmers take when it comes to land as well: "Our land and our water is what we commonly get attacked for." She motioned to the back of the creamery, where a large, pristine pond connected the yard to the fields. To keep that pond unpolluted there is manure management plus crop consultants who test and monitor the entire farmstead. To keep the cows healthy and happy, a vet supervises the care given to each animal and makes surprise visits to ensure the animals' well-being. When I showed skepticism about factory farms taking the same care, Alise told me that larger dairies are monitored even more closely.

As for farmers and dairy farmers in particular, Alise said, "We understand more aspects of being alive on this earth because we know about our food."

Deep-Fried Cheese Curds

SERVES 6–8 (IF YOU AREN'T A GREEDY GLUTTON LIKE ME)

¾ cup all-purpose flour, plus ½ cup for dusting
1½ teaspoons baking powder
2 teaspoons dried dill
1 large egg
½ cup soda water
vegetable oil for frying
8 ounces Redhead Creamery fresh cheddar
    cheese curds, very cold
hot sauce and honey for serving

In a large mixing bowl, combine ¾ cup of the flour, baking powder, and dill. In a separate mixing bowl, whisk together egg and soda water. Add liquid to dry ingredients and stir until just combined.

In a heavy-bottomed pot, bring oil to 375 degrees over medium-high heat. (Alternatively, use a deep fryer to heat the oil.) Set a wire rack over a paper towel–lined baking sheet.

Add remaining ½ cup flour to a small mixing bowl. Dust individual curds with the flour, then dip in batter to coat. Fry in small batches in hot oil, turning so that curds cook evenly. Remove from oil when the batter is a deep golden brown and drain on cooling rack. Eat while hot; serve with your favorite hot sauce and honey.

Jerry's Kids

We spent Labor Day weekend in anticipation of Sunday night's Jerry Lewis telethon. Throughout the night we willed our bodies to stay awake while Jerry begged and beguiled his audience to send money for kids with muscular dystrophy. He was joined onstage by old celebrities we'd mostly never heard of and kids in wheelchairs or with crutches. Jerry told their stories about living with MD, and near the end of the nearly twenty-four-hour-long broadcast, Jerry's voice would start to quiver as he put an arm around one of the kids and he'd erupt with exhausted tears. His annual breakdown was probably the most luridly fascinating thing about the program.

Every year my sister Susan watched Jerry with pen and paper at the ready so she could jot down the address for sending away to receive a free Muscular Dystrophy Association Carnival Kit. Months later when the carnival kit finally arrived, we'd practically forgotten it was coming. Susan would secure the package, call her best friends, and block me from entering her bedroom so she could begin planning in secret.

The kit contained every imaginable thing a kid needed to throw an amazing backyard carnival and raise money for Jerry's Kids: an activities booklet, signs to guide guests to the various carnival events, badges for VIP carnival volunteers, and tickets to sell for carnival entrance and games.

By the time she was eleven years old, Susan had established a reputation for running the best MDA Carnival in town. Most years she held the carnival in the open lot across the street from our house, explaining that our big backyard was just too small to hold her extravaganza. We'd pack her Red Flyer with everything we needed, hauling loads of stuff across busy Main Street and then setting up.

Susan had many roles, including but not limited to marketing, local businesses liaison (asking for donations), acting carnival director, CEO of admissions and sales. She also acted as the bouncer, ringmaster, and Boss. Susan's friends got exciting tasks like running the ring toss or selling refreshments. One year there was a fortune teller! (The medium was actually Susan or one of her friends disguised in flowing scarves and speaking with a mysterious accent.)

I was relegated to the Clothespin Drop, aka the baby game:

1. Have kid kneel on chair with hands over backrest.
2. Blindfold kid.
3. Hand kid clothespins one at a time and direct kid to drop clothespin into wide-mouth Mason jar on ground.
4. Kids who successfully drop three clothespins into jar win a small prize.

My true passion was for the concessions stand, where we sold popcorn and drinks. Once I was called in to substitute for one of Susan's friends during a tween emergency (likely something having to do with boys). I snuck handfuls of fresh buttered popcorn and guzzled Kool-Aid directly from the pitcher. Eventually my telltale grape mustache gave me away, and Susan directed me back to Clothespin Drop purgatory.

We did our best to raise money for Jerry's Kids, although none of us can remember how much was sent back to the MDA.

Microwaved Popcorn on the Cob

MAKES ABOUT 2 CUPS POPPED CORN

We didn't have microwaves in the early 1970s. We made our popcorn right over the stovetop and added enough butter and salt that it soaked through the bottom of the paper grocery bags we used to hold it.

Microwaving a single popcorn cob is pretty exciting. You can buy the ears from farmers markets and online.

1 cob popcorn
1 teaspoon butter
salt
1 small paper lunch bag

Rub dried corn on the cob with butter and season with salt. (Alternatively, you can season your popcorn with melted butter after it pops.) Place in the paper bag. Fold the bag top over twice so that opening is secured. Place in the microwave and cook on high until popping slows to between 2 and 3 seconds, about 2½ to 3 minutes. Discard cob and eat directly from bag.

Apples

Our front yard was shaded by the branches of a huge tree so heavy with apples that by the time summer was over the limbs nearly swept the ground. We'd fill paper grocery bags with fallen apples that littered the lawn and trek them into the kitchen, where my mom stood for days peeling endless ropes of apple skins. Every surface of the kitchen was covered with crocks and pots filled with apples that went into applesauce and canned apple butter. The house smelled like cinnamon and sweet baked apples, and the occasional pie. We collected bags and bags of apples, setting them just inside the back porch door, until finally Mom said we'd gathered enough apples and she didn't have room for any more.

Neil's Great Aunt Hazel's Knobby Apple Cake

SERVES 12–16   HAZEL (JENKINS) MUKA VIA DR. NEIL O. ANDERSON

My friend Neil is known in our circles for his cooking. His themed dinner parties are acclaimed, and we all jostle for invites. His tarts, pies, and cakes are legendary. We all joke about his canning disorder, because he spends every waking moment from spring harvest through fall preserving the bounty that grows in his gardens and fruit tree orchard. Neil taught me to make æbleskiver and pastry crust, and gifts me frequently with his excess produce.

Neil isn't originally from Minnesota, but his aunt Hazel's cake tastes like home wherever you land. Use local apples for a local flavor.

3 cups all-purpose flour
1 teaspoon salt
1 teaspoon baking powder
1 teaspoon ground cinnamon
2 large eggs
1½ cups sugar
1 cup oil (avocado, olive, walnut)
2 teaspoons vanilla extract
½ cup whole milk
3 cups chopped apples, peeled and cored
½ cup chopped nuts (walnuts)
1 tablespoon sugar mixed with 2 teaspoons ground
   cinnamon (optional)
whipped cream or ice cream for serving

Heat oven to 350 degrees. Grease and flour a 13x9–inch cake pan. In a large mixing bowl, whisk together flour, salt, baking powder, and cinnamon. Set aside.

Beat eggs and sugar together until they are light, about 3 to 5 minutes. Stir in oil, mixing well. Add vanilla. In 3 batches, add the dry mix and the milk, beating into batter completely before adding next batch. Stir in apples and nuts and spread batter into prepared pan. Sprinkle top of cake evenly with cinnamon sugar (if using).

Bake for 50 minutes or until wooden pick comes out clean. Serve warm with whipped cream or ice cream.

Grannie's Apple Crisp

SERVES 6　　　　　　　　　　　　　　　　　　**NATALIE SATTER**

Natalie chefs at one of our favorite grocery stores, and I love visiting to see what special recipes she comes up with. When she told me about her grandmother's apple crisp, I promptly asked for the recipe. This crisp is deceivingly simple and packs a punch of complex flavor.

Natalie says, "Grandma's recipe for brown sugar, if you didn't have any: regular sugar and 2 tablespoons of molasses. Great-grandma was a huge fan of cardamom, so Grandma added it to the crisp just for her."

4 Granny Smith apples, cored and finely chopped
¾ teaspoon ground cinnamon
¼ teaspoon nutmeg
¼ teaspoon ground cardamom
⅓ cup granulated sugar

¾ cup packed brown sugar
½ cup all-purpose flour
½ cup oats
⅓ cup butter, softened
cinnamon or vanilla ice cream for serving

Heat oven to 375 degrees. Generously grease a deep-dish pie pan or 9x9–inch baking dish.

In a large bowl, combine apples, spices, and granulated sugar. Pour into prepared baking dish. In a separate bowl, combine brown sugar, flour, oats, and butter. Mix thoroughly and sprinkle over apples. Bake for 30 to 35 minutes and serve warm with cinnamon (or vanilla) ice cream.

Apple Cider Donut Muffins

MAKES 36 MINI MUFFINS   SUSAN JOHNSON SCHMIDT

If you live in Minnesota, you probably make a trip to the apple orchard each autumn. Everyone has their favorite — orchard *and* apple. We bring home a bag or two of Honeycrisp, SweeTango, and Zestar!, a half gallon of cider, and at least a dozen apple cider donuts.

These muffins replicate apple cider donuts when a trip to the orchard isn't in the cards.

¾ cup plus 2 tablespoons sugar
1 large egg
¼ cup vegetable oil
¾ cup apple cider
1 teaspoon vanilla extract
1½ cups all-purpose flour

2 teaspoons baking powder
¼ teaspoon salt
½ teaspoon nutmeg, divided
1 teaspoon ground ginger
1 teaspoon ground cinnamon

Heat oven to 350 degrees. Prepare miniature muffin tins with liners.

In a large mixing bowl, use electric mixer to beat ¾ cup of the sugar and egg together until light and frothy. Blend in oil, apple cider, and vanilla.

In a separate mixing bowl, whisk together flour, baking powder, salt, and ¼ teaspoon of the nutmeg. Pour liquid mixture into dry ingredients and whisk together until just blended.

In a small mixing bowl, whisk together remaining 2 tablespoons sugar, remaining ¼ teaspoon nutmeg, ginger, and cinnamon.

Fill prepared tins three-quarters full with batter and sprinkle sugar-spice mixture evenly over tops of muffins. Bake for 15 to 18 minutes or until inserted wooden pick comes out clean.

Back to School Biscuits

The year we moved to Worthington, only three of us sisters remained at home, the older two girls having moved on to adulthood. Candi, Susan, and I gathered around the kitchen table after school each afternoon with the AM transistor radio playing songs that sometimes made Candi cry, like "Wildfire," a sad song about a runaway horse.

Junk food was not a Johnson family staple, and my sisters made snacks like saltine crackers sandwiched around peanut butter and jelly. When they had the brilliant idea to pull out Mom's trusty container of biscuit mix, I was treated to warm biscuits loaded with melting butter and jam.

All these years later I cannot eat a biscuit without thinking about my sister Candi, and Wildfire the runaway horse and his sad teen owner who searched for him and became lost in a blizzard.

Biscuits

MAKES ABOUT 13 CUPS, FOR ABOUT 50 (¼-CUP) PORTIONS

SUSAN JOHNSON SCHMIDT

Susan said, "I remember very well making the biscuits. We had a Tupperware with the mix. I think we just added shortening and water. Happy, fun memories … as long as we cleaned up the kitchen before Mom got home! Maybe they just tasted so good because they were made with love."

For the biscuit mix

9 cups sifted flour
⅓ cup baking powder
¼ cup sugar

1 tablespoon salt
1 cup nonfat dry milk
2 cups shortening

Sift together flour, baking powder, sugar, salt, and dry milk 3 times in large mixing bowl. Cut in shortening until the mixture looks like coarse cornmeal. Store refrigerated in a tightly covered container and use within 2 months.

To make biscuits

Heat oven to 375 degrees. In a mixing bowl, stir together 3 parts mix with 1 part water. Drop ¼- to ⅓-cup portions onto parchment-lined baking sheet and bake until biscuits are risen and tops are golden brown, about 20 minutes.

Double Hot Fudge Pudding Cake

SERVES 9

My mom used her trusty Better Crocker cookbook to bake a special hot fudge pudding cake a few times each month. It was my favorite dessert because it felt so special and smelled like a Dairy Queen where you could order anything you wanted. My mom said she loved this recipe because a decent pantry always contained the ingredients needed to make the cake. I loved the recipe because somehow the fudge and the cake magically traded places as the cake baked.

Mom, being an ice cream–aholic, sometimes topped our warm pudding cake with a generous scoop of vanilla ice cream. I waited for the cream to melt into the hot cake, cooling the lava-like innards so that I could safely take a large bite without burning my mouth. It was a way to contain/time/temper(?) my greed. Milk and half-and-half made good toppings on nights when there was no ice cream in the freezer.

This updated version of Mom's (and Betty's) pudding cake substitutes chocolate morsels for nuts, but you could also use fresh or frozen (thawed and drained) cherries.

For the cake batter

1 cup all-purpose flour
½ cup granulated sugar
2 tablespoons unsweetened
    cocoa powder
2 teaspoons baking powder

½ teaspoon salt
½ cup whole milk
2 tablespoons butter, melted
2 teaspoons vanilla extract
¾ cup bittersweet chocolate morsels

Heat oven to 350 degrees. Grease an 8x8–inch cake pan (or 1½–quart casserole). In a large mixing bowl, whisk together flour, granulated sugar, 2 tablespoons cocoa, baking powder, and salt.

Combine milk, butter, and vanilla in liquid measuring cup and add to the dry ingredients, mixing just until batter forms. Stir in chocolate morsels. Spread batter over bottom of prepared baking dish.

For the hot fudge layer

1 cup packed brown sugar
¼ cup unsweetened cocoa powder

1¾ cups boiling water

In a small mixing bowl, whisk together brown sugar and ¼ cup cocoa. Evenly sprinkle the top of the batter with mixture, then gently pour boiling water over the entire cake. Bake for 45 minutes. Serve warm with ice cream or cream and berries.

Diwali

Late in September my friend Paurvi extends invitations for her family's annual Diwali celebration. She sends the invites out a month early as a save-the-date effort to make sure we all can attend. As the years roll by, we do our best to be there.

Diwali, the festival of lights, symbolizes a spiritual victory of light over darkness, good over evil, knowledge over ignorance. Hindus, Buddists, Jains, and Sikhs clean and decorate their homes before throwing festive parties. We lucky participants are welcomed into the homes of loved ones and dear friends to feast on sweets and other delicious treats.

When we arrive at Paurvi's home, the front porch is adorned with orderly rows of shoes belonging to guests. Coming from inside the house we hear laughter and conversations, and we smell the aromas of food, much of which Paurvi's mother, Rekha, cooks for days in advance of the party. My Indian friends are decked out in their finest sari and shalwar kameez. There is color everywhere, and the occasion has become a joyful reunion for many of us. We inch through the crowd, greeting dear friends and meeting new ones. The dining room table is so full I have to shuffle platters and serving trays around to find room for my contribution, and a buffet behind the table holds another full stash of sweets: cakes, tarts, candy, mini-Bundts, and dozens of other goodies that symbolize the sweet taste of light's victory over darkness.

While I know the importance of sweets on Diwali, I cannot help but fill my plate with every bite of savory goodness laid out. There are fried morsels, rice and legumes, salads, dips, and flatbreads. Happily, roti also makes an appearance on the Diwali table. Roti is an unleavened bread that is a staple of Indian cuisine. It is eaten with everyday curries, dal (spiced lentils), potatoes and vegetables, and meat. Rekha has been rolling roti her entire life, and her roti are perfectly round and soft. I cannot help myself and always take more than my fair share. I tuck stolen rounds beneath some curry and dal and pretend I'm not a greedy roti glutton.

Once at a lefse party, Paurvi told us that the rituals around making lefse reminded her of Indian roti. She invited us to learn to make them with her mom, and we were enthralled as Rekha and her friend Ila demonstrated how to make the flatbread. It was a dance: first making the dough out of nothing more than flour, salt, and water; then kneading it into a supple ball and using a thin tapered rolling pin to roll out small pieces of the dough into rounds. Each bread was

charred over an open flame
on the gas stovetop, and
Ila used her bare fingers to
deftly rotate the bread and
flip it as it got just the right
amount of char. Cooked roti
received a spoonful of ghee
that soaked into the bread as it
cooled, softening and flavoring the
bread until at last we were allowed to
spread a bit of chutney over the warm
rounds and indulge.

Since that afternoon in Rekha's kitchen,
roti tastes to me like the stories of immigration
and love that Rekha and Ila shared. Rekha told us
about marrying Paurvi's father after meeting him and
knowing him for a brief time. Rekha's Indian parents arranged
the marriage before Harshad immigrated to America and attended graduate school in Tennessee. After earning his graduate degree in engineering, he sent
for Rekha. Having been apart for two years, Rekha finally joined Harshad in Chi-
cago. A year later Paurvi was born, and as Paurvi says, "Our family was complete."

When Rekha arrived in the United States during the late 1960s, our grocery
stores were limited in the items they carried. Indian foods were rare, and Rekha
became adept at creating substitutes for essential ingredients. An example is
Rekha's tamarind chutney. Chutney in many forms is common in most grocery
stores now, yet Rekha continues to use the recipe she came up with when she was
a young bride and new to America. Rekha combines apple butter, lemon, and
spices, and it tastes almost identical to the chutney it imitates.

I have all of these thoughts as I sneak away from the Diwali table with my pil-
fered roti hidden under a mound of rice. I imagine Rekha as a young woman, in
a world so different from the one she left. She came to the Midwest, eventually
Minnesota, for love and a new life. She had the determination and savvy to create
familiarity out of unexpected ingredients. Light over darkness; courage over
complaint.

Roti

MAKES 12 (5-INCH) ROUNDS, ABOUT 6 SERVINGS

REKHA BHATT AND ILA PATEL

2 cups whole wheat atta or
    bread flour
½ teaspoon salt

2 teaspoons vegetable oil
¾–1 cup lukewarm water
ghee or clarified butter, melted

In a medium mixing bowl, stir together flour and salt. Add the oil and slowly add water while using hands to knead. Add only as much water as needed to form a craggy mixture that pulls away from the side of the bowl. Turn dough out onto a well-floured surface and knead until smooth and silky. Cover with kitchen cloth and let rest 10 minutes.

(Alternatively, add flour and salt to food processor fitted with a metal blade; add oil and pulse while very gradually adding enough of the water so that the mixture begins to pull away from the sides of the bowl and forms a smooth dough. Remove from bowl and cover with a kitchen cloth; let rest 10 minutes.)

Divide dough into 12 equal parts, about the size of a walnut. Form each piece into a smooth ball and flatten slightly with the palm of your hand. On a well-floured surface, roll each flattened ball into a 5-inch round.

To cook over gas flame: with flame on medium to medium-low, place roti directly on flame. Use tongs or chopsticks to turn for even cooking. After about 30 seconds, the bread will begin to char; flip and cook the other side in the same manner.

To cook on grill: place roti over direct high heat. Use tongs to turn for even cooking. After 1 to 2 minutes, the bread will begin to char; flip and cook the other side in the same manner.

To cook on skillet or griddle: preheat skillet over medium-high heat. Place roti on ungreased surface about 1 to 2 minutes; flip and cook the other side.

Cooked roti should have some dark brown spots when finished. As you remove each roti from the heat, place the darker side down on a plate and generously spoon a teaspoon or two of melted ghee over the top. Serve warm.

NOTE *Roti is commonly made with whole wheat atta, which is a high-gluten flour and consists of 11.5 to 13 percent protein. The gluten makes the dough pliable and easier to roll very thin. Atta can be found at Indian grocery stores. Use whole wheat bread flour when atta is not available. For added flavor, stir ½ teaspoon of ground ginger, garlic, or coriander into the flour before making the dough.*

Faux Tamarind Chutney

MAKES ABOUT 1 CUP   REKHA BHATT

1 cup apple butter
1 teaspoon ground cinnamon
½ teaspoon ground cumin
¼ teaspoon salt

pinch cayenne
zest of ½ lemon plus 2 tablespoons fresh lemon juice

In a small mixing bowl, whisk together all ingredients. Let sit at room temperature for 30 minutes before serving; store refrigerated for up to 1 week.

Chana Masala (GARBANZO BEAN CURRY)

SERVES 6

Traditional garbanzo bean curry does not include pumpkin, but I like how pumpkin adds a creamy texture to curry, and it marries masala to the Midwest.

½ pound dried garbanzo beans, soaked in 5–6 cups cold water overnight
2 thumb-size pieces fresh ginger, peeled
5–6 cloves garlic
juice of 1 lemon (about 3 tablespoons)
2 teaspoons garam masala
1 teaspoon ground cumin
1 teaspoon ground coriander
1 teaspoon turmeric
½ teaspoon ground cardamom
½ teaspoon paprika

2–3 tablespoons hot chili paste (such as sambal oelek)
2 tablespoons vegetable oil
1 onion, chopped
1 (16-ounce) can crushed tomatoes
1 cup pumpkin puree
salt and pepper
pure maple syrup
rice or naan for serving
plain yogurt and cilantro for serving

Drain beans and discard any stones or odd peas. In a large stockpot, bring beans and 3 to 4 cups of water to a boil; reduce heat and simmer, uncovered, 30 minutes. Check beans to see if they are becoming tender. Continue simmering until beans are al dente. Remove from heat.

Add ginger, garlic, lemon juice, and spices (garam masala through chili paste) to food processor fitted with metal blade and puree.

Add oil to a large skillet over medium-high heat. Add onions and cook, stirring, until translucent. Add puree and cook while stirring constantly for 1 to 2 minutes, or until the kitchen fills with an amazing aroma. Stir in tomatoes, pumpkin, and beans with their cooking water.

Simmer over medium-high heat, stirring occasionally, for 15 to 20 minutes. Season with salt and pepper. Taste and add enough maple syrup to balance acidity. Serve over rice or naan with plain yogurt and cilantro relish.

Honey

Gary Reuter is my bee guy. We met through our work at the University of Minnesota, where Gary researches pollinators and teaches the public about beekeeping. At the St. Paul campus Bee Lab, we sat down one blustery, sunny autumn afternoon to talk about honey life.

Gary started cooking when his mom taught him to make french toast. She told him he was so much better at it than she was, probably as a way to get out of making it herself. "I fell for it!" he says. Gary's mom also taught him to make rosettes when she swore she just couldn't do them anymore. But she always told him he didn't put enough powdered sugar on them: "I'd look at her while she was eating a cookie, and she'd have powdered sugar all over her blouse." (Side note: Gary gifts me with a package of his rosettes every holiday season, and they are the best rosettes I've ever had.)

Thanks to his beekeeping dad, Gary says, "All through junior high and high school I'd have a honey sandwich for lunch every day: butter and honey on white bread. To this day my lunch is Wonder Bread! Dad quit beekeeping because he thought I was allergic to beestings. I broke out in a rash once when I was stung." Ironically, Gary's wife, Ginger, encouraged him to get into beekeeping as an adult and later they discovered *she* was allergic. He began taking classes on beekeeping at the university and eventually kept two hundred colonies. "I never thought I'd end up teaching that class someday."

After spending a year teaching high school shop class, Gary decided that with four kids he couldn't afford to be a public school teacher. He began contract work on alarm systems, always longing to get back into teaching. When the bee position opened up at the university, Gary applied and got the job. Thirty years later, he says, "I like honey. To be honest, that was my main attraction to bees. Now I'm interested in their behavioral [activities]." When it comes to honeybees, Gary says, "Lucky for us they don't know how much honey they need to make to survive the winter, so they make too much and we can take it. I'm okay with stealing honey."

I asked Gary about colony collapse and other issues related to bee decline. "There have always been issues," he told me. "About the time I started, Varroa mites came. They act like a wood tick, sucking and spreading viruses which affect the bees. Bees have always had some issues. What we work with here is bee health, not specifically colony collapse, but good bee health."

At the Bee Lab native bees are an important part of research. Native pollinators do not produce honey and as a result are often ignored when laws protecting honeybees are made. Pesticide-treated seeds that aren't allowed near areas where honeybees pollinate might be liberally used where native bees do. "Native bees do a lot of pollinating. We don't know how bad things are for them right now because no one paid attention to them for many years. A lot of native bees are so small, you don't really see them. At the Bee Lab we ask, 'What is the status of the bee population now? Can and how do we assess if they are in trouble?'" While we enjoy the honey that bees produce, we often forget that wild, native bees are responsible for feeding us a majority of our pollinated fruits and vegetables.

I asked Gary about the future of our pollinators based on the research being done at the University of Minnesota and other institutions. "I feel positive that the bees are going to be okay," he replied. "But there is something we are missing. All of the attention has been valuable. People are getting sensitive about pesticides. I'm not an anti-pesticide person; it's necessary for some of our pests. On the other hand, we shouldn't be out there spraying willy-nilly. Pesticide instructions are written for saving honeybees. But this isn't true for native bees. They are living out there in the environment. They are at risk."

Gary spoke about the hundreds of people who take his bee classes each year. He isn't sure how many actually become beekeepers. "People want to know what they can do to help the bees. They say, 'I want to get bees.' But the more important thing to do is to plant native flowers. Being a beekeeper takes a lot of work. We'd rather have no keeper than a poor keeper. Plant flowers; send money."

Gary's Honey Sandwich

SERVES 1   GARY REUTER

2 slices white bread   waxed paper
butter, softened   potato chips
honey

Carefully butter each slice of bread on one side, being sure to cover completely. It does not have to be thick, but any holes will allow honey to soak through and make a real mess. Spread honey evenly over butter on one piece of bread, then cover with second piece, butter side down. Cut in half diagonally; wrap with waxed paper. Let mellow for at least 2 hours. Best when eaten with potato chips.

Buckwheat Softies

MAKES 88 COOKIES   **GINGER REUTER**

Ginger Reuter is Gary's wife. She said, "This was originally a standard spice cookie, and I substituted buckwheat honey for molasses. Buckwheat honey is pretty common in Minnesota but pricy. There is usually a good supply at the honey booth at the state fair. I worked a number of years at the Bee & Honey exhibit. I did the cooking demos, answered questions, and whatever else was needed from open to close. I also helped with setup and judging.

"One year, on the day when we were taking in the food entries, I made a big batch of buckwheat softies for the setup staff. (It can be kind of frustrating to be looking at and smelling all these wonderful things and not taste them.) ["Blue Ribbon Baker"] Marjorie Johnson always came with a ton of entries, and checking her in was pretty time-consuming. She tried one of my cookies and asked for the recipe. It didn't fit the criteria (too much sugar versus honey), but she wanted to play with it. She always sat through my cooking demos, too; right in the front row, dressed in red, taking notes. She said there was always something new to learn."

1 cup margarine, or substitute butter
    for firmer cookies
1 large egg
1⅓ cups sugar, plus more for rolling
½ cup buckwheat honey
2 tablespoons milk

4 cups all-purpose flour
2 teaspoons baking soda
2 teaspoons ground cinnamon
1½ teaspoons ground ginger
1½ teaspoons ground cloves

Heat oven to 350 degrees. In a large mixing bowl, beat together margarine, egg, and 1⅓ cups sugar until light and fluffy. Add honey and milk and beat until well combined.

In a large mixing bowl, whisk together flour, baking soda, cinnamon, ginger, and cloves. Add dry ingredients to wet and mix well. Add a cup of sugar to a large, shallow dish. Shape dough into balls and roll in sugar. Place on parchment-lined baking sheets at least 1 inch apart, and bake for 12 minutes.

Snack Mix

MAKES 16 (½-CUP) SERVINGS (IF YOU CAN RESTRAIN YOURSELF)

GINGER REUTER

Ginger said, "This is another standby demo recipe. Add spices or different cereal."

Patrice says, "Stay away from the snack mix. It is so addictive I made three batches in one weekend and ate them all by myself." You might choose Annie's Organic Cheddar Crackers in place of the Goldfish; any cheese cracker will work. Add 1 teaspoon of rosemary and a pinch of red pepper flakes: it is shockingly delicious.

8 tablespoons butter, melted
½ cup honey
1½ cups Crispix cereal
1½ cups Cheerios cereal

1½ cups Life cereal
1 cup plain Goldfish crackers
1 cup pretzels
1 cup cashews

Heat oven to 325 degrees. In a very large mixing bowl, whisk together butter and honey. Toss with remaining ingredients to coat everything well. Spread mixture onto 1 or 2 parchment-lined baking sheets and bake for 30 to 45 minutes, stirring every 10 minutes and checking to be sure mixture doesn't burn.

NOTE
Be especially careful toward the end of baking. Let the color of the Goldfish guide you, as it is easy to jump from "done" to "burned."

Booya

There was a big Gophers football game that afternoon, and I frowned when my husband came into the living room dressed in a Green Bay Packers sweatshirt and a red Motion "W" baseball cap from his alma mater, the University of Wisconsin. We were meeting friends at a dive bar on the other side of town, and I told him, "You cannot wear that. The Gophers have a huge game today, and you don't know what the crowd at that bar might be like. You could get beat up in the parking lot." Grudgingly, he returned to the bedroom and changed into a Twins jersey.

My worry was unjustified. The bar patrons were friendly and cheerful, and far too interested in the booya being served that day to pay any attention to some guy dressed in a rival's gear. The booya was to be served from 11 AM until it ran out. "Last year we ran out before 2," I was warned when I called the day prior, so we arrived early.

For the uninitiated, *booya* is both a stew and the community gathering where booya is prepared and eaten. Booyas are held all summer long and into autumn. Personally, I prefer cold weather booya. Hot burly booya fortifies us during long winters.

We found our friends and searched for a table. I ordered a Bloody Mary garnished with pickled asparagus, cubed cheese, and a meat stick. The bartender didn't blink when I asked for a snit, setting a beer back next to my cocktail. (I'm told that a mini beer served with your brunch Bloody is a midwestern thing, but I have not indulged in enough tomato cocktails outside of Minnesota to provide any personal research and opinion.)

A folding table in the corner of the main bar stood lined with compostable bowls and spoons, two large cookie jars filled with oyster crackers, and quart-size booya buckets for take-home. I asked to speak to the cooks and was introduced to a woman who invited me outside to a cozy tent shelter. Inside the tent, an enormous electric kettle bubbled in one corner. Its belly held a thick, pale stew, and when our proud hostess lifted the lid and used a boat oar to stir the booya, an aromatic steam misted my face. "Our booya is the best in town!" she told me, and I believed her.

Back in the bar we stood in a line ten people deep and waited to pay five bucks for a bowl of booya (cash and checks only, please). A man behind us held an already used bowl, ready for another helping. "It is really peppery this year," he complained. A woman behind him nodded in agreement. "Too much pepper." Still, both were more than happy to plunk down another five dollars for a second serving.

. . .

After our booya bash I spoke with Therese Linscheid, whose family has been in the booya business for nearly one hundred years. Therese says booya is part of her heritage on both sides of the family. She explained that most booya recipes are top secret, known to only a few (usually male) cooks who rise up through the ranks before being allowed such an honor.

Therese told me that when she grew up in St. Paul, there were always church and local organizations throwing booyas at the Highland Park Pavilion. "Before people used Highland Park, they would borrow booya kettles from each other so that they could make enough. Eventually the kettles were donated to the city and they built the booya shack at Highland Park and now they are all hooked up to gas. The first business day in January people line up to get their permits for their date. You will seldom see a female stirring the kettles up at Highland Park. It's a rite of passage for the men to learn to do it.

"My heritage is Czech, Slovak, and Polish. The booya traditions we are involved with are through the Sokol organization, an ethnic fraternal organization which embraces Czech/Slovak heritage. My parents both belonged to Sokol as children and brought all eleven of us [Therese and her siblings] up in Sokol. We were involved in gymnastics and folk dancing through Sokol.

"Pine City is where the organization built a summer camp in 1929 on beautiful Cross Lake. The following summer they started the booya picnic as a celebration and fundraiser for the camp. We still make our booya over a wood fire. Setting up the kettles so that they are level is a major undertaking. They have to be level, and the kettles themselves are lovingly cared for. They are cast iron and hold about seventy-five gallons each. We have two large and one fifty-gallon one. My siblings and I all know how to stir the booya; scorching the soup isn't an option—the money! I have seven sisters and three brothers. When you have that big of a family everybody works at the booya, and so we are a valuable asset to our organization when it comes time to volunteer. All my kids started out the way I did: cutting and peeling vegetables, helping grandpa stir the booya and clean the kettles, and working the kids' games, bingo, and folk dancing."

She continued, "We are unusual in two ways. First, the females stir booya with the men. Second, five of my siblings are blind. My oldest sister, Bobbie Jo, helps prepare the vegetables and meat and also makes meat loaf, halusky [thick, soft noodles or dumplings], and cabbage rolls for the event. She is totally blind. One benefit from having blind people help with preparing the meat is when we have to debone the cooked meat. They find a lot of small bones people who are sighted miss." Therese's brother Ray Vanyo is the head cook at the Sokol Camp Booya in Pine City now and has been for several years.

Therese shared the family's former booya recipe, published in an old cookbook from Sokol, Minnesota. Their recipe has changed over the years, and for the better, Therese said. I asked advice about cooking a homemade version of booya, and Therese said, "Crock-Pots work well for homemade booya. When I had a chest freezer I used to put leftover beef, chicken, and canned vegetables into an ice cream bucket until it was close to full. Then buy oxtails to get the broth and make a batch. Just not the same without the oxtails."

The Sokol Camp Booya recipe, credited to Angela Pavlicek and Bessie Smolik, includes 120 pounds of chicken, 100 pounds of oxtails, 170 pounds of soup bones, and 90 pounds of boneless beef. The recipe instructs cooks to begin on Saturday morning by quartering and then boiling the chicken. An hourly step-by-step listing brings the cook all the way to Sunday noon, when the booya is "Ready to serve!"

Booya for a Crowd (but not a throng)

MAKES ABOUT 20 (1-CUP) SERVINGS

My version, while providing less volume, riffs on the flavors of Angela and Bessie's two-day stewing event (see page 178). The original recipe calls for the addition of barley. Add a cup of uncooked pearl barley to the stew with the cabbage, tomatoes, and turnip if you like. To make this recipe, you need a really, really big stockpot or the biggest slow cooker you can find. I had to break my booya into two batches once all of the ingredients were added.

vegetable oil
3½–4 pound fryer chicken, cut into pieces
1 pound beef oxtail
salt and pepper
1 pound soup bones
1 cinnamon stick
1 teaspoon allspice berries
1 teaspoon mustard seeds
1 teaspoon coriander seeds
1–2 bay leaves
1 thumb-size piece fresh ginger, finely chopped
½ teaspoon whole cloves
½ teaspoon ground cardamom
¼–½ teaspoon hot red pepper flakes (optional)
⅛ teaspoon ground mace
3 stalks celery, roughly chopped

1 apple, quartered
1 pound stew meat, cut into ½-inch cubes
1 yellow onion, finely chopped
1 teaspoon dried marjoram
1 teaspoon dried parsley
1 turnip, chopped into ½-inch pieces
2–3 carrots, chopped into ½-inch pieces
½ small head green cabbage, cored and shredded
15–20 ounces strained tomatoes
2 pounds yellow potatoes, chopped into ½-inch pieces
1 (14-ounce) can corn, drained
1 cup frozen peas, thawed
1 cup frozen green beans, thawed
crackers for serving

Add oil to a very large Dutch oven or heavy-bottomed stockpot over high heat. Season chicken and oxtails generously with salt and pepper. Work in batches to sear meat on all sides. Set aside oxtail; place chicken in stockpot and add 4 cups water. Bring to a boil, reduce heat to simmer, and cover. Simmer until internal temperature reaches 165 degrees, about 30 minutes. Remove chicken from stockpot (do not drain) and set aside to cool. When chicken is cool enough to touch, remove meat from bones and skin. Reserve bones; place meat in covered container and refrigerate.

While chicken cooks, heat oven to 400 degrees. Place soup bones on parchment-lined baking pan with 1-inch lip. Season generously with salt and pepper and roast 20 minutes.

Add soup bones, oxtails, and chicken bones to cooking liquid in stockpot or slow cooker. Add 2 additional cups water, seasonings (cinnamon stick through mace), celery, and apple. Place over high heat to bring to a simmer, then reduce heat to keep at simmer; cover and cook 1½ hours. (Alternatively, cook on high in slow cooker for 4 hours.)

Discard chicken carcass. Transfer oxtail and soup bones to plate. When cool enough to handle, shred meat into bite-size pieces and discard fat and bones. Rest soup for 1 hour to cool. Pour stock through fine-mesh strainer and discard solids. Allow stock to settle and then skim and discard fat.

Generously season stew meat with salt. Add 1 tablespoon oil to clean stockpot set over high heat. Add meat and sear on all sides. Add onions and continue cooking an additional 3 minutes. Add 6 cups of the stock, marjoram, and parsley and simmer 30 minutes. Check meat for tenderness. Add turnip, carrots, cabbage, and tomatoes and return to simmer an additional 15 minutes. Add potatoes and cook an additional 20 minutes. Add chicken and shredded meat, corn, peas, and green beans and heat thoroughly, 2 to 3 minutes. Season to taste with salt and pepper. (Alternatively, add seared meat and onions and all remaining ingredients to slow cooker and cook on high for 4 hours.)

Traditionally served with oyster crackers, but saltines are worthy as well.

Commercials

As we move through life if we are lucky we will hang out with people who wield wonderful and great influence over us. In my case I've been profoundly influenced by two Danish chefs I met in Minot, North Dakota. Every year we are the hired help, demonstrating our kitchen savvy at the Nordic Kitchen during Minot's annual Norsk Høstfest, aka North America's largest Scandinavian festival.

Chef Stig Hansen is our leader. He flies in from Denmark, often accompanied by his equally accomplished wife, Rita, and Chef Stig delights the crowds with his dry humor and mouthwatering food. His open-face sandwiches are so popular with our audiences that he demos them every single day. Chef Stig's smørrebrød are works of art.

A few years ago, a new chef joined us. Chef Mari Harries is a Danish American whose restaurant, River City Eatery, brings modern diner dishes to Windom, Minnesota. Recently she added The Danish Table: Hygge Kitchen in Elk Horn, Iowa, to her plate. She runs the second restaurant as a loving, living memory of her mother's Danish cooking. Of course, Danish meatballs are included on the menu.

As a self-proclaimed Nordic food geek and meatball historian, I pride myself in my intimate understanding of Nordic meatballs, and although I proclaim Swedish meatballs to be the best, I have a soft spot in my heart for Danish meatballs. I've even conceded a few times that I occasionally like (love?) Danish meatballs a little bit more than Swedish ones. But I will never, ever admit that in public, so you didn't read it here.

Swedish meatballs, köttbullar, are traditionally a beef and pork mixture flavored with allspice and onions, made tender with the addition of cream and soft breadcrumbs, and rolled tiny to demonstrate the delicate hand that made them.

Danish meatballs are an entirely different beast. Frikadeller are a simple mix of pork, milk, and flour flavored with a bit of onion. The mix is formed into a quenelle, or football shape, by using two spoons. The meatballs are fried in butter and often served with brunede kartofler (caramelized browned potatoes) and red cabbage. My first taste of this feast made me understand that Danes are spectacular and creative in the kitchen.

When Chef Mari created a Danish meatball commercial for The Danish Table, I got her to agree to share the recipe. As I tested her recipe, I channeled my inner Danish chef (although I am nether Danish nor a chef) and recalled the dozens of times I watched Chefs Stig and Mari shaping the meatballs, then searing and basting them in butter. I also recalled the story Chef Stig tells of his cooking apprenticeship when his instructor made each cook taste frikadeller mix raw to make sure the spices were exactly right. That kind of commitment to a meatball is probably why frikadeller are so darned tasty.

You may know commercial sandwiches by their other various names: open-face sandwich, hot beef, hot commercial, and hot beef or hot turkey commercial. There is a theory that commercials are named for the traveling salesmen who were known as commercial (as in commerce, or business) travelers. These traveling salesmen were especially fond of the hot sandwich that included bread, protein, potatoes, and gravy. Another theory designates the name to the grade of beef used in the original sandwiches.

Chef Mari's recipe makes four to six commercials, and you will have leftover potatoes to enjoy once the frikadeller are gone. Mari serves her commercials with a side of Danish red cabbage, but you'll have to visit one of her restaurants to enjoy that full meal because, as Mari told me, "I am not giving that recipe away!"

I've gotten to know and love many Danes over the years, and one thing I admire about their food aesthetic is the amount of butter they spread over bread. Chef Mari's commercials are the only sandwiches I've ever witnessed being served on nonbuttered bread coming out of a Dane's kitchen.

Frikadeller (Meatball) Commercial

MAKES 12–14 MEATBALLS, ENOUGH FOR 3–4 SANDWICHES

MARI HARRIES

For the meatballs

1 pound ground pork
1½ teaspoons salt
¼ cup whole milk
¼ cup all-purpose flour

1 large egg
½ onion, minced
½ teaspoon pepper
butter and oil for frying

In a large mixing bowl, mix ground pork and salt together using a spoon or spatula. Stir in milk, flour, egg, onion, and pepper until well blended. Refrigerate mixture for at least 1 hour as it is much easier to form when mixture is cold.

Put 1 tablespoon of butter and 1 tablespoon of oil in a large skillet over medium-high heat. Use two large spoons to form oval or egg-shaped meatballs (quenelle) and place in skillet. Dip spoons in warm water between meatballs to easily remove mixture from spoons.

After a few minutes and when one side of the meatball has browned, flip to cook on opposite side.

For the gravy

2 tablespoons drippings
    from meatballs
2 tablespoons all-purpose flour
1½ cups beef broth, warm or at room
    temperature
½ teaspoon Worcestershire sauce
2 tablespoons heavy cream
salt and pepper

In a saucepan over medium heat, whisk together drippings and flour until mixture forms a well-blended paste. Slowly add in about ¼ cup beef broth at a time, continuously whisking. When mixture starts to thicken, add remaining broth. Add Worcestershire sauce and blend well. Stir in cream, and season with salt and pepper to taste.

For the mashed potatoes

5 pounds potatoes, peeled
    and quartered
2 tablespoons plus ½ teaspoon salt
4 ounces cream cheese

8 tablespoons butter
1 teaspoon minced garlic
¾ cup heavy cream
½ teaspoon seasoned salt

In a very large stockpot, add potatoes, 2 tablespoons of the salt, and enough water to completely cover the potatoes. Place over high heat and bring to a boil. Reduce heat and simmer until you can easily put a fork through the potato, about 15 minutes. Drain potatoes.

Using either a standing mixer or a large mixing bowl with a hand mixer, add cream cheese, butter, garlic, cream, seasoned salt, and remaining ½ teaspoon salt to the potatoes and blend until smooth. (Alternatively, push warm potatoes through a ricer and gently fold in remaining ingredients.)

To assemble

Make a meatball sandwich using a soft white bread—no need to get fancy here. I like to use Texas toast–style bread. It should be a soft bread to "soak up" the gravy. Place 3 to 4 meatballs between bread, add a scoop of mashed potatoes and cover entire meatball sandwich and potatoes with gravy.

Friends Thanksgiving

For twenty-five years we junior and high school friends have reunited the Saturday before Thanksgiving, gathering with gratitude for the longevity of our friendships. Our Friends Thanksgiving began as a way to feed those of us returning from college as vegetarians and complaining that there was nothing to eat at their family Thanksgivings: "Even the mashed potatoes are made with turkey stock."

Our first meal was a vegetarian version of a traditional Thanksgiving. Tofurky was making the rounds, introduced in the mid-nineties as packaged vegan roast turkey alternative. But tofurky was expensive, and a scratch version was a better alternative for young college grads on a budget. Our tofurky was pressed seitan (always and forever referred to as Satan) covered in pastry dough. Of course, as one of two nonvegetarians in the group, I was the only one who loved the tofurky and brought home all of the leftovers.

Our dinners have evolved over the years. While I gravitate to typical Thanksgiving themes, the others in our group are inclined to follow more exciting food trends. The past few years we've dined out, monopolizing the private room at a favorite restaurant and enjoying a menu created especially for us by the chef. We've cooked chef-y meals from popular cookbooks, potlucked a hodgepodge of courses, and catered in tapas and paella with the chef making our feast tableside.

We feel like we pretty much invented the holiday and take full credit for the abundance of similar friend get-togethers during Thanksgiving. In fact, we are pretty snobby about the whole thing, and would never refer to our event as Friendsgiving. Way too millennial for our group of Gen Xers.

Friends in Sidecars

MAKES 1 COCKTAIL

One year we greeted guests as they arrived with this signature cocktail, a riff on a traditional sidecar that tastes like the season.

2 ounces brandy
1 ounce cranberry maple juice
   (recipe follows)

1 ounce orange-flavored liqueur (such
   as Tattersall Orange Crema)
orange zest
confectioners' sugar

Pour brandy, cranberry maple juice, and orange liqueur into cocktail shaker with plenty of ice. Shake well. Strain and serve in coupe glass rimmed with orange zest and confectioners' sugar.

Cranberry Maple Juice

MAKES ABOUT 3–3½ CUPS

2 cups fresh cranberries
2 cups water

¼–½ cup pure maple syrup
juice from 2 small lemons

Simmer cranberries and water in a medium saucepan for 30 minutes. Cool, then puree. Pour through a wire mesh strainer and discard solids. Sweeten to taste with maple syrup; stir in lemon juice. Refrigerate before using.

Cranberry Focaccia

SERVES 8–12

For the dough

4 cups all-purpose flour

2 tablespoons olive oil

1 packet instant yeast (about 2¼ teaspoons)

2 teaspoons pure maple syrup

1½ teaspoons salt

1 cup warm water

nonstick cooking spray

¼ cup cornmeal

Add flour, 2 tablespoons oil, yeast, maple syrup, salt, and water to bowl of standing mixer fitted with dough attachment. Turn machine to low and mix until sticky dough forms. Switch machine to medium and continue mixing for an additional 5 minutes. (Alternatively, combine dry ingredients in a very large mixing bowl and slowly mix in wet. Stir with a wooden spoon to form sticky dough, then turn dough out onto a floured surface and knead until smooth, adding additional flour if necessary.)

Use hands to form dough into a ball and place ball in large oiled bowl. Cover with plastic wrap and let rise for 1 hour, or until doubled in size.

Heat oven to 400 degrees. Line a baking sheet with parchment, then cover parchment generously with nonstick spray. Sprinkle cornmeal over parchment. Roll the dough onto the parchment and press to stretch across the surface of the baking sheet. Cover with plastic wrap and rest for 30 minutes.

For the toppings

3 tablespoons olive oil

5 tablespoons cranberry mustard sauce (recipe follows)

1 tablespoon finely minced rosemary

pepper and flake salt to taste

Use fingertips to poke holes over crust. Spread 2–3 tablespoons olive oil over entire surface. Spread cranberry mustard sauce along holes; sprinkle with rosemary. Season generously with pepper and flaked salt. Bake 25 to 30 minutes.

Cranberry Mustard Sauce

MAKES ABOUT 1½ CUPS

½ cup fresh cranberries

¼ cup cider vinegar

¼ cup water

¼ cup pure maple syrup

¼ cup coarse-ground mustard

¼ cup honey

zest of 1 orange

salt and pepper

Combine cranberries, vinegar, water, and maple syrup in a saucepan and bring to a rolling boil. Reduce heat and simmer 15 minutes. Stir in mustard, honey, and zest. Season with salt and pepper to taste.

Pumpkin Lasagna

SERVES A CROWD

Don't let the multiple steps of this lasagna keep you from making it. Good things sometimes take time. In this case, it is worth the work and the wait. Serve with fried sage leaves and lots of cranberry sauce.

For the pumpkin

about 3 pounds pumpkin or assorted
    winter squash, peeled, seeded,
    and cut into ½-inch cubes
5 cloves garlic, peeled

several bunches fresh sage
    and rosemary
salt, pepper, olive oil

Heat oven to 375 degrees. Spread pumpkin, garlic, and herbs in a single layer on a large baking sheet; season with salt and pepper and drizzle with olive oil. Roast until tender but not mushy, about 30 minutes. Remove rosemary and discard. When cool enough to touch, mince garlic.

For the onions

1 large red onion, sliced in thin strips
2 tablespoons butter
1 tablespoon olive oil

2 tablespoons white wine
1 tablespoon sugar
salt and pepper

Combine onion, butter, oil, wine, and sugar in a large skillet over low heat and cook, stirring every few minutes, until onion are caramelized, about 45 minutes. Season with salt and pepper.

In a large mixing bowl, toss pumpkin and caramelized onions together. Set aside.

For the béchamel

3 tablespoons butter
5 tablespoons flour
5 cups whole milk, warmed
3 sage leaves (or 2 teaspoons
    minced sage)

5 ounces (about 1¼ cups) Parmesan
    or Romano cheese
nutmeg, salt, pepper

In a large pot, melt butter over medium heat; whisk in flour and cook roux, whisking constantly, about 3 minutes. Stream in milk while continuing to whisk, then bring to a simmer. Simmer 10 minutes, whisking occasionally. Remove from heat and stir in sage, cheese, and nutmeg, salt, and pepper to taste.

For the ricotta filling

16 ounces (2 cups) ricotta cheese

2 large egg yolks

5 ounces (about 1¼ cups) Parmesan
   or Romano cheese

2–3 tablespoons finely chopped
   fresh basil

nutmeg, salt, pepper

Blend ingredients together in a small mixing bowl.

Additional ingredients for assembly

several cups shredded mozzarella,
   provolone, Parmesan cheese

1 (9-ounce) package no-boil
   lasagna noodles

¼ cup chopped fresh basil

1–2 cups half-and-half

Heat oven to 375 degrees. Grease a lasagna pan or deep 16x12–inch casserole. Layer ingredients in pan: half of the pumpkin-onion mixture, pasta sheets, half of the shredded cheese, a third of the béchamel, pasta sheets, all of the ricotta, a third of the béchamel, pasta sheets, remaining pumpkin-onion mixture, remaining shredded cheese, pasta sheets, remaining béchamel, basil. Pour half-and-half along sides of lasagna until liquid just reaches the top layer. Cover with greased foil.

Bake 30 minutes. Remove foil and bake an additional 15 minutes, until golden and bubbly. Let lasagna rest for 15 to 20 minutes before slicing.

Coconut Ginger Pumpkin Pie

SERVES 8–10

The crust is inspired by Lola Perpich's oil and milk crust from her apple pie recipe in Eleanor Ostman's *Always on Sunday* (see page 125). Serve pie with coconut sorbet.

For the crust
½ cup vegetable oil
¼ cup whole-fat coconut milk or
    cream, cold (see note)
2 cups all-purpose flour
1 teaspoon salt

In a liquid measuring cup, combine oil and coconut milk; do not stir. In a mixing bowl, combine flour and salt; add oil and milk, mixing until dough forms. Shape into ball and press evenly into a 9-inch pie plate. Refrigerate 1 to 2 hours.

For the filling
1 (15-ounce) can pumpkin
1⅓–1½ cups whole-fat coconut
    milk or cream
½ cup packed brown sugar
¼ cup granulated sugar
2–3 teaspoons ground ginger

1 teaspoon ground cinnamon
½ teaspoon salt
¼ teaspoon ground allspice
¼ teaspoon ground nutmeg
¼ teaspoon ground cloves
2 large eggs plus 1 yolk

Heat oven to 425 degrees. Use a food processor, standing mixer, or whisk to combine all filling ingredients until smooth. Pour into uncooked pie shell, being careful not to spill over the edges (pour any extra filling into a ramekin and bake alongside pie). Bake 15 minutes; reduce heat to 350 degrees and continue baking an additional 45 to 50 minutes or until pie is just set.

NOTE *Recipe calls for a 15-ounce can of whole-fat coconut milk: ¼ cup goes into the crust, and the remaining portion goes into the filling.*

Wild Rice

In Minnesota we add wild rice to everything from hotdish to stuffing. We eat it cold and savory in salad, and hot and sweet in porridge. For information on finding and purchasing true wild rice, contact Ojibwe Tribal Offices, or visit sites like White Earth's nativeharvest.com or Red Lake's redlakenationfoods.com.

Wild Rice Blini with Smoked Trout

MAKES 24 (2-INCH) CAKES

1 teaspoon yeast
3 teaspoons warm water
2 teaspoons pure maple syrup
1 cup whole milk
2 large eggs, separated
½ cup hazelnut flour
½ cup all-purpose flour
pinch salt
1 cup cooked wild rice

2 tablespoons melted butter

For garnish
crème fraîche (see page 128)
smoked trout, skin and bones
    removed, shredded
herring or salmon roe
minced chives

In a large mixing bowl, whisk together yeast, water, and maple. Set aside until mixture gets foamy, about 5 minutes. Whisk in milk, egg yolks, flours, and salt. Cover and let rest in warm place about 1 hour. Mix in wild rice. Beat egg whites to stiff peaks and fold into batter. Stir in melted butter.

Heat a very large nonstick skillet over medium heat. Work in small batches to fry tiny cakes (about 1 tablespoon each), adding butter to surface if cakes stick at all. Cakes cook quickly: about 2 minutes on the first side and 1 additional minute once flipped. Keep cooked blini in low oven (200 degrees) until serving.

To serve, top each blini with a teaspoon of crème fraîche, a bit of the smoked fish, and a garnish of roe and chives.

Wild Rice Chicken Potpie

SERVES 6–8

Wild rice potpie is a great way to incorporate leftovers into a meal that will excite everyone at the table. I like to make this pie the day after we've dined on rotisserie chicken; I make a stock for the sauce with the leftover carcass and use leftover chicken meat in the filling. After your pie crust is filled, you may have extra filling; save it for lunch the next day, as it makes a delicious thick, gravy-like soup. This recipe can also be made with turkey or any other poultry. Serve with cranberry sauce on the side.

3 tablespoons butter
½ cup finely chopped white or yellow onion
½ cup finely chopped celery
2 teaspoons dried thyme
1 teaspoon dried rosemary
1 teaspoon dried sage
¼ cup all-purpose flour
3 cups warm chicken broth
½ cup dry white wine
1–2 teaspoons balsamic vinegar

salt and pepper
2 carrots, chopped
1–1½ cups cooked wild rice
1–1½ cups cooked chicken, shredded or roughly chopped
8 ounces mushrooms, chopped and cooked in butter
1 cup chopped green beans
pastry for double-crust pie

Melt butter over medium heat in a large skillet. Add onions, celery, thyme, rosemary, and sage. Cook, stirring often, until vegetables are just tender, about 4 minutes. Add flour and whisk for 2 minutes; roux should become golden in color and form a paste. Slowly whisk in broth and wine. Bring sauce to a simmer and continue cooking over medium to medium-high heat for 10 minutes, whisking often. Sauce will begin to thicken and reduce slightly. Stir in vinegar and season to taste with salt and pepper. Stir in carrots and simmer an additional 5 minutes.

Remove from heat and stir in wild rice, chicken, mushrooms, and green beans. Taste again and add salt or pepper if needed. Cool 30 minutes.

Heat oven to 425 degrees. Press one pie crust into a 9-inch pie dish. Spoon the cooled filling into the crust. Top with second pie crust and crimp to seal the edges of the crust together. Cut several slits in top of crust to allow steam to escape. Place pie dish on a parchment-lined baking sheet (to catch any drips). Bake for 35 to 45 minutes, or until crust is golden brown and baked through. Cool pie for 20 minutes before slicing.

Hope

We were feeling pretty down about the state of the world and looking for inspiration, finding ourselves at the annual Wild Rice Festival in Roseville, Minnesota. The event is a few blocks from our house, across from the park where we spend plenty of hours running, biking, and walking. Sprawling out east of the park is a wildlife preserve where we can walk on docks throughout the restored wetlands. Whenever we enjoy this lush and hidden area of our neighborhood, we marvel at how we scored such a gift to live close to both city and nature.

We approached an area at the festival where experts demonstrated ricing techniques. Harvesting wild rice is a lengthy process, beginning with hand harvesting the seeds by using a pole to steer canoes through the shallow waters where the rice grows. The seeds are knocked into the canoe floor, where they rise up like a lawn of needles reaching toward the sun. The harvested wild rice is laid out to dry on canvas sheets (in the old days birch bark was used), allowing the rice to ripen and also encouraging any bugs and spiders caught in the wild rice to crawl away. After raking, the rice is either parched over fire or the seeds are packed into balls of mud for reseeding. Parched rice is then jigged by dancing or treading on it to loosen hulls. Finally, the rice is winnowed. At the winnowing station, a large blue tarp on the ground caught stray rice that fell from a basket as a couple practiced winnowing: aerating the seeds so that the hulls rise out of the rice and drift into the air and the chaff blows away.

Hope Flanagan introduced herself, and her name struck me as a good sign. She began telling us the key to sustaining a healthy harvest: "We take one-third for humans to eat, the birds and animals take one-third to eat, and we leave one-third to reseed for next year." A simple but important rule, this balance of human and nature respect is the way to assure everyone has enough, always.

· · ·

Hope and I chatted a month later, after the ricing season and well into cranberry harvesting. "It is a good cranberry year," she told me. "The water levels this year meant good cranberries. The peat bogs [where the cranberries grow] don't seal up fast, so I follow the deer tracks to pick snowberries, and blueberries too at different times." It was on such an outing that she found the cranberries she had just returned from harvesting.

A Native woman, Hope was born outside the Tonawanda Indian Reservation in New York. "I was raised on wild lands," she said. "My sister and I were always picking. One of my first memories is my mom telling me about wild carrots, or Queen Anne's lace. We picked cherries, plums, hazelnuts, wild grapes. You'd see groups of Native people picking. That's how things were back then."

She riced for the first time when she moved to Minnesota to attend the University of Minnesota: "I remember going out with friends to Leech Lake, knocking rice. More people were out in the woods surviving on what they could find."

I asked if she saw a lot of Native people ricing. "You don't see very many young people. You see older people. We want to get the young ones to remember. They call it blood memory." Hope described foraging as soothing and healing. It reminds her of where she comes from.

At Dream of Wild Health, Hope teaches youth in the Native community about their Indigenous history and the Ojibwe language, restoring blood memories. The mission at Dream of Wild Health is "to restore health and well-being in the Native community by recovering knowledge of and access to healthy Indigenous foods, medicines, and lifeways."

Wild rice plays a major role in that mission as it not only embodies the symbiotic relationship between humans and nature but also nurtures the body: "You can survive on wild rice." Hope described visits to the homes of elders up north where a pot of rice is always on the stove: "Usually when you go to a Native home there is an understanding you harvested it, or you traded for it. It is still traded for all sorts of stuff. I love to visit the older people, the elders up north, and I always bring rice."

"Rice is picky. It won't grow with people around. It doesn't like dirty motorboats. It wants a clean and stable home with not a lot of houses. People are too dirty!" Hope laughed and went on to tell me about foraging. Her enthusiasm is contagious: "I love to forage. I look for medicinal plants. I just love all plants." She learned which plants to pick from elders and others who showed her what to look for. "It is part of being aware of how things are connected. Like how the Clean Water Act encouraged wild rice to grow. Then the swan, muskrats, geese populations picked up. All sorts of life can thrive as the wild rice returns."

"Before there was anything there was a Creator and the Spirit World. The Spirits looked away from the fire and an explosion caused Earth to form. The moon became the Mother and the sun became the Father. The Creator thought Earth was cold and needed something to warm her and so gave her a covering of hair, which are all the plants. The plants are dependent on Mother Earth for their life. The grass comforted Earth, but she was lonesome. The animals came, and they were even more dependent on Mother. Finally, the youngest and most foolish children came to Earth. People are the most likely to topple off. They are too young to pay attention to Mother, who gives us everything. Our job is to pay attention to her, and to our elders, the plants, and animals."

"In Australia I met some Aboriginal men. They don't look like me but one man heard I am from the Turtle Clan and he said, 'Hey, I am Turtle Clan too! This man is Eagle Clan,' and I told them I know his relatives." Hope says the two Indigenous groups share much, and that when we go back far enough in human history, we see all of our commonalities: "The Old Ways of living on earth was in harmony."

Native people continue to gather for important rituals like wild ricing. "We always do a thank-you ceremony before we take anything, and there is a thank-you feast for major events." Hope described typical regional Ojibwe fare as ceremonial foods that echo how to eat with the seasons. In autumn when ricing occurs, the feast includes wild rice, blueberries, smoked fish and venison, and maple sugar. "We always follow the earth's seasons. There is a lot of food out there if we don't kill it all off. There is such variety out there."

"Our old method is to always be grateful. When you thank your food, it comes closer to you. If you ignore it and act like it isn't important, it leaves. There is a trickster legend about every plant and animal providing a gift to humans. But humans need to be grateful or those gifts will disappear."

"In Ojibwe way of being, there are the wild ones and the enslaved ones. The wild ones are rice, grasses, wild potatoes, rose hips, deer. The enslaved ones are corn, the cow, the pig. The enslaved ones are never going to give the same nutritional value as plants and animals that choose partners that support them in the wild. Depleted soil does not provide the same food value as food growing wild. Domesticated food is subjected to pesticides, herbicides, GMO alteration, and unnatural fertilizers."

Hope went on to talk about the University of Minnesota's discussion of wild rice alteration: "We don't want the University of Minnesota messing with the genetics of the rice. We don't want paddy rice pretending to be wild rice." Indeed, the proliferation of domesticated paddy rice is an example of appropriation not only of the ricing tradition but of the rice itself, as thick-stemmed, black-seeded grasses cross-pollinate with the native species. Today many non-Natives don't know the difference between the paddy rice sold as wild and true wild rice, or manoomin, the "food that grows on water."

Hope's favorite way to eat rice is at its most simple: "Straight up with salt and butter."

Wild Rice Straight Up with Salt and Butter

SERVES 6

This recipe honors Hope Flanagan (whose Native name is Noodinesiikwe, which means Little Wind Woman) and the Native people who continue working to ensure manoomin's enduring heritage.

6 cups water
1 cup wild rice, rinsed
1 teaspoon salt

butter
pepper

Add water to stockpot and bring to a boil. Add wild rice and salt and bring back to boiling. Reduce heat to simmer. Cook until wild rice is tender, about 45 minutes. Add enough butter to make you happy. Season with pepper.

Passing Seasons

I love Minnesota. I love her seasons, her landscapes, and her people. I love her food.

And there is so much more I want to tell you. I want you to see my earnest husband when the freeze arrives, pulling branches off our massive silver maples to feed the deer that live in our neighborhood. I want you to admire our rural roads in winter, bordered by endless loops of snowmobile tracks in the deep snow. I want you to smell spring when it arrives, wet and slowly swelling to that familiar verdant opulence. I want you to sit with me on the dock where a friend's cabin rests and listen as the fish swim up in the shallows. They sound like skipping stones as they find their breakfast on the lake's surface before the Jet Skis and water-skiers behind speedy boats show up and pump wakes onto the shore. I want you to swat mosquitoes and recite "bunny bunny" to keep the veil of smoke from our backyard firepit from swathing your head, right before you take a bite of the world's most perfect s'more and are permanently encased in sticky. I want you to fall asleep with the windows open while the cricket chirps calm you into soft dreams. I want you to walk with me through heavy woods on a crisp autumn afternoon, dead leaves crunching beneath our feet, talking quietly about the whole wonderful circle of seasons.

I want you to feel the gratitude that comes from living in the North.

This place is our Mother. Her Dakota name, Mnisota, means "sky-tinted water." (A meaning appropriated by St. Paul's Hamm's Brewery to sell beer in their catchy jingle that began with drums invoking Native dance and the words "From the Land of Sky Blue Waters." I remember well the Hamm's Beer scrolling scene-o-rama light propped up on my dad's or maybe someone else's home bar with the waterfalls, a canoe, teepee tent, and campfire. Was the bear paddling the canoe?) Keep Mnisota's rivers, streams, and ten thousand lakes (actually, the count is closer to twelve thousand) clean and blue.

During a span of two months in spring 2019, a common theme emerged. I was at several conferences, mostly for history and communications specialists (of which I am neither), attended mostly by white women (of which I am both). At each event we acknowledged the Dakota peoples upon whose land we gather and dwell. We recognized their rich culture and thanked them for the care they give to the land. That simple assertion seemed hollow, and I internalized that oft-used defense, "But what can I do? I'm only one person."

When it comes to living sustainability, I look to the Natives, who have been living on this land in this place for countless generations before my people ever thought of leaving their own lands.

I get overwhelmed with divisive politics, climate crises, and dire predictions. Every time I want to throw my hands in the air and proclaim all hope is lost, the Universe in Her wisdom sends someone who reminds me that all is not lost as long as we work toward improvement and, in my case, keep a cool head and remember to be grateful. Count your blessings, as my mother often reminds me.

Don't wait for your neighbors or employer or church or government to make changes. Resolve to take action as an individual. Start with doable activities. Make peace in your own small borrowed place in this world. Plant a pollinator garden. Plant a tree. Recycle. Be kind to one another. Take a walk in the park and admire the birds, squirrels, flowers, and ponds. Take part in your community's ice fishing competition or Jell-O cook-off, eat your Lenten suppers at an unfamiliar venue, buy organic raspberries and Native-harvested wild rice at the farmers market, hang out at a meat raffle or booya or pizza farm, and for goodness sake get yourself to the Minnesota State Fair.

Start the tough conversations by beginning where we all agree. When all else fails, sit down together over a delicious hotdish.

Acknowledgments

A decade ago, I took a documentary seminar from Margot Fortunato Galt. The class inspired me to look at my small part of the world with new curiosity, and my final for class was a literary piece about a neighborhood meat raffle. That story became the bones of this book as I looked back on my life in Minnesota, from my childhood at the family dining room table to my first job busing dishes at a crummy breakfast diner.

For a year my husband, foodie friends, and I spent weekends traveling across Minnesota to share food with strangers who quickly became friends. Something magical happens when we break bread together. The people who spoke with me about their traditions and generously contributed recipes taught me much about how our landscape and culture determine our meals.

The research and writing became a panicked compulsion to document my beloved state, her people, and her food before global warming and climate change finally caught up to us. During the months that passed since the draft of this book was due, our world imploded. Pandemic, unrest, division: we are reaping a damaged harvest of continued disregard for Earth and her inhabitants.

Early in 2020, we woke up to the realities of pandemic life and shelter-in-place measures long enough to ponder sourdough starters and yeast shortages. Just as we were easing into daily rituals of breadmaking, homeschooling, and videoconferencing, we collectively witnessed the horror of George Floyd's murder in Minneapolis.

Too late, white Minnesotans clearly saw the disparity between Black, Brown, and Native lives and our own. While I—and many others—prefer to believe Minnesota is a progressive state, we hide our bigotry under the guise of Minnesota Nice. Reality is forcing me to examine how my white experiences differ from those of my Black neighbors and to question what I can do to alter the disparity.

Our land, people, and foods are not represented by the white plate of potatoes, lutfisk, and cream sauce so often assigned to us via the Nordic people who settled here more than a hundred years ago. As I interviewed Minnesotans for this book I was proud of our diversity, and my goal for this collection of stories and recipes is to showcase that rich diversity, which happens to be one of the reasons I love this state so much.

Book acknowledgments are a tricky thing to write even in the best of times. A writer, or in this case a recipe and story collector, is entirely indebted to the people who and places that teach and inspire her. For me, that list is endless. Below is just a start.

This is my second book published with Minnesota Historical Society Press and with my editor, Shannon Pennefeather (whose cookies deserve blue ribbons at the Minnesota State Fair every year), and designer Susan Everson (who found exactly the right way to set Minnesota's table). Many thanks to MNHS Press, Shannon, and Susan.

Minnesota is a better place because of organizations like American Swedish Institute. ASI reaches out to neighbors with messages of hope and community and as a gathering place to share experiences in culture, migration, environment, and the arts. Their unflagging belief in me and my aspirations, as well as the generous opportunities they continue to gift me, help to keep me humble.

I am grateful also to my coworkers at University of Minnesota. They patiently ate their way through an endless array of hotdishes and Crock-Potted fare on Reject Mondays. Reject Mondays (and sometimes Tuesdays) happened after recipe testing and photo shooting weekends. My coworkers gave thoughtful feedback and lavish encouragement, and several of them contributed recipes.

Oliver: thank you for being such a perfect tour guide as we made our way through Washington, DC, to eat all the good hotdish. Perhaps one of my favorite experiences in writing this book, and no one better to share it with than you.

My high school buddies, my work friends, and my coffee hour Millennials: your willingness to Zoom nearly every week during pandemic check-ins sustains me. I cannot wait to hug you all.

Neil and Diego: for feeding us, making us laugh, and providing colorful flowers when it snowed on Easter.

Tiffany and Chris (and Cyrus): whether we are eating pizza on a farm, photographing our fondue party in your dining room because the lighting is superb, or sitting twenty feet apart in the backyard for a physically distant happy hour, you give me faith that the world is made up mostly of beautiful, kind people who value the lives of others.

My mom, dad, and sisters: my entire life I've been chasing childhood memories because when we were all together you spoiled me with the safety that comes from unconditional love.

The Not-So-Golden Girls: thank you for taking care of my daughter during our time apart. Nothing gives a mother more comfort than knowing her child is safe and cherished.

Ted and Pooh: the world is a better place because you are in it. You challenge and inspire me, and I adore you both. Ted, you are an amazing video producer, director, and technical advisor. I couldn't have done a single Zoom cooking class without your wicked skills.

And my friend Robert, aka Noonie: you left too soon to see the power and dignity that comes from this uprising. You are gone but never forgotten. Because you are not here to tell your story: this one's for you.

We have a long road ahead. The abomination of George Floyd's murder as well as the murders of countless other men, women, and children of color expose the inequity that continues to divide our state and our country. George Floyd's murder was not the way Minnesotans wanted the world to see us. It was not the way we wanted to see ourselves.

Now we are recognizing the bigotry we attempt to keep concealed. Minnesotans must step up and lead the way with demands and plans to end the systems that keep racism alive. I am deeply grateful to the Minnesotans who are leading us in the change that is coming. We will begin to see, hear, value, and celebrate all of our neighbors. Diversity is strength.

In Minnesota we thrive, regardless of season, when we celebrate and eat together. As I write these words popular restaurants are closed, markets are limited, and food gatherings are canceled—at least temporarily. It would be impossible to write this book today.

Yet I have faith that we will gather again and share a hotdish, or perhaps wander the fairgrounds enjoying food on a stick.

A

Æbleskiver, Cheese Curd, 151
Always on Sunday (Ostman), 125, 189
American Pie Pizza Dough, 132
Ancho Mama's Chili, 54
Anderson, Neil O., 163
Anoka County Historical Society, 85
apples: about, 162; Apple Cider Donut
    Muffins, 165; Faux Tamarind Chutney, 171;
    Fennel Apple Slaw, 41; Grannie's Apple
    Crisp, 164; Neil's Great Aunt Hazel's Knobby
    Apple Cake, 163; Oven-Roasted Butternut
    Hash with Pan-Fried Walleye and Dill
    Hollandaise, 48–49
arugula, in House Salad, 141
Asparagus Pasta Salad, Radish Greens
    Pesto and, 67
A to Z, 137–38
atta, in Roti, 170

B

bacon: Bacon-Wrapped Roasted Radishes, 66;
    Double Chip Bacon Cookies, 45
bananas: Banana Cream, 91; Bourbon
    Banana Flip, 91
barley: Beef Barley Stew, 35; Booya for a
    Crowd, 179–80
bars: Coffee Toffee Bars, 95; Erma's Special
    Lingonberry Bars, 94; Graduation
    Caramel Bars, 93
Bartz, Bill, 137–40
basil: Basil-Infused Olive Oil, 140; Pesto, 135;
    Pumpkin Lasagna, 187–88; Radish Greens
    Pesto and Asparagus Pasta Salad, 67;
    Tomato Pie (Tomat Paj), 128
beans: Ancho Mama's Chili, 54; Chana Masala
    (Garbanzo Bean Curry), 171
beans, green: Booya for a Crowd, 179–80; Wild
    Rice Chicken Potpie, 191
beef: Beef Barley Stew, 35; Bison Lucy, 101–2;
    Booya for a Crowd, 179–80; Danny's Awe-
    some World-Famous Onion Burgers, 32;
    Little Moga-hot-dishu, 27–28; Meatball
    Pinwheel Hotdish, 22–23; Meatball
    Stroganoff, 36–37; No-Can Tater Tot Hotdish,
    19; Pasty, 123–24; Pot Roast with Parsnip
    and Potato Puree and Horseradish Sour
    Cream, 33–34; Reuben Soup, 59; Sunday
    Gravy, 38–39
beer: Blonde Ale Cheese Soup, 61; Crayfish
    with Dill (Kräftor med Dill), 129; Deep-Fried
    Pickles, 155
bees, 172–73
Better than Bouillon, 29
Bhatt, Rekha, 168–71
The Big Lebowski, 100–101, 103–4
Bilberry Soup (Blåbärssoppa), 52
Biscuits, 166
Bison Lucy, 101–2
Blåbärssoppa (Bilberry Soup), 52
Blonde Ale Cheese Soup, 61
blueberries, in Blåbärssoppa
    (Bilberry Soup), 52
booya: about, 47, 176–78; Booya for a
    Crowd, 179–80
Bourbon Banana Flip, 91
brandy, in Friends in Sidecars, 185
Bread Pudding, Farmers Market, 121
Buckwheat Softies, 174
burgers: Bison Lucy, 101–2; Danny's Awesome
    World-Famous Onion Burgers, 32
Butternut Hash with Pan-Fried Walleye and Dill
    Hollandaise, Oven-Roasted, 48–49

C

cabbage: Booya for a Crowd, 179–80; Colorful
    Coleslaw, 75; Fennel Apple Slaw, 41; Hotdish
    A-Hmong Friends, 26
cakes: Chocolate Hazelnut Sheet Cake, 79;
    Double Hot Fudge Pudding Cake, 167; Neil's
    Great Aunt Hazel's Knobby Apple Cake, 163;
    Parsnip Almond Cake, 125
Candied Lemon Peel, 135
Candied Rhubarb, 68
Caramel Bars, Graduation, 93

caraway seeds: Colorful Coleslaw, 75; Pickled Ramps, 83; Rye Pretzel Bites with Caraway, 76

carrots: Beef Barley Stew, 35; Blonde Ale Cheese Soup, 61; Booya for a Crowd, 179–80; Colorful Coleslaw, 75; Hotdish A-Hmong Friends, 26; Japanese Curry Rice Minnesota Style, 42; Minnesota Hmong Hotdish, 7; Pasty, 123–24; Pot Roast with Parsnip and Potato Puree and Horseradish Sour Cream, 33–34; Sort-of Jan Doerr's Shrimp and Carrot Salad, 107; Sunday Gravy, 38–39; Wild Rice Chicken Potpie, 191

cashews, in Snack Mix, 175

cassava, in Liberian Inspired Hotdish, 29

cereal (various): Parsnip Almond Cake, 125; Rhubarb Pudding, 68; Snack Mix, 175

Chana Masala (Garbanzo Bean Curry), 171

Cheddar cheese: Cheese Enchiladas, 78; Meatball Pinwheel Hotdish, 22–23; SPAM Potato Hotdish, 21; Susan's Cheese Crackers, 58; Swedish Cheese Tart (Västerbottensostpaj), 127; Tomato Pie (Tomat Paj), 128; Walleye Macaroni and Cheese, 50

cheese. *See specific types of cheese*

cheese curds: Cheese Curd Æbleskiver, 151; Deep-Fried Cheese Curds, 159

Cheese Enchiladas, 78

cherries: Old-Fashioned Jell-O Shots, 87; Strawberry-Cherry Pretzel Jell-O Salad, 114–15

Cheryl's Jell-O Salad, 86

chicken: Booya for a Crowd, 179–80; Chicken Katsu, 43; Fried Chicken, 112; Maple Wings, 82; From Monrovia with Love: Liberian Inspired Hotdish, 29; Wild Rice Chicken Potpie, 191

Chicken-Fried SPAM-n-Waffle Bites, 154

Chocolate Hazelnut Sheet Cake, 79

chocolate morsels: Coffee Toffee Bars, 95; Double Chip Bacon Cookies, 45; Double Hot Fudge Pudding Cake, 167; Graduation Caramel Bars, 93

Christensen, Linda, 147, 156

Chutney, Faux Tamarind, 171

cilantro: Chana Masala (for serving), 171; Cheese Curd Æbleskiver, 151; Cheese Enchiladas (for serving), 78; Cilantro Gremolata, 55; Little Moga-hot-dishu, 27–28; Minnesota Hmong Hotdish (for serving), 7

climate change, 4, 10–11

coconut cream/milk: Chocolate Hazelnut Sheet Cake, 79; Coconut Ginger Pumpkin Pie, 189; Minnesota Hmong Hotdish, 7; Sweet Corn Ice Cream, 143

coconut flakes, in Parsnip Almond Cake, 125

Coen, Joel and Ethan, 84, 100

Coffee Toffee Bars, 95

Colby-Jack cheese, in Egg Bake with Hash Browns, 118

Colorful Coleslaw, 75

Comstock, Erma, 94

cookies: Buckwheat Softies, 174; Double Chip Bacon Cookies, 45; Sarsaparilla Snaps, 104

Coriander Chutney, 28

corn: Booya for a Crowd, 179–80; creeping, 142; Farmers Market Bread Pudding, 121; Sweet Corn Ice Cream, 143

Crackers, Susan's Cheese, 58

Craig, Angie, 25

cranberries: about, 192; Cranberry Focaccia, 186; Cranberry Maple Juice, 185; Cranberry Mustard Sauce, 186

crayfish: about, 126; Crayfish with Dill (Kräftor med Dill), 129

cream cheese: Blonde Ale Cheese Soup, 61; Cream Cheese Frosting, 125; Four-Ingredient Tortellini Soup, 60; Frikadeller (Meatball) Commercial, 182–83; Gjetost and Hard Cider Fondue, 14; Strawberry-Cherry Pretzel Jell-O Salad, 114–15

cream-of-something soups: about, 17; Cream-of-Something Soup Substitute, 18

Crème Fraîche, 128

Croutons, Rye, 59

Curry Dip, 13

D

Danish meatballs: about, 181–82; Frikadeller (Meatball) Commercial, 182–83

Danny's Awesome World-Famous Onion Burgers, 32

Dayton's Popovers, 71

Deep-Fried Cheese Curds, 159

Deep-Fried Pickles, 155

Dill Hollandaise, 49

Diwali, 168–69

Doerr, Jan, 107

Donuts, Not-So-Mini Ginger Pinchy, 153

Double Chip Bacon Cookies, 45

Double Hot Fudge Pudding Cake, 167

Dream of Wild Health, 193

dressings. *See* sauces and dressings

E

Easy Tomato Soup, 57

eggs: Dayton's Popovers, 71; Egg Bake, 117; Egg Bake with Hash Browns, 118; Farmers Market Bread Pudding, 121; Potato Salad, 113; Swedish Cheese Tart (Västerbottensostpaj), 127; Sweet Corn Ice Cream, 143

Emmenthal cheese, in Blonde Ale Cheese Soup, 61

Erma's Special Lingonberry Bars, 94

F

Farmers Market Bread Pudding, 121

farmers markets, 120

Faux Tamarind Chutney, 171

Fennel Apple Slaw, 41

Ferrari, Luciano, 88

fish: Crayfish with Dill (Kräftor med Dill), 129; Gary's Famous Fish and Chips, 119; No-Can Fish and Noodle Hotdish, 20; Oven-Roasted Butternut Hash with Pan-Fried Walleye and Dill Hollandaise, 48–49; Salmon Croquettes with Dill and Peas Sauce, 72–73; Tempura-Fried Pickled Herring with Lingonberry Hot Sauce, 152; Walleye Macaroni and Cheese, 50; Wild Rice Blini with Smoked Trout, 190

fish frys, 69–70

Flanagan, Hope (Noodinesiikwe, Little Wind Woman), 192–95

fondue: about, 12; Gjetost and Hard Cider Fondue, 14; Steak Fondue, 13

Food Scientists Podcast, 31

Four-Ingredient Tortellini Soup, 60

Franco, Delores "Lola," 77

Franken, Al, 24

Fried Chicken, 112

Fried Onions, 102

Friends in Sidecars, 185

Friends Thanksgiving, 184

frikadeller (Danish meatballs): about, 181–82; Frikadeller (Meatball) Commercial, 182–83

frosting: Cream Cheese Frosting, 125; Seven-Minute Frosting, 79

G

Garbanzo Bean Curry (Chana Masala), 171

Gary's Famous Fish and Chips, 119

Gary's Honey Sandwich, 173

Gaylord United Church of Christ, 56

Gjetost and Hard Cider Fondue, 14

Goldfish crackers, in Snack Mix, 175

Gouda cheese: From Monrovia with Love: Liberian Inspired Hotdish, 29; Savory Pudding with Roasted Cherry Tomatoes and Radishes, 122

Graduation Caramel Bars, 93

Grannie's Apple Crisp, 164

Gruyère cheese: Blonde Ale Cheese Soup, 61; Gjetost and Hard Cider Fondue, 14; Savory Pudding with Roasted Cherry Tomatoes and Radishes, 122; SPAM Potato Hotdish, 21; Susan's Cheese Crackers, 58; Swedish Cheese Tart (Västerbottensostpaj), 127; Tomato Pie (Tomat Paj), 128; Walleye Macaroni and Cheese, 50

H

Hamline Church Dining Hall, 88–89

Hammel, Lara, 88

Hansen, Stig, 102, 181

Hard Cider Fondue, Gjetost and, 14

Harries, Mari, 181–82

Hash Browns, Egg Bake with, 118

hazelnuts: Chocolate Hazelnut Sheet Cake, 79; Ramp Pesto, 82; White Russian Float (for garnish), 104

"Helan Går," 129

Herring with Lingonberry Hot Sauce, Tempura-Fried Pickled, 152

Hmong food and culture, 4–6

Holland, Alison, 51

Hollandaise, Dill, 48–49

honey: Buckwheat Softies, 174; Cranberry Mustard Sauce, 186; Gary's Honey Sandwich, 173; Snack Mix, 175

Hot Chocolate, 16

hotdish: about, 17; Hotdish A-Hmong Friends, 26; Little Moga-hot-dishu, 27–28; Meatball Pinwheel Hotdish, 22–23; Minnesota Hmong Hotdish, 7; From Monrovia with Love: Liberian Inspired Hotdish, 29; No-Can Fish and Noodle Hotdish, 20; No-Can Tater Tot Hotdish, 19; SPAM Potato Hotdish, 21

House Salad, 141

Hush Puppies, 74

I

ice cream: Ice Cream Jell-O, 90; Sweet Corn Ice Cream, 143; White Russian Float, 104

ice fishing, 46–47

Ingraham, Christopher, 10–11

Italian Cream Soda, St. Anthony Main's American Pie, 136

Izzy's Jell-O Salad ice cream, 88–89

J

jalapeños, in Little Moga-hot-dishu, 27–28

Japanese Curry Rice Minnesota Style, 42

Jarlsberg cheese, in Blonde Ale Cheese Soup, 61

Jell-O: about, 84–85; Cheryl's Jell-O Salad, 86; Old-Fashioned Jell-O Shots, 87; Orange Push-Up Jell-O Shots, 108; Strawberry-Cherry Pretzel Jell-O Salad, 114–15; Yummy Jell-O Mold, 90

Jell-O Salad Cook-Off, 85–86

Jerry's Kids, 160–61

Johnson, Jill, 85

Johnson, Marjorie, 148, 174

K

Kahlúa, in White Russian Float, 104

Keepsake Cidery, 14

kielbasa, in Four-Ingredient Tortellini Soup, 60

Knudsen, Emily, 137–40

Kräftor med Dill (Crayfish with Dill), 129

kräftskiva, 94, 126

Kratzke, Amelia, 60

Kratzke, Dawn, 59

L

lamb, in Little Moga-hot-dishu, 27–28

Lasagna, Pumpkin, 187–88

lemons: Candied Lemon Peel, 135; Cranberry Maple Juice, 185

Lewis, Jerry, 160

Liberian Inspired Hotdish, 29

Linde, Lillian, 86

lingonberries: Erma's Special Lingonberry Bars, 94; Lingonberry Hot Sauce, 152; Lingonberry Maple Syrup, 103; Lingonberry Pancakes, 103; Tempura-Fried Pickled Herring with Lingonberry Hot Sauce, 152

Linscheid, Therese, 176–78
liqueur, flavored: Friends in Sidecars, 185; Orange Push-Up Jell-O Shots, 108; White Russian Float, 104
Little Moga-hot-dishu, 27–28
Lola, 140

The Main (Sausage, Pepperoni, Green Pepper, and Onion Pizza), 133
Makela, Joanne, 53–54
maple syrup: Cranberry Focaccia, 186; Cranberry Maple Juice, 185; Cranberry Mustard Sauce, 186; Lingonberry Maple Syrup, 103; Maple Wings, 82; Orange-Maple Vinaigrette, 81; Ramp Pesto, 82; Wild Rice Blini with Smoked Trout, 190
marshmallow crème, in Banana Cream, 91
Mayonnaise Dressing, 155
McCauley, Stephanie, 117
McCollum, Betty, 25–26
meatballs: about, 181; Frikadeller (Meatball) Commercial, 182–83; Meatball Pinwheel Hotdish, 22–23; Meatball Stroganoff, 36–37
meat raffles, 30–31
merkén (Chilean chili powder): about, 53; Ancho Mama's Chili, 54
Messner, Cheryl, 117
Microwaved Popcorn on the Cob, 161
Minnesota Congressional Delegation Hotdish Competition, 24–29
Minnesota Hmong Hotdish, 7
Minnesota State Fair, 4, 7, 31, 40, 88–89, 146–49, 153, 156–57
From Monrovia with Love: Liberian Inspired Hotdish, 29
Monterey Jack cheese, in No-Can Tater Tot Hotdish, 19
Morrissey, Molly, 24
Muffins, Apple Cider Donut, 165
Muka, Hazel (Jenkins), 163
mushrooms: Ancho Mama's Chili, 54; Egg Bake, 117; Japanese Curry Rice Minnesota Style, 42;

Meatball Stroganoff, 36–37; No-Can Tater Tot Hotdish, 19; Wild Rice Chicken Potpie, 191

Native people and culture, 192–94, 197
Neil's Great Aunt Hazel's Knobby Apple Cake, 163
Nilsson, Magnus, 129
No-Can Fish and Noodle Hotdish, 20
The Nordic Cookbook (Nilsson), 129
Norsk Høstfest, 181
Northern Clay Center Chili Cook-off, 54
Not-So-Mini Ginger Pinchy Donuts, 153

O'Brien, Kathryn, 120–21
Ode to St. Anthony Main American Pie Pizza Dough, 132
O'Donnell, Lori, 118
Ojibwe culture, 193–94
Old-Fashioned Jell-O Shots, 87
Omar, Ilhan, 25, 27
Onions, Fried, 102
"ope," 84–85
Orange Crush BBQ Sauce, 111
Orange-Maple Vinaigrette, 81
Orange Push-Up Jell-O Shots, 108
Ostman, Eleanor, 125, 189
Our Lady of Guadalupe, 77
Oven-Roasted Butternut Hash with Pan-Fried Walleye and Dill Hollandaise, 48–49

pancakes: Cheese Curd Æbleskiver, 151; Lingonberry Pancakes, 103
pancetta, in Sunday Gravy, 38–39
parsnips: Minnesota Hmong Hotdish, 7; Parsnip Almond Cake, 125; Pot Roast with Parsnip and Potato Puree and Horseradish Sour Cream, 33–34
Pasty, 123–24

Patel, Ila, 168–70

Pavlicek, Angela, 178

peas: Booya for a Crowd, 179–80; Salmon
    Croquettes with Dill and Peas Sauce, 72–73

Perpich, Lola, 189

Pesto and Shrimp Pizza, 134–35

Peterson, Carol, 95

Phillips, Dean, 25, 29

Pickled Mustard Seeds, 150

Pickled Ramps, 83

Pickles, Deep-Fried, 155

pine nuts: House Salad, 141; Pesto, 135

pizza farms, 137–39

pizzas: Lola, 140; The Main (Sausage, Pepperoni,
    Green Pepper, and Onion Pizza), 133; Pesto
    and Shrimp Pizza, 134; pizza dough, 132;
    SPAM Lefse Pizza, 150

Pizzeria, 130–31

plantains, in Liberian Inspired Hotdish, 29

Pleasant Grove Pizza Farm, 137–40

Popcorn on the Cob, Microwaved, 161

Popovers, Dayton's, 71

pork: Frikadeller (Meatball) Commercial,
    182–83; Meatball Pinwheel Hotdish, 22–23;
    Pasty, 123–24; Trautmueller Meat Pie, 44

potato chips: Double Chip Bacon Cookies, 45;
    No-Can Fish and Noodle Hotdish, 20

potatoes: Blonde Ale Cheese Soup, 61; Booya
    for a Crowd, 179–80; Frikadeller (Meatball)
    Commercial, 182–83; Japanese Curry
    Rice Minnesota Style, 42; Oven-Roasted
    Butternut Hash with Pan-Fried Walleye
    and Dill Hollandaise, 48–49; Pasty, 123–24;
    Potato Salad, 113; Pot Roast with Parsnip and
    Potato Puree and Horseradish Sour Cream,
    33–34; SPAM Potato Hotdish, 21

potatoes, sweet: Ancho Mama's Chili, 54;
    Japanese Curry Rice Minnesota Style, 42;
    From Monrovia with Love: Liberian Inspired
    Hotdish, 29

Pot Roast with Parsnip and Potato Puree and
    Horseradish Sour Cream, 33–34

pretzels: Rye Pretzel Bites with Caraway, 76;
    Snack Mix, 175; Strawberry-Cherry Pretzel

Jell-O Salad, 114–15

Princess Kay, 157–58

prosciutto, in House Salad, 141

pumpkin: Chana Masala (Garbanzo Bean
    Curry), 171; Coconut Ginger Pumpkin Pie,
    189; Pumpkin Lasagna, 187–88

Q

queso, in Cheese Enchiladas, 78

R

radishes: about, 65; Bacon-Wrapped Roasted
    Radishes, 66; Radish Greens Pesto and
    Asparagus Pasta Salad, 67; Savory Pudding
    with Roasted Cherry Tomatoes and
    Radishes, 122

ramps: Pickled Ramps, 83; Ramp Pesto, 82

Redhead Creamery, 156–57

Reishus, Elizabeth, 56

Reuben Soup, 59

Reuter, Gary, 119, 172–73

Reuter, Ginger, 174–75

rhubarb: Rhubarb Juice, 68; Rhubarb
    Pudding, 68

ricotta cheese: Lingonberry Pancakes, 103;
    Pumpkin Lasagna, 187–88

Rooney-Welsch, Maureen, 90

roti: about, 168–69; Roti, 170

Rousseau, Maggie, 24

rutabaga, in Pasty, 123–24

Rye Croutons, 59

Rye Pretzel Bites with Caraway, 76

S

Sabako, Tara, 59

St. Anthony Main American Pie Pizza Dough,
    Ode to, 132

St. Anthony Main's American Pie Italian
    Cream Soda, 136

salads: Cheryl's Jell-O Salad, 86; House Salad,
    141; Potato Salad, 113; Radish Greens Pesto

and Asparagus Pasta Salad, 67; Sort-of
Jan Doerr's Shrimp and Carrot Salad,
107; Strawberry-Cherry Pretzel Jell-O
Salad, 114–15
Salmon Croquettes with Dill and Peas
Sauce, 72–73
sambal oelek (Indonesian chili paste):
Chana Masala (Garbanzo Bean Curry),
171; Maple Wings, 82; Orange Crush BBQ
Sauce, 111
Samuelson, Daisy, 52
Sarsaparilla Snaps, 104
Satter, Natalie, 164
sauces and dressings: Cranberry Mustard
Sauce, 186; Curry Dip, 13; curry sauce, 7;
dill and peas sauce, 73; Dill Hollandaise,
48–49; Lingonberry Hot Sauce, 152;
maple "gravy," 154; Mayonnaise Dressing,
155; Orange Crush BBQ Sauce, 111;
Orange-Maple Vinaigrette, 81; Pesto,
135; Ramp Pesto, 82; Special Sauce
Spread, 102; Steak Sauce, 13; Sunday
Gravy, 38–39; tartar sauce, 119; Tomato
Sauce, 133
sausage: Egg Bake, 117; Egg Bake with Hash
Browns, 118; Meatball Pinwheel Hotdish,
22–23; Minnesota Hmong Hotdish, 7;
Sunday Gravy, 38–39
Savory Pudding with Roasted Cherry
Tomatoes and Radishes, 122
Schmidt, Susan Johnson, 58, 109–10,
160–61, 165–66
Seven-Minute Frosting, 79
shrimp: From Monrovia with Love: Liberian
Inspired Hotdish, 29; Pesto and Shrimp
Pizza, 134–35; Sort-of Jan Doerr's Shrimp
and Carrot Salad, 107
Sibley County Food Shelf, 56
Sibley County Heavenly Soup and Chili
Cook-Off, 56, 59–60
Sjostrom, Alise, 156–58
skyr, in Fried Chicken, 112
Slow Cooker Pulled Turkey, 40

Smolik, Bessie, 178
Snack Mix, 175
SNAP (Supplemental Nutrition Assistance
Program), 27
snow days, 15
Sommers, Jeff, 88–89
Sort-of Jan Doerr's Shrimp and Carrot
Salad, 107
soups and stews: Ancho Mama's Chili, 54;
Beef Barley Stew, 35; Blåbärssoppa
(Bilberry Soup), 52; Blonde Ale Cheese
Soup, 61; Easy Tomato Soup, 57;
Four-Ingredient Tortellini Soup, 60;
Reuben Soup, 59
SPAM: Chicken-Fried SPAM-n-Waffle Bites,
154; SPAM Lefse Pizza, 150; SPAM Potato
Hotdish, 21
SPAM Lefse Pizza, 150
SPAM Potato Hotdish, 21
Special Sauce Spread, 102
spinach: Four-Ingredient Tortellini Soup,
60; Little Moga-hot-dishu, 27–28
squash: Oven-Roasted Butternut Hash with
Pan-Fried Walleye and Dill Hollandaise,
48–49; Pumpkin Lasagna, 187–88
Steak Fondue, 13
Steak Sauce, 13
Strawberry-Cherry Pretzel Jell-O
Salad, 114–15
Sunday Gravy, 38–39
Susan's Cheese Crackers, 58
Sussman, Danny, 31–32
Svenskarnas Dag (Scandinavian
Summer Fest), 51
Swedish Cheese Tart
(Västerbottensostpaj), 127
Swedish meatballs (köttbullar), about, 181
Sweet Corn Ice Cream, 143
Swenson-Klatt, Erin, 83
Swiss cheese: Blonde Ale Cheese Soup, 61;
Reuben Soup, 59

T

tater tots: Hotdish A-Hmong Friends, 26; Little
    Moga-hot-dishu, 27–28; Minnesota Hmong
    Hotdish, 7; No-Can Tater Tot Hotdish, 19
Tellström, Richard, 129
Tempura-Fried Pickled Herring with
    Lingonberry Hot Sauce, 152
Tofu Katsu, 43
tofurky, about, 184
tomatoes: Booya for a Crowd, 179–80; Farmers
    Market Bread Pudding, 121; Lola, 140; Savory
    Pudding with Roasted Cherry Tomatoes
    and Radishes, 122; Tomato Pie (Tomat Paj),
    128; Tomato Sauce, 133
Tortellini Soup, Four-Ingredient, 60
Trautmueller Meat Pie, 44
Trout, Wild Rice Blini with Smoked, 190
turkey: Four-Ingredient Tortellini Soup, 60;
    Slow Cooker Pulled Turkey, 40
turnips: Booya for a Crowd, 179–80; Minnesota
    Hmong Hotdish, 7

V

Vang, Yia, 4–6, 25
Vanyo, Ray, 178
Vasaloppet, 51–52
Västerbottensostpaj (Swedish Cheese Tart), 127

vodka: Orange Push-Up Jell-O Shots, 108;
    Tempura-Fried Pickled Herring with
    Lingonberry Hot Sauce, 152; White Russian
    Float, 104
Volkenant, Cheryl, 86

W

Wagner-Harkonen, Jennifer, 123–24
walleye: Oven-Roasted Butternut Hash with
    Pan-Fried Walleye and Dill Hollandaise,
    48–49; Walleye Macaroni and Cheese, 50
Walz, Tim, 25
weather, 10–11
White Russian Float, 104
"Wildfire," 166
wild rice: about, 192–94; Wild Rice Blini with
    Smoked Trout, 190; Wild Rice Chicken
    Potpie, 191; Wild Rice Festival, 192; Wild Rice
    Straight Up with Salt and Butter, 195

Y

Yummy Jell-O Mold, 90

Z

zucchini: Farmers Market Bread Pudding, 121;
    No-Can Tater Tot Hotdish, 19

....

Land of 10,000 Plates was designed and set in type by Susan Everson
in St. Paul, Minnesota. The typefaces are Coquette, Mr. Eaves, and Mrs.
Eaves. The book was printed by Versa Press in East Peoria, Illinois.